README FIRST FOR A USER'S GUIDE TO
Qualitative Methods
Third Edition

Lyn Richards
RMIT University

Janice M. Morse
University of Utah

Los Angeles | London | New Delhi
Singapore | Washington DC

Los Angeles | London | New Delhi
Singapore | Washington DC

FOR INFORMATION:

SAGE Publications, Inc.

2455 Teller Road

Thousand Oaks, California 91320

E-mail: order@sagepub.com

SAGE Publications Ltd.

1 Oliver's Yard

55 City Road

London EC1Y 1SP

United Kingdom

SAGE Publications India Pvt. Ltd.

B 1/I 1 Mohan Cooperative Industrial Area

Mathura Road, New Delhi 110 044

India

SAGE Publications Asia-Pacific Pte. Ltd.

3 Church Street

#10-04 Samsung Hub

Singapore 049483

Acquisitions Editor: Vicki Knight

Associate Editor: Lauren Habib

Editorial Assistant: Kalie Koscielak

Production Editor: Laureen Gleason

Copy Editor: Megan Granger

Typesetter: C&M Digitals (P) Ltd.

Proofreader: Kate Macomber Stern

Indexer: Wendy Allex

Cover Designer: Garon Kiesel

Marketing Manager: Nicole Elliott

Permissions Editor: Adele Hutchinson

Printed in the United States of America

Library of Congress Cataloging-in-Publication Data

Richards, Lyn.

Readme first for a user's guide to qualitative methods / Lyn Richards, Janice M. Morse. — 3rd ed.

p. cm.
Includes bibliographical references and index.

ISBN 978-1-4129-9806-2 (pbk.)

1. Social sciences—Research—Methodology.
2. Qualitative research. I. Morse, Janice M. II. Title.
III. Title: Read me first for a user's guide to qualitative methods.

H62.M6612 2013
001.4´2—dc23   2012001310

This book is printed on acid-free paper.

Certified Chain of Custody
SUSTAINABLE Promoting Sustainable Forestry
FORESTRY   www.sfiprogram.org
INITIATIVE   SFI-01268
SFI label applies to text stock

13 14 15 16 10 9 8 7 6 5 4 3 2

Brief Contents

Preface   xvii

About the Authors   xix

1. Why *Readme First?*   1

PART I. THINKING RESEARCH   21

2. The Integrity of Qualitative Research   23

3. Choosing a Method   49

4. Qualitative Research Design   87

PART II. INSIDE ANALYSIS   117

5. Making Data   119

6. Coding   149

7. Abstracting   169

8. From Method to Analysis: Revisiting
   Methodological Congruence   185

PART III. GETTING IT RIGHT   213

9. On Getting It Right and Knowing if It's Wrong   215

10. Writing It Up   231

PART IV. BEGINNING YOUR PROJECT   253

11. Groundwork for Beginning Your Project   255

12. Getting Started   269

Appendix 1. Qualitative Software: Where to Go Next   281
   by Lyn Richards

Appendix 2. Applying for Funding   285
  by Janice M. Morse

References   287

Author Index   295

Subject Index   299

Detailed Contents

Preface   xvii

About the Authors   xix

1. Why *Readme First?*   1
    Goals   4
    Methods and Their Integrity   4
    Methodological Diversity and Informed Choice   5
    No Mysteries!   7
    Learning by Doing It: Qualitative Research as a Craft   7
    Qualitative Research as a Challenge   9
    Using *Readme First*   10
        Terminology   10
    The Shape of the Book   11
    Doing Qualitative Research: What to Expect   14
    Resources   19

PART I. THINKING RESEARCH   21

2. The Integrity of Qualitative Research   23
    Methodological Purposiveness   23
        Why Are You Working Qualitatively?   25
            The Research Question Requires It   25
            The Data Demand It   26
        Should You Be Working Qualitatively?   27
        How Should You Be Working Qualitatively?   29
        From Selecting a Method to Making Data   30
        From Choosing Sources and Sorts of Data to
            Managing and Analyzing Data   32
    Methodological Congruence   34
        Seeing Congruence by Doing It   34
    The Armchair Walkthrough   36
    And Now—Your Topic?   36
        How to Find a Topic   38
            You Are Already There   39
            There Is a Gap in the Literature   39

Another Way of Looking Is Needed 40
What's Going on Here? 40
Supplementing Quantitative Inquiry 41
Now, Consider the Research Context 41
Considering What You Want to Know 41
Considering What You Are Studying 42
Considering the Setting 43
Considering What You Want to Do 43
Considering Issues in Finding Participants 44
Considering Ethical Constraints 44
From Topic to Researchable Question:
Focusing Qualitative Inquiry 45
What Can You Aim For? 46
Summary 46
Resources 47

3. **Choosing a Method** **49**
Description and Interpretation 50
Starting Simple 52
Five Methods 54
Ethnography 54
What Sorts of Questions Are Asked? 54
The Researcher's Stance 55
What Sorts of Data Are Needed? 57
What Do the Results Look Like? 58
Different Approaches Within Ethnography 59
Grounded Theory 61
What Sorts of Questions Are Asked? 61
The Researcher's Stance 62
What Sorts of Data Are Needed? 63
What Do the Results Look Like? 63
Different Approaches Within Grounded Theory 64
Phenomenology 67
What Sorts of Questions Are Asked? 68
The Researcher's Stance 69
What Sorts of Data Are Needed? 70
What Do the Results Look Like? 70
Different Approaches Within Phenomenology 70
Discourse Analysis 72
What Sorts of Questions Are Asked? 72

Case Study Method 205
   Working With Data 205
   Strategies of Analysis 207
Summary 208
Resources 208

PART III. GETTING IT RIGHT **213**

9. On Getting It Right and Knowing if It's Wrong **215**
Ensuring Rigor in the Design Phase 216
   Appropriate Preparation 216
   Appropriate Review of the Literature 217
   Thinking Qualitatively, Working Inductively 218
   Using Appropriate Methods and Design 220
Ensuring Rigor While Conducting a Project 221
   Using Appropriate Sampling Techniques 221
   Responsiveness to Strategies That
      Are Not Working 222
   Appropriate Pacing of the Project 222
   Coding Reliably 223
When Is It Done? 224
   Project Histories 224
   Audit Trails 226
   Your Findings and the Literature 226
Demonstrating Rigor on Completion of the Project 227
   Triangulating With Subsequent Research 227
   Reaffirming Through Implementation 227
Summary 228
Resources 229

10. Writing It Up **231**
Ready to Write? 231
   Who Is It for, and Where Will It Appear? 232
   Writing Qualitatively 232
   Using Your Data 233
      When Do You Use Quotations? 234
      Editing Quoted Material 234
      Using Yourself 235
   Brevity and Balance 235
Re-revisiting Methodological Congruence 236

Protecting Participants   237
Evaluating Your Writing   238
Polishing   239
Using Your Software for Writing   239
    Approaches   239
    Advances   240
    Alerts   240
Writing Your Thesis or Dissertation   241
    Beginning to Write   242
Writing an Article for Publication   244
    Beginning to Write   245
After Publication, Then What?   249
    Findings Used Alone   249
       Use the Theory as a Framework for Practice   249
       Bring the Implicit and the Informal to the Fore   250
       Delimit Scope or Boundaries of
         Problems or Concepts   250
       Describe the Problem and Aid in
         Identification of the Solution   250
       Provide an Evaluation of
         Nonmeasurable Interventions   251
    The Cumulative Effect of Research Results   251
Summary   251
Resources   252

PART IV. BEGINNING YOUR PROJECT   **253**

11. Groundwork for Beginning Your Project   **255**
Writing Your Proposal   255
    Using the Literature Review   256
    Writing the Methods Section   257
    Estimating Time (and Related Resources)   258
    Developing a Budget   258
    A Note on Dealing With Available Data   260
Ensuring Ethical Research   261
    The Challenge of Anonymity   261
    Permissions   262
    Participant Assent and Consent   263
Summary   266
Resources   267

12. Getting Started   **269**

  Why Is It So Hard to Start?   270

  How Do You Start?   271

    Start in the Library   271

    Start With an Armchair Walkthrough   272

    Start Thinking Method   273

    Start With Yourself   273

      What Role Should the Researcher's

        Personal Experience Play?   274

      Hidden Agendas   274

    Start Small   275

    Start Safe   276

    Start Soon   276

    Start With a Research Design   277

    Start Skilled   277

    Start in Your Software   278

  Congratulations, You've Started!   278

  Resources   279

Appendix 1. Qualitative Software: Where to Go Next   **281**
  by Lyn Richards

Appendix 2. Applying for Funding   **285**
  by Janice M. Morse

References   **287**

Author Index   **295**

Subject Index   **299**

Preface

Qualitative research is rapidly expanding, constantly changing, and becoming increasingly accepted in areas where, until very recently, it was derided. The problems we and our students faced a decade ago are quite different from the new challenges, yet much of the literature is unchanged. Where qualitative methods previously were a minority activity in most disciplines, learned as a craft in apprenticeship to experienced researchers, they are now often attempted without training, and researchers may have difficulty finding mentors. Where data handling was a gross clerical load and data access limited by human memory, computer software now provides ways of handling and analyzing data that were impossible to achieve by manual methods. The widespread use of specialist software has made qualitative research more attractive and more accessible to those without qualitative training. Just as a decade ago, however, it remains difficult to begin a qualitative project, make sense of methodological choices, and get *thinking*—let alone started—on the right track. The researcher facing these difficulties is much more likely now to be facing them alone.

We wrote this book in recognition that these changes have altered the qualitative research world forever. Since the first edition, this book has been used by researchers at many levels of experience and translated into several languages. As change continued, we prepared a second and now a third revised edition reflecting on new pressures on researchers and new opportunities for them.

We share a conviction that if the changes are merely ignored or regretted, damage is done to both the researchers and the methods. New researchers need to get over those preliminary obstacles, to understand the language of qualitative inquiry, and to know what questions to ask, where to look for information, and how to start thinking qualitatively. They also need to challenge myths and false expectations and to know what to expect before they start the "real thing." This involves placing the wonderful promises of qualitative research in the context of the methods that make them work, and facing up to the processes of choosing methods appropriate for your research. It also involves placing the promises of technology in the context of tasks and techniques.

This book is intended to be read *first* by those who are thinking about becoming qualitative researchers—before they acquire data; before they preemptively choose a method, let alone a software package; and before they commit to a project. It may be used as a text for an introductory course, or it may be used by those who are simply interested in qualitative inquiry and want to get a feel for the qualitative research process. This new edition includes an overview of what software can now do for you. On our new companion website you will find advice on choosing software appropriate to your method and links to sites carrying up-to-date reviews of software and tutorials so that you may try out the computer tools and learn what they offer—and what they don't—before you propose your own project. Above all, the aim of this book is not to teach a single method but to map the range of methods, not to commit you to one sort of research but to show you why there are so many ways of working qualitatively. As we wrote these chapters, we discovered how different our own methods were. Readers who know our work will recognize one voice or another as that of the first author of particular chapters. But all our diverse experiences pointed to the same need—a need for a book that would meet the approaching researcher at the beginning of the path into the methodological maze.

The idea for this book grew from our shared frustration with the resources to help novice researchers see into the fascinating jungle of qualitative methods, and find their way through it. It draws on our separate and different attempts to teach qualitative methods to students and professionals and to assist with their research. We thank our students, colleagues, and friends for their questions and challenges, for sharing their confusions and insights, and for providing opportunities to explain abstract and complicated concepts and techniques. We thank our husbands, Bob Morse and Tom Richards, for their support and assistance. At SAGE, thanks to our editor, Vicki Knight, for her enthusiastic help in making this edition happen and to the copy editor, Megan Granger, for her fine attention to its final details.

—Lyn Richards & Janice Morse

SAGE and the authors gratefully acknowledge the contributions of the following reviewers: Rhonda R. Buckley, Texas Woman's University; Matthew A. Eichler, Texas State University–San Marcos; Sandra Mott, Boston College; Cheryl L. Nosek, Daemen College; Ruth Segal, Seton Hall University; Mona Shattell, DePaul University; and Irina L. G. Todorova, Northeastern University.

About the Authors

Lyn Richards, BA Hon. (political science), MA (sociology), is a qualitative research writer and consultant and adjunct professor in the Graduate School of Business at RMIT University in Melbourne. As a family sociologist, she published four books and many papers on Australian families and women's roles. As a methodologist, she taught graduate and undergraduate qualitative research at La Trobe University and went on to write for and teach the teachers. Her tenth book is *Handling Qualitative Data* (second ed., 2009). In university research with Tom Richards, she developed the NUD*IST software and founded QSR International, Melbourne. In interaction with the researchers using the software, and later development teams at QSR, she worked on the design of the subsequent versions (to N6) and then NVivo, as a principal member of the QSR software-development teams and author of the software's documentation. She was an invited speaker at all the conferences in the first decade of qualitative computing and a leading teacher and trainer internationally in qualitative computing and the handling of qualitative data. Richards has taught qualitative methods and qualitative software to some 4,000 researchers in 15 countries, and has learned from them all.

Janice M. Morse, PhD (nursing), PhD (anthropology), FAAN, is a professor and Presidential Endowed Chair at the University of Utah College of Nursing and Professor Emeritus at the University of Alberta, Canada. From 1991 to 1996, she also held a position as professor at Pennsylvania State University. From 1997 to 2007, she was the founding director and scientific director of the International Institute for Qualitative Methodology, University of Alberta; founding editor of the *International Journal of Qualitative Methods*; and editor of the Qual Press monograph series. She remains the founding editor of *Qualitative Health Research* (now in Volume 2, SAGE) and is currently editor of the monograph series *Developing Qualitative Inquiry* and *Essentials of Qualitative Inquiry* (Left Coast Press). Her research programs are in the areas of suffering and comforting, preventing patient falls, and developing qualitative methods. In 2011, she was awarded the Lifetime Achievement in Qualitative Inquiry from the International Center for Qualitative Inquiry, was an inaugural inductee into the Sigma

Theta Tau International Nurse Researcher Hall of Fame (2010), and was the fifth recipient of the Episteme Award (also Sigma Theta Tau). She received honorary doctorates from the University of Newcastle (Australia) and Athabasca University (Canada). She is the author of 460 articles and chapters and 19 books on qualitative research methods, suffering, comforting, and patient falls.

1

Why *Readme First?*

Why *Readme First?* Why should a researcher, new to qualitative inquiry, begin by reading a book on the range of ways of doing qualitative analysis? Why not just start by collecting the data and worry later about what to do with them?

The answer is simple. In qualitative research, collecting data is not a process separate from analyzing data. The strength of qualitative inquiry is in the integration of the research question, the data, and data analysis. There are many ways of gathering and managing data, but because qualitative research is always about discovery, there is no rigid sequence of data collection and analysis. If you collect data and later select a method for analyzing them, you may find that the method you have chosen needs different data. To start with a *method* and impose it on a research question can be equally unhelpful. Good qualitative research is consistent; the question goes with the method, which fits appropriate data collection, appropriate data handling, and appropriate analysis techniques.

The challenge for the novice researcher is to find the way to an appropriate method. A researcher new to qualitative inquiry who evaluates the possible paths well and makes good choices can achieve a congruence of research question, research data, and processes of analysis that will strengthen and drive the project. However, this may seem an impossible challenge. The process of qualitative inquiry all too often appears as a mystery to the new researcher, and the choice of an appropriate method of analysis is obscured. The embattled researcher too often resorts to collecting large amounts of very challenging data in the hope that what to do with them will later become apparent. Some researchers end projects that way, still wondering why they were doing this or what to do with all the data they collected.

Readme First is an invitation to those who have a reason for handling qualitative data. We see qualitative research as a wide range of ways to explore and understand data that would be wasted and their meaning lost if they were preemptively reduced to numbers. All qualitative methods seek to discover understanding or to achieve explanation *from* the data instead of from (or in addition to) prior knowledge or theory. Thus, the goals always include learning from, and doing justice to, complex data. In order to achieve such understanding, the researcher needs ways of exploring complexity.

Qualitative data come from many sources (e.g., documents, interviews, field notes, and observations) and in many forms (e.g., text, photographs, audio and video recordings, and films). Researchers may analyze these data using very many, very different methods. But each method has integrity, and all methods have the common goal of making sense of complexity, making new understandings and theories about the data, and constructing and testing answers to the research question. This book is an invitation to new qualitative researchers to see many methods—to see them as wholes and as understandable unities. This makes the choice of method necessary but also makes the process of choosing enabling rather than alarming.

> In this book we use the term *method* to mean a collection of research strategies and techniques based on theoretical assumptions that combine to form a particular approach to data and mode of analysis.

This book provides the beginning researcher with an overview of techniques for making data and an explanation of the ways different tools fit different purposes and provide different research experiences and outcomes. Our goal is not to present a supermarket of techniques from which the researcher can pick and choose arbitrarily; rather, we aim to draw a map that shows clearly how some methodological choices lead more directly than others to particular goals. We see all qualitative methods as integrated and good qualitative research as purposive. Until the researcher has an idea of the research goal, sees from the beginning the entire research process, knows the contents of the appropriate analytic toolbox, and recognizes from the start of the project what may be possible at the finish, it is not advisable to begin.

This book is not intended to be a sufficient and complete sourcebook but, rather, a guide to what it would be like to do a project. Indeed, it is intended to be read before a researcher begins a project. The book is about how ways of collecting and making data are connected to ways of handling data skillfully, and how qualitative methods allow researchers to understand, explain, discover, and explore. Our intention is to inform readers of the research possibilities, direct them to the appropriate literature, and help them on their way to trying out techniques and exploring the processes of analysis. By informing themselves about the possibilities for analysis and the range of methods available, new researchers can critically select the methods appropriate to their purposes.

We wrote this book because as researchers, teachers, mentors, and advisers, we have suffered from a vast gap in the qualitative research literature. Most texts describe a single method, often not explaining how purpose, data, and analytic technique fit together. A few display the range of qualitative methods, but a novice researcher is seldom helped by such displays if they include no explanation of how and why choices can be made. The confusion is worsened if the researcher is led to believe that one method is required for reasons of fashion, ideology, alleged superiority, or pragmatic necessity (for example, when only this one method can be supervised or approved in the research site). A researcher may be caught between instructions for a particular method and research reports that offer no sense of how those who did the research got there. In this volume, we offer to bridge at least some of these gaps. In Part I, we discuss the very wide range of methods and how to select among them. Then Part II takes the reader inside a project, showing what it would be like to construct and conduct a project.

The present literature rarely helps readers envision, at the beginning, the completion of a project. Researchers approaching qualitative inquiry need to be able to see the end before they start. In the chapters in Part III, we advise the reader on the goals to aim for, on rigor and reliability, and on the processes of finishing and writing it up. In the final two chapters, we deal with getting the reader started on his or her own project and smoothing the challenges of the startup.

Readme First is neither a substitute for experience nor an instruction manual for any particular method. Researchers who want to use the techniques we describe here on their own data are directed to methodological literature that offers fuller instruction in particular methods. Nor do we intend this book to be a substitute for the new researcher's learning how to think qualitatively alongside an experienced mentor. We are both sure that qualitative research, like any other craft, is best learned this way. But many researchers do not have the opportunity to work with mentors, and sometimes the learning experience can be confining even while it is instructive. In this book, we present some practical ways new researchers can try out various techniques so they may develop their skills. Exploiting these practical examples will give researchers insights into why they should use certain procedures and build their confidence to try them. Our goals are to demystify analysis, to promote informed choice, and to assist researchers in test-driving techniques while avoiding generalizing across methods or smudging the differences.

∭ GOALS

In the development of this volume, we identified five related goals:

1. To emphasize the integrity of qualitative methods

2. To present methodological diversity as requiring informed choice

3. To demystify qualitative methods

4. To introduce qualitative research as a craft and to provide researchers with information on ways in which they can gain experience before launching their projects

5. To present qualitative methods as challenging and demanding

∭ METHODS AND THEIR INTEGRITY

A strong message in this book is that although there is no one (or one best) approach to handling and analyzing qualitative data, good research is purposive and good methods are congruent with a fit among question, method, data, and analytic strategy. There are common strategies and techniques across all methods. It is these commonalities that make it sensible to talk about "qualitative methods." But techniques and strategies make methodological sense only in the context of particular methods, and the method is what molds how the strategies and techniques are used. Therefore, although informed and debated innovation strengthens and changes methods, researchers do not gain by picking and choosing among techniques and incorporating them out of their methodological context.

Qualitative research helps us make sense of the world in a particular way. Making sense involves organizing the undisciplined confusion of events and the experiences of those who participate in those events as they occur in natural settings. Qualitative methods provide us with a certain type of knowledge and with the tools to resolve confusions. Behind the selection of method is often, but not always, an explicit or implicit theoretical framework that carries assumptions about social "reality" and how it can be understood. Various qualitative methods offer different prisms through which to view the world, different perspectives on reality, and different ways in which to organize chaos. Further, they use different aspects of reality as data, and the combination of these different data, different perspectives, and different modes of handling the data give us different interpretations of reality.

Because the method the researcher uses influences the form the results will take, the researcher must be familiar with different kinds of qualitative methods, their assumptions, and the ways they are conducted before beginning a qualitative project. Such preparation will ensure that the researcher's goals are achieved, that the assumptions of the research have not been violated, and that the research is solid.

To argue for *methodological integrity* is not to argue for rigidity in methods. Methods rarely stay unchanged, and it is essential that they evolve over time. Researchers develop new techniques when confronted by challenges in their data, and if these techniques are consistent with the methods, they are drawn into other researchers' strategies. We both find excitement in methodological change and debate and have both been actively involved in it. However, we argue that innovations must be evaluated and critiqued within a method and developed with caution by seasoned researchers. Researchers who approach analysis by mixing and matching techniques derived from different methods without understanding them in their context commonly end up with a bag of techniques unlinked by strategies and uninformed by method, techniques that have nothing in common except that they are in the same project bag. Specifically, we want to warn researchers against using all the tools that particular computer programs provide without asking whether these techniques fit the research question, the research method, and the data.

〰 METHODOLOGICAL DIVERSITY AND INFORMED CHOICE

Our second goal is to display the diversity of qualitative methods and, in so doing, help the new researcher in choosing a method. As we noted above, the literature is dominated by texts that teach one particular way of doing qualitative research. Those texts are essential in that they provide the detail researchers need to work with particular methods, but in our experience, newcomers need an overview of the range of methods to help them envision the possibilities and outcomes of using alternative methods. Just as automobile manuals tell you little about the processes of driving, the menus in a software package do not tell you how to *analyze data* or how to use the software with different qualitative methods.

We begin with the assumption that no one method is intrinsically superior to others; each method serves a different purpose. For any given project or purpose, there may well be no method that is obviously best suited. However, the researcher needs to identify which method is *most* appropriate and then go to the relevant texts—hence, the title of this book. This volume is intended not as a substitute for the texts on particular methods but, rather, as a tool to help researchers access those texts. Like the README files that come with computer applications, it is intended to be read before the researcher commences the research process. We hope that researchers will be led from this book to particular methods and that what they learn here will help them make informed choices concerning what they do during the research process.

We start with a sketch map of a few qualitative methods. This particular methodological map may puzzle those familiar with the qualitative literature because it deliberately ignores disciplinary boundaries. We strongly believe that the development of qualitative methods has been hindered by narrow debates and the inability of many researchers to learn from, or even read about, the methods used in other disciplines. For instance, although ethnography was developed within anthropology (and often best answers questions asked by anthropologists), researchers from other disciplines (e.g., education) often ask ethnographic types of questions and are thus best served by ethnographic method. But research methods have been subject to waves of fashion so that, for instance, in health sciences, the relevance of ethnography is often ignored in favor of other methods that may be less suited to particular projects, such as grounded theory or phenomenology. Disciplines do not "own" methods, and researchers are deprived of resources if they are prevented from looking beyond the current trends in their own disciplines.

Our methodological map is designed only for orientation; it is not complete, and it gives relatively little detail. We do not attempt to map all forms of qualitative inquiry; rather, we want to distinguish major methods in order to show and encourage methodological diversity, integrity, versatility, and respect for the many ways of making sense of data and making theory from data.

𝕸 NO MYSTERIES!

Our third goal is to demystify qualitative methods. Each method provides a cluster of approaches or techniques to use with data—techniques requiring plenty of skill but no magic. New researchers who are awed by the great mysteries of analysis are inhibited from trying their hands at making sense of data, even when they urgently wish to do so.

Demystifying is always dangerous, as it risks trivializing. Good qualitative research certainly summons—and deserves—amazement, awe, and excitement for the complex processes involved in constructing new understandings and arriving at explanations that fit. We do not intend our discussion in this book to remove that excitement. But we see qualitative research as a craft, not a mystery, and as cognitive work, not miraculous and instantaneous insight. The processes of good qualitative analysis are exciting—not because they are mysterious, disguised by the wave of the magician's wand, but because, like the work of the sculptor, they are the result of skilled use of simple tools, practiced techniques, focus and insight, concentrated work, and a lot of hard thinking.

This book, then, is about agency. Researchers make data and work with data as they attempt to derive from them accounts and theories that satisfy. We offer no "black box" from which theory "emerges." To do justice to qualitative analysis, researchers have to be able to see how messy data can be transformed into elegant understanding and that this is something normal folk can attain. In this, they will be helped by practical accounts of how it has been done and hindered by passive-voice accounts of how themes are "discovered" and assertions that a theory "emerged." We believe good qualitative research requires not only that researchers be actively involved in data making and interpreting but that they account for and describe their progressive understanding of their data and the processes of completion. This is an active and intentional process, one that researchers control, develop, shape, and eventually polish. It is, therefore, enormously exciting and rewarding.

𝕸 LEARNING BY DOING IT: QUALITATIVE RESEARCH AS A CRAFT

Like any craft, qualitative research is best learned by doing it and talking about the experience. We have learned that teaching qualitative methods in abstraction, without involvement in data, works for very few students.

Yet most introductory texts offer rules rather than experiences. Our fourth goal is to offer learning by doing. In this book, we offer few rules; instead, we offer many explanations of techniques and the way they fit methods, as well as suggestions for test-driving the techniques discussed.

Of course, we cannot attempt to teach all the aspects of the major craft of qualitative analysis, with its long history and rapidly changing techniques, in this small volume. Our goal is to give a sense of what competent qualitative craftsmanship can do to data. Therefore, this book is not a "dummy's guide"; we do not provide abbreviated instructions that result in trivial projects. We do not spoon-feed readers, and we do not give instructions regarding sequential steps they should take. Rather, we offer readers ways of exploring the aims and effects of the central qualitative techniques and of getting a sense of what these techniques do to data in the context of particular methods.

To see qualitative research as a craft is to resist trends toward qualitative inquiry that stops at description, merely reporting selected quotations. Whilst all projects describe what the researcher discovers, the craft of analysis is grounded in a theoretical context. Qualitative research is an intellectual activity firmly based on the cumulative intellectual activities of those who have come before and their respective disciplines. In Part I, we discuss the different emphases of different methods on description and analysis. Our aim is not only to assist researchers in trying out techniques but to help them see those techniques as making sense in the context of a given method with a theoretical framework, a history, and a literature.

We tackle this goal with attention to the software tools currently available for handling qualitative data. These are changing rapidly, and we share a concern that technological advances should not further obscure or replace the craft of analysis. Whether researchers handle their data using index cards or sophisticated software, the essential first step is to learn to think qualitatively. When data handling is done with software, the researcher must understand that software does not provide a method.

Selection of *some* tools for doing analysis requires an understanding of how analysis might be done with *other* tools. It is now common for researchers to use specialized software tools for at least some qualitative research processes, but the qualitative methods literature has handled the discussion of computer techniques poorly, if at all. Computer programs may come to dominate the ways researchers handle data and probably have contributed to the explosion of qualitative research. Yet novice researchers often see such programs as offering a method. For that reason, this book will look at what qualitative researchers can and cannot do with computers.

Managing Abstraction   177
    Documenting Ideas: Definitions,
        Memos, and Diaries   178
    Growing Ideas   178
    Managing Categories: Index Systems   179
    Models and Diagrams   180
Using Your Software for Managing Ideas   180
    Approaches   180
    Advances   181
    Alerts   182
Summary   183
Resources   183

8. From Method to Analysis: Revisiting
Methodological Congruence   **185**
Ethnography   186
    Working With Data   186
        First-Level Description   186
        Thick Description   188
        Comparison   189
    Strategies of Analysis   190
Grounded Theory   191
    Working With Data   192
        Memos and Their
            Importance   193
        Data Preparation   193
    Strategies of Analysis   193
        Strategies That Facilitate the
            Identification of Process   194
        Strategies for Coding   194
        Strategies With Memos   196
        Theory-Building Strategies   196
        Changing Grounded Theory   198
Phenomenology   198
    Working With Data   199
    Strategies of Analysis   200
Discourse Analysis   202
    Working With Data   203
    Strategies of Analysis   204

6. Coding   **149**

  Getting Inside the Data   152

    A Reminder: The Distinctiveness of Qualitative Methods   152

    Storing Ideas   153

  Doing Coding   153

    Descriptive Coding   154

      What Is It Used For?   154

      How Is It Done?   155

      Where Is It Used?   155

    Topic Coding   156

      What Is It Used For?   156

      How Is It Done?   156

      Where Is It Used?   157

    Analytic Coding   157

      What Is It Used For?   158

      How Is It Done?   158

      Where Is It Used?   159

  Theme-ing   160

  Purposiveness of Coding   160

  Tips and Traps: Handling Codes and Coding   161

    Code as You Learn   162

    Always See Coding as Reflection   162

    Never Code More Than You Need   162

    Manage Your Codes   163

    Monitor Coding Consistency   164

  Using Your Software for Coding   164

    Approaches   165

    Advances   165

    Alerts   166

  Summary   167

  Resources   167

7. Abstracting   **169**

  The First Step: Categorizing   171

    Categorization and Coding   171

    Categorization as Everyday Strategy   172

  The Next Step: Conceptualizing   173

  Doing Abstraction   174

    When Does It Happen?   174

    How Is It Done?   176

Using Your Software for Research Design   110
    Approaches   110
    Advances   111
    Alerts   112
Summary   113
Resources   114

PART II. INSIDE ANALYSIS   **117**

5. Making Data   **119**
What Data Will Your Study Need?   120
What Will Be Data (and What Will Not)?   120
    The Researcher in the Data   121
    Good Data/Bad Data   122
Ways of Making Data   123
    Interviews   126
        Interactive Interviews   126
        Semistructured Questionnaires   127
        Conversations   128
        Group Interviews   128
    Observations   129
    Online Sources   130
    Video Recording   131
    Photography   131
    Documents   132
    Diaries and Letters   132
    Indirect Strategies   132
Who Makes Data?   133
Transforming Data   134
Managing Data   135
    Managing Focus Group Data   137
The Role of Data   138
Yourself as Data   140
    You and Those You Study   141
    Your Experience as Data   142
Using Your Software for Managing Data   143
    Approaches   143
    Advances   144
    Alerts   144
Summary   145
Resources   146

The Researcher's Stance   74
What Sorts of Data Are Needed?   74
What Do the Results Look Like?   75
Different Approaches Within Discourse Analysis   75
Case Study Method   75
What Sorts of Questions Are Asked?   76
The Researcher's Stance   77
What Sorts of Data Are Needed?   77
What Do the Results Look Like?   78
Different Approaches Within Case Study Method   79
Summary   79
Resources   81

4. **Qualitative Research Design**   **87**
The Levels of Design   88
Planning Design   88
The Scope of the Project   89
Designing the Scope   90
The Nature of the Data   91
Doing Design   93
Designing for Validity   94
Project Pacing   96
Conceptualizing Stage   96
Entering the Field   96
Setting Up and Managing a
Data Management System   97
Sampling and Theoretical Sampling   98
Analysis   98
Designs Using More Than One Study   98
Mixed Method Designs   99
Combining Qualitative Studies   99
Combining Qualitative
and Quantitative Studies   100
Multiple Method Designs   101
Synthesizing Multiple Studies   101
Using Different Ways of Looking   102
Comparative Design   102
Triangulated Design   103
Taking an Overview   104
Choosing Your Software   105

An overview of what software does is provided in Chapter 4, to assist you in choosing the appropriate software tools for your project. Four tables summarize what all programs do, then the variety available and when this will matter. They are designed to help the researcher see software choice, like methods choice, in terms of the requirement for methodological congruence.

Each of the chapters about techniques of handling data (Chapters 4, 5, 6, and 7) and writing up your study (Chapter 11) concludes with a summary of what you can expect from your software and advice and warnings to help you use it well. Qualitative software tools are developing rapidly, and the software in turn changes methods, since it allows researchers to handle data and ideas in ways not feasible without computers. So these chapter sections do not describe the range of current software. Any printed account of particular functions of available software would be immediately out of date. To learn about the range of qualitative software available to you, and the functions and tools that different software packages offer, you must turn to websites. This is easily done via the University of Surrey's CAQDAS Networking Project, whose website (http://www.surrey.ac.uk/sociology/research/researchcentres/caqdas/) provides up-to-date summaries of current software and links to the websites of all qualitative software developers.

The sections on software in this book offer something different. Rather than comparing current software functionality, they explore the ways qualitative work can be supported and inevitably changed by use of software tools—and how these can challenge or even obstruct research efforts. Our new companion website develops these themes and offers links to resources and tutorials in current packages and to further material. For more on these questions, see Richards's (2009) companion book, *Handling Qualitative Data: A Practical Guide,* and the web resources at www.sagepub.co.uk/richards.

⟍ QUALITATIVE REJEARCH AJ A CHALLENGE

Our fifth goal concerns the public relations of various qualitative methods. We confront the widespread assumption that qualitative research is simple and that to "do qualitative" is easier than conducting quantitative research because you do not need statistics and computers. It never was simple or easy, and now, like any research activity, it requires computers. With the assumption that these are "soft methods for soft data," we present qualitative methods as challenging and demanding, made so because they can (and must) be rigorous and can (and should) lead to claims for defensible and useful conclusions.

The challenge is not in doing it "one right way" but in achieving coherent, robust results that enhance understanding. We present our readers with principles rather than hard-and-fast rules to be followed. We conclude the book by addressing the issues of rigor and the ways in which it is achieved, assessed, and demonstrated.

There is also a challenge in reconciling the sometimes opposing requirements of different methods. We emphasize, rather than obscure, what we consider to be the essential paradoxes inherent in qualitative research. Central among these paradoxes are the opposing requirements of simultaneous pursuit of complexity and production of clarity.

We explore and discuss the built-in contradictions that texts often submerge, dodge, or totally ignore. It is our experience that novice researchers find sometimes insurmountable barriers in unexplained paradoxes. Too often, they are left puzzled and paralyzed, feeling responsible for their inability to progress toward analysis. If understood as an integral part of analysis, however, these are challenges, not barriers. Meeting these challenges is a normal and necessary part of coping with complex data. Confronted, they offer hurdles that can and must be cleared, and all qualitative researchers know the pleasure of clearing such methodological obstacles. Once a researcher has acquired the proper tools, these obstacles become exciting challenges rather than reasons for giving up.

≫ USING README FIRST

Warning: This book is designed to be read like a novel—it has a story. If you skip a section, later parts may not make sense; our best advice is that you skim read before you jump in fully.

Terminology

We use specific terms in specific ways. When we use the term *method*, we refer to a more-or-less consistent and coherent way of thinking about and making data, interpreting and analyzing data, and judging the resulting theoretical outcome. Methodological principles link the strategies together. These methods are clearly labeled and have their own literatures. We have chosen five methods to sketch and compare throughout this book: ethnography, grounded theory, phenomenology, discourse analysis, and case study. Many others will appear in the discussions as we show how methods vary in their emphases and completeness. A great amount of qualitative research is done without traditional methods. We share a concern that researchers feel coerced to stick a traditional label on less complete methods.

A research *strategy* is a way of approaching data with a combination of techniques that are ideally consistent with the method the researcher has chosen to use. Strategies, therefore, are based on, and consistent with, the assumptions and procedures linked in each particular method. We will argue that strategies made up of techniques that have been haphazardly and arbitrarily selected from different methods are problematic.

We also use the term *technique* to refer to a way of doing something. In our context, research techniques are ways of attempting or completing research tasks. If you see someone using a particular technique (e.g., coding data), that technique might not tell you which method the researcher is using—everyone codes data. But if you look more closely at the ways in which the researcher is applying that technique and at where it takes the researcher, you will be able to determine the method the researcher is using. Coding does different things to data when it is done by researchers using different methods.

We aim to map commonalities while explaining diversity and to present methodological techniques in ways that will help researchers arrive at coherent strategies within understood methods. Our overall goal is to help readers develop a sense of methodological purpose and appropriateness, and, at the same time, provide an evaluation and critique of qualitative research. We hope this book will help those readers who go on to do their own research to know what they are trying to do and why they are doing it one way rather than another. We want to help our readers achieve the most satisfying answers to their research questions, the strongest sense of discovery and arrival, and the best new understanding with the most efficiency and expediency.

⚙ THE ∫HAPE OF THE BOOK

We begin by establishing the integrity of methods and then approach, in turn, the different dimensions of qualitative research that researchers have to understand in order to be able to start their own research projects. In each section, we aim to give an idea of how it would be to work in a specific way.

At the end of each chapter for which software skills are relevant, we discuss how it will feel to work with software, and we advise on the use of computer tools. Each chapter concludes with a list of resources to direct readers to the literature on each of the methods discussed, to wider literature, and to completed examples of relevant research. This literature deals with the processes of thinking qualitatively, preparing for a project, relating to data, and creating and exploring ideas from the data and theories about the data.

The chapters in Part I, "Thinking Research," address our first two goals: to establish the integrity of qualitative methods and to present methodological diversity as a choice, not a confusing maze. They provide a view from above, to be used as one would use an aerial photograph to scan a particular terrain and understand possible routes to a given destination.

In Chapter 2, which deals with the integrity of qualitative research, we set out what we see as core principles—the *purposiveness* of method and the methodological *congruence* of qualitative research. We show how different methods fit different sorts of qualitative data and how they have different implications for analysis. This very general overview informs the discussion in later chapters about the range of ways of meeting and handling data and the range of analysis processes and outcomes.

We compare five methods in Chapter 3 as we present the case for methodological congruence, showing how the question, data, and analysis fit together in each of the five methods introduced. These are all widely used: ethnography, grounded theory, phenomenology, discourse analysis, and case study method. Although there are many variants within each method, each is identified by characteristic ways of addressing questions through data. Each method is appropriate to particular types of questions, each directs researchers to make particular research designs and data, and each leads researchers to use particular techniques for handling data and discovering and analyzing meanings.

Chapter 4 is about research design, and it has a simple message: A researcher absolutely needs a research design. We discuss why design is often demoted or ignored in qualitative research and urge that researchers take the opposite approach. Like the methods they express, research designs should not be seen as fixed or holy. However, careful consideration and planning set a project on the path to its intended goals and maximize the likelihood of getting there. We explore what researchers can and cannot plan, and we emphasize the design of the *scope* of the project and the *appropriateness* of the data. At the end of the chapter, we discuss designs that combine more than one method and the risks and benefits of these.

The chapters in Part II, "Inside Your Project," are concerned with what doing qualitative research is like. Chapter 5 is about data: the range of ways of making data, the role of the data at the beginning of the project, the sources and styles of qualitative data, data required for different methods, and when data will be useful and when not. We emphasize the agency of the researcher in making data collaboratively with "subjects," and the ways data are crafted to meet the research goal from the beginning of the project.

All methods share the goal of deriving new understandings and making theory out of data. But novice researchers are often unable to get a sense of the research experience behind these goals. What is a category? How would I know one if I found one? What should coding *do* for you? What is it *like* to create theory? In the remaining chapters in Part II, we discuss and demonstrate the tools for handling and coding data and for theorizing. Starting with abstraction, we move to the common processes of using and developing categories and linking them to data through coding. In Chapter 6, we examine the central and varied processes of coding and the different ways in which researchers can use coding to move between data and ideas. Chapter 7 deals with the goal of abstracting and "theme-ing," or "thinking up" from the data, which is common to all methods. In Chapter 8, we return to the theme of methodological fit. We revisit the same five methods, focusing now on what working in that method is like. For each, we discuss the ways of working with data and the analytic strategies most commonly used in that method, as well as the differences within it.

The chapters in Part III, "Getting It Right," are concerned with the process of completing qualitative analysis so that it works for the researcher's purposes. In Chapter 9, we discuss what is involved in getting analysis right, as well as the ways researchers can know if it is wrong. Chapter 10 deals with reporting results and writing them up, ensuring that a qualitative project will be credible and persuasive, and ways in which researchers can aim for these goals.

Thus, this book ends with a beginning. Chapters 11 and 12 in Part IV, "Beginning Your Project," end the book by describing the groundwork researchers need to do to begin their own projects once they have understood the choice of method and the tasks of research to follow.

We recommend that while researchers wait for the permissions they need to begin their projects, they "get skilled" by selecting and learning to use appropriate software for their analysis. We finish with encouraging words to get the new researcher started.

Appendix 1 is a guide to finding software tools. Appendix 2 discusses how to apply for funding.

☒ DOING QUALITATIVE RESEARCH: WHAT TO EXPECT

This book is intended to be read at the inception of a project and reread as needed until writing is completed. We recommend that you consult it when you wonder why you are doing this or that or where your current path is taking you.

So what will it be like? Qualitative researchers differ greatly from quantitative researchers in the way they approach research. Usually, qualitative researchers start with *areas of interest* or general, rather than specific, research questions. They may not know very much about the topic at the start, and even if they do, they seek to learn more through the data. To do this, they must be flexible. You need to start with a broad understanding about the general area, be receptive to new ideas and willing to relinquish old—but unsupported—favorite ideas, and obtain a notion of the boundaries from the phenomenon studied. In all qualitative methods, one goal is to create categories and linkages systematically from the data, confirm these linkages, and create theory. You will find it is easier to achieve this objective if you understand the entire research process and have an overview of the entire project, knowing what steps come next.

If you are approaching qualitative research with no idea of what it will be like, this book offers a sketch. It is not, of course, a picture of an ideal project (or any real project), but an impression of the ways things tend to develop. It gives a simple overview of the research process and the ways in which you might interface with *Readme First*. If this sketch were to represent reality, it would be a mess of loops and double-headed arrows— qualitative research is more often cyclical than linear. But although you cannot expect a tidy procession of stages, qualitative research usually has some predictable progress; during most projects, there are series of periods during which a few things happen simultaneously. We revisit this picture in the final chapter.

Even before selecting a research topic, you must understand the nature of qualitative methods. You must know what qualitative methods *can do* and *cannot do*, where and for what kinds of problems and questions they should be used, and what kind of information is obtained through the use of various qualitative methods. We start with this point in the next chapter.

The process of learning to think qualitatively—to think like a qualitative researcher—can be challenging. If you do not have training, our best advice is that you read basic introductory texts, take an introductory course, talk to researchers about their experience and read their studies, and find and read *critically* a wide range of published works by researchers who have employed different qualitative methods. Such a broad overview will give you a feel for the field. Ask yourself: What kinds of questions are best answered using qualitative methods? What kinds of qualitative methods are best used with certain questions? What is the relationship between the data and the emerging results? What does "good" research look like? Explore how research results vary in their level of theoretical development, from simply reporting and organizing quotations to creating sophisticated and elegant theories. Ask yourself why some research seems satisfying and some less so. You should be asking all these questions simultaneously.

Becoming Focused

Read *Readme First.* Learn to think qualitatively.

Read other texts, take a course, and talk to researchers. Reflect on, refine, and define a topic area. Start to shape a research question.

Where will you start? Once an area of interest has led to existing research, a qualitative researcher usually locates a *topic*—not a specific question and very rarely a research location or sample. This is not a methodological or moral imperative, but if you start, for example, with a particular group you wish to study, you may find it hard to broaden your vision to a wider context. So resist the temptation to move directly to research design or, worse, to make a list of the questions you are going to ask your study participants.

If you approach the topic from a broad perspective, it will lead you to the literature. There, you can examine and analyze other studies critically, both within the context of the proposed research and within the context of the researchers' disciplines. But, most important, you should examine the literature *qualitatively*. It is not enough to summarize or synthesize others' results. Rather, you need to examine the theoretical perspective and method of each study, looking for overt and covert assumptions, beliefs, and values that contributed to the researcher's perspective, questions, selection of hypotheses, and interpretations of results. For a while, you should combine these tasks.

Becoming Competent Methodologically

Read extensively around the topic. Read extensively on the possible methods. Develop and learn the ways you will handle data. Narrow down your methodological options. Choose your software and learn it.

Such a critical appraisal of the literature is a student's first step in qualitative inquiry—and in qualitative analysis. This may also be your first step in handling qualitative data. You should treat the literature review as a data-managing exercise. As you work through this book, consider how each method we discuss might be applied to making sense of your reading (which, just like interview data, builds up in unstructured text records).

Now is the time to start *managing data* skillfully. If you are planning to use a computer program to handle your data, learn it *now* and use it to organize your notes and any discussions arising from the literature. Things move fast once you have located your study methodologically, and competence with your software will help you maintain the pace and maximize the exploration of data as they accumulate.

Your new understanding of the literature, and the acquired understanding of qualitative methods in general, will direct you toward the research question, the appropriate qualitative method, and, thus, the start of a research design. Resist the temptation to narrow the research question too far; you will refine and delimit it during the process of data collection. Resist any pressure to select your method until you are sure you know where your study fits.

Shaping the Study

Locate the study methodologically. Locate the study in the research field. Work on and rework a research design. Start making some appropriate data. Start data analysis *now*. Manage data and ideas.

Every researcher experiences this stage as a flurry of activity and impending chaos. Reading about method is imperative if you are to be sure-footed in your entry into the research field. The importance of learning to think theoretically will be evident as soon as you begin data collection. Any observation or piece of text can be seen in two ways: It can be taken at face value, or it can be viewed as theoretically rich, linked to other pieces of data, linked to existing theory, and linked to your ideas. Our best advice is that you take this stage of interlocking tasks carefully and slowly. Never allow the excitement and demands of the impending project to distract you from *designing* your research.

It is important at this point that you develop a systematic and simple means of documenting, linking, sorting, and storing these ideas. The system must be fluid so that the developing codes and categories remain malleable as the ideas change and evolve with your increasing comprehension. If you are using a computer program, talk to other users and partake in online discussions to gain a sense of what tools the program offers you and which ones you can use.

Note that you have now commenced analysis work: active, hard, deliberate cognitive work. You are not mindlessly gathering data as if picking apples; your analysis should be ongoing and never delayed until all data are in. If you are working qualitatively, it is the data-driven analysis that will tell you when the data are adequate.

Conceptualizing and Theorizing

Actively seek theory. Constantly check data. Explore complexity and context. Simplify and integrate. Sift, sort, and play with data.

Processes of making data and making the analysis continue. Your early ideas and data sortings look simplistic, but the "right" solutions often appear beyond your grasp. Although this is an intriguing and exciting stage, it can also be the most frustrating and most difficult one. Return to this volume for overviews of the data-handling and theory-generating processes. Ensure that you keep analyzing as you make data and that you allow the data to direct you to ideas that surprise you and that you had not previously thought to explore.

Explore your data from different perspectives. Play with your data. Pursue hunches and think outside of the tidy explanations. Write, write, write, and rewrite. Create models and discuss them. Confirm ideas in your data or collect additional data. Discuss your theories with anyone who will listen. Compare the emerging theory with the theories in the literature. And, most important, think! Consider the research as a puzzle to be solved, a solution as always possible, and the process as active mind work. Theory does not emerge overnight; data never "speak for themselves."

Molding and Writing

Arrive at a best account of the data or theory to make sense of the data.

Tidy up and polish.

Write, present, and publish.

It may happen suddenly that all your research will come together and integrate in a flash of discovery, or it may happen slowly over a period of time. But, eventually, your research will make sense. The growing web of ideas and theory will be strong enough to support a story, an account, or an explanation that makes sense of the data. Your familiarity with the literature will have given you a sense of the final product but perhaps not of something achievable by you. Like all extraordinary experiences, it will be different from what you expected, and you will be astonished when it happens. You can *tell* your study. You have arrived at a solution—a beautiful, elegant solution—that is supported with data, connects with the literature, and makes sense in the research context. Your study, *if* tidied up and polished, will make an important contribution to the literature.

Keep the momentum going until your study is published and accessible to all. And when that is done, with great pomp and ceremony, give *Readme First* to a friend.

RE*J*OURCE*J*

Read widely among the available basic texts to get a feel for how to approach qualitative analysis.

Major Resources

Creswell, J. W. (2009). *Qualitative inquiry and research design: Choosing among five traditions* (2nd ed.). Thousand Oaks, CA: Sage.

The five approaches covered in this text are biography, phenomenology, grounded theory, ethnography, and case study.

Denzin, N. K., & Lincoln, Y. S. (Eds.). (2011). *The SAGE handbook of qualitative research* (4th ed.). Thousand Oaks, CA: Sage.

Each chapter is a solid review of a pertinent topic; a comprehensive overview of qualitative inquiry.

Mason, J. (2002). *Qualitative researching* (2nd ed.). London: Sage.

This text gives an overview of qualitative methods and clear discussion of many of the current issues students confront.

Mayan, M. (2009). *Essentials of qualitative inquiry.* Walnut Creek, CA: Left Coast Press.

An excellent overview for doing qualitative inquiry.

Munhall, P. L. (2012). *Nursing research: A qualitative perspective.* Sudbury, MA: Jones & Bartlett.

Richards, L. (2009). *Handling qualitative data: A practical guide* (2nd ed.). London: Sage.

This is a companion work to *Readme First,* the present book. It advises on what to do when you have data, with detailed advice on the tasks and techniques described in the next chapters. On the companion website (http://www.sagepub.co.uk/richards/) there are case studies of methods in practice, detailing the researcher's experience, and advice on starting to work with qualitative software.

Additional Resources

Bernard, H. R. (2000). *Social research methods: Qualitative and quantitative approaches.* Thousand Oaks, CA: Sage.

Creswell, J. W. (2009). *Research design: Qualitative, quantitative, and mixed method approaches* (3rd ed.). Thousand Oaks, CA: Sage.

Ezzy, D., Liamputtong, P., & Hollis, D. B. (2005). *Qualitative research methods.* Oxford, UK: Oxford University Press.

Grbich, C. (1999). *Qualitative research in health: An introduction.* Sydney, Australia: Allen & Unwin.

Lewins, A., & Silver, C. (2007). Using qualitative software: A step-by-step guide. London: Sage.

Marshall, C., & Rossman, G. B. (1999). *Designing qualitative research* (3rd ed.). Thousand Oaks, CA: Sage.

Prasad, P. (2005). *Crafting qualitative research: Working in the post positivist tradition.* Armonk, NY: M. E. Sharpe.

Ritchie, J., & Lewis, J. (Eds.). (2004). *Qualitative research practice: A guide for social science students and researchers.* Thousand Oaks, CA: Sage.

Seale, C., Gobo, G., Gubrium, J., & Silverman, D. (2004). *Qualitative research practice.* London: Sage.

Part I

THINKING RESEARCH

Chapter 2. The Integrity of Qualitative Research

Chapter 3. Choosing a Method

Chapter 4. Qualitative Research Design

2

The Integrity of Qualitative Research

When commencing a qualitative research project, it is essential that the researcher understand not only the variety of methods available but also that in each there is a relationship between research question, method, and desired results. In this chapter, we introduce the researcher to choosing a topic, and, considering context, how this leads to a method. Choice of method will locate the project, indicating what is possible for the research to achieve, what the researcher can ask and hope to have answered, and how it is to be done. Thus, question, method, data, and analysis fit together. Once a researcher recognizes this fit, the choice of a method for any particular study is never arbitrary, and qualitative research, although a venture into the unknown, is purposeful and goal directed.

Not all qualitative methods integrate all aspects of the project in the same manner, and most contain considerable variety. In this overview, we stress the two principles of qualitative methods that inform the rest of this book: methodological *purposiveness* and methodological *congruence*. We illustrate these by comparing five very different and widely used qualitative methods.

※ METHODOLOGICAL PURPOSIVENESS

There is almost always a best way to do any research project, a particular method best suited to each particular problem. The choice of best method always comes from the research purpose.

method comes from purpose

Of course, the choice is never entirely open. It is always constrained by something—the researcher's familiarity with methods, the researcher's resources, or sometimes the data themselves. Researchers starting from the availability of particularly interesting data will quite normally have their methodological options predetermined. Although this can be restricting, such researchers may well be envied by others confronting too many choices: a general topic area, many possibilities for making data, and no methodological direction. Researchers in the latter group, in turn, may be tempted to claim constraint ("I have to do a grounded theory study because that's the only sort of qualitative research accepted in my school"). But that's where the danger lies—in a topic shoehorned into a particular method. Some seasoned researchers work the other way around, through commitment to one method, which means they ask only (even, it might appear, *can* ask only) certain sorts of questions. But they start with questions, and they must always be open to the possibility that a question requires a different method.

Especially when choice of method seems constrained, it is important to understand the process by which a method is selected, and to see the selection as *deliberate* and as reflecting research purpose. The purpose may be to learn about a specific problem (e.g., "Why do residents not use the facilities?") or to understand a situation ("I wonder what the experience of . . . is"). Or the purpose may be no more specific than to learn more about a particular topic or to do justice to those interesting data that suddenly became available. In such a project, exploring the literature and spending time in the setting will help the researcher focus on a clearer problem and frame a sharper research question, and the data will direct further inquiry. A decision about method does not just happen by default. A purpose, however unspecific, guides the researcher to a more focused research question and, hence, to a choice of method.

The researcher actively creates the link between purpose and method through a process of reflecting on purpose, focusing on a researchable question, and considering how to address it. That link is never, of course, a simple one-way causal connection. It is helpful to commence with an opening *armchair walkthrough,* considering several routes and several methodological vehicles. The appropriate approach may not be a qualitative method. Sometimes the research purpose opens out to several research questions, each requiring a different qualitative method, or the interplay of qualitative and quantitative methods. But, however it is arrived at, the link of purpose to method is what gets a project going.

Why Are You Working Qualitatively?

Why did you select a qualitative method? Often, the researcher has a very practical goal for beginning the project. It may be to understand an unanticipated problem area in the classroom or a particularly puzzling patient situation that the experts seem unable to explain. It may be to throw light on an area in which patterns of behavior are statistically clear (changes in the birthrate, for instance) but researchers can only guess at reasons for these patterns without an understanding of people's own accounts of their behavior. It may be to inform a policy area (such as urban planning) where the best-laid plans are thwarted by apparently irrational choices (incredibly, the slum dwellers didn't want to be relocated!). In each of these cases, the researcher chose to work qualitatively, with complex unstructured data from which new understandings might be derived. Below, we summarize the two major reasons for working qualitatively—the research question requires it, and the data demand it.

The Research Question Requires It

For many of us, the first really good moment in a project occurs when we see how the research purpose can be pursued by one but not another means. In retrospect, this may be blindingly obvious. For instance, you need to understand what children *mean* to parents in this society before you can predict fertility rates, so what you must do is listen to parents' stories of parenthood rather than ask predetermined questions about birth control. The only way of making sense of classroom problems is to get an understanding of the latent processes of power—observe, listen to what is said in the classroom and the staff room, and examine the words and their meanings rather than simply distribute a questionnaire. What if the apparently irrational behavior of slum dwellers makes sense to them? The only way to find out is to hang around and observe their daily life, rather than assume that the condition of their housing is their top priority. Each of these purposes points toward one of the methods we compare throughout this book.

Researchers who are brought (sometimes kicking and screaming) to a qualitative method driven by the topic often combine qualitative with quantitative methods. They may recognize their need to understand and to develop meaning prior to or subsequent to, rather than instead of, a quantitative study. Perhaps they require a larger-scale inquiry or systematic testing of hypotheses. In such situations, a qualitative component may precede a quantitative project and provide different types of findings for richer results, or input into the questions to be asked in a subsequent survey. Or results of the quantitative study may be explored in detail through qualitative study of particular cases. (We address ways in which qualitative and quantitative methods can be combined in Chapter 5.)

The Data Demand It

It may be, however, that you have no such research purpose directing you to work qualitatively. What, then, might lead you to a method? A powerful push can come from recognition of what data you can possibly, and properly, use. Some data can be obtained only through the use of a particular strategy. For example, it is not possible to interview some participants; very young children who cannot talk or elderly persons with Alzheimer's disease may not be able to provide coherent responses. In these situations, researchers may use observational strategies, obtaining data in the form of field notes or video recordings. This will be the first of many times in the project when data seem to be driving the study. Recognizing such imperatives will always take you forward, because qualitative methods are properly responsive to discoveries in data.

Many quantitatively trained researchers first started working qualitatively because they recognized that the statistical analyses of particular survey responses did not seem to fit what those in the situations of interest said or what people wrote in their open-ended answers. In avoiding the temptation to dismiss their participants' open-ended responses or to use them merely to illustrate the reports, perceptive researchers sought ways to analyze them. Action researchers might be brought to qualitative methods by complex social or political situations in which understanding all sides of a controversy is essential but the available documents and discussions defy neat categorization. For a study to be useful, the researcher must make sense of such a situation. Practitioners might observe and record the complexities of clinical situations that seem to be denied by tidy reports of patient compliance; in seeking an understanding of that complexity, they find they need ways of doing justice to the data.

Coming to a qualitative method because your data require it provides high motivation but often high stress, too. The survey must be reported, the action group informed, the patients helped; it seems that you must become an instant qualitative researcher. If this is your situation, we recommend that you go carefully through the nine points we list in Chapter 13 under the heading "How Do You Start?"

Should You Be Working Qualitatively?

The obvious first question is whether the research purpose is best answered by qualitative methods. We hope we have made it clear that we see nothing morally or methodologically superior about qualitative approaches to research. Other things being equal, a quantitative project will often be faster, easier for a researcher lacking qualitative training, and arguably more acceptable in many research contexts. Moreover, the research world is replete with questions that are properly and effectively answered quantitatively and that will be badly answered, or not answered at all, if a qualitative method is imposed on them. Forcing such questions into qualitative methods has the same effect on projects and researchers as Cinderella's ugly stepsisters' forcing the glass slipper onto their feet had on their marriage prospects—it won't work, it will hurt a lot, and the result is a loss of credibility.

Our goal in this book is not to examine the philosophical origins of qualitative methods or the approaches to evidence and "reality" behind different methodologies, but it is important to note that we see no chasm between qualitative and quantitative techniques. In our experience, many qualitative projects involve counting at some stage, and many questions are best answered by quantification. But given that we aim here to give those embarking on qualitative research an understanding of what it will be like, we assume that you, the reader, are about to embark. Thus, the obvious first question is whether you should do so.

Qualitative methods are the best or only way of addressing some research purposes and answering some sorts of questions, as in the following cases:

1. If the purpose is to understand an area where little is known or where previously offered understanding appears inadequate (thin, biased, partial), you need research methods that will help you see the subject anew and will offer surprises. Put bluntly, if you don't know what you are likely to find, your project requires methods that will allow you to learn what the question is from the data.

2. If the purpose is to make sense of complex situations, multicontext data, and changing and shifting phenomena, you need ways of simplifying and managing data without destroying complexity and context. Qualitative methods are highly appropriate for questions where preemptive reduction of the data will prevent discovery.

3. If the purpose is to learn from the participants in a setting or a process the way *they* experience it, the meanings they put on it, and how they interpret what they experience, you need methods that will allow you to discover and do justice to their perceptions and the complexity of their interpretations. Qualitative methods have in common the goal of generating new ways of seeing existing data.

4. If the purpose is to construct a theory or a theoretical framework that reflects reality rather than your own perspective or prior research results, you may need methods that assist the creation of theory from data.

5. If the purpose is to understand phenomena deeply and in detail, you need methods for discovery of central themes and analysis of core concerns.

Each of these suggestions has a flip side. If you know what is being hypothesized and what you are likely to find, if you do not need to know the complexity of others' understandings, if you are testing prior theory rather than constructing new frameworks, or if you are simply describing a situation rather than deeply analyzing it, it is possible that you should *not* be working qualitatively. Perhaps the research question you are tackling with in-depth interviews would be more properly addressed with a survey. In such a case, our best advice is that you review your general purpose and ask yourself if it can be addressed better that way. Many purposes are perfectly served by survey data, and very many purposes require surveys. Important examples are research questions seeking to establish the associations among easily measured factors across a group or setting. If your goal is to establish that women in the paid workforce use neighborhood services less than do women who don't work outside the home, a survey will do it. But maybe what you really need to ask is how women in the paid workforce perceive neighborhood relations.

Or perhaps the research purpose can be addressed through the use of more straightforward techniques, such as quantitative content analysis. If you wish to know which words dominate discussions of medical treatments, rather than the meanings the participants give those words, a qualitative approach is likely to delay your answer. But maybe you want to find out more—for example, maybe you want to discover whether dominant discourses underlie those discussions.

On reflection, in either of the above cases there might be aspects of the research topic that would be best addressed through a combination of qualitative and quantitative data. As we will show in Chapter 5, such combinations fit easily with many qualitative methods.

Qualitative research is a proper response to some, but not all, research needs. We have both learned to be alert to risk in projects where the researcher is working qualitatively for the wrong reasons. These include reasons that are negative rather than positive ("I hate statistics" or "I can't use computers"). We warn against assumptions that qualitative research is more humanistic, moral/ethical, worthy, feminist, radical, or admirable. The techniques we describe in the chapters that follow are often invasive, intrusive, and morally challenging; the only good reason a researcher should consider using them is that the research problem requires them.

Our point here is not just that you need a good reason for working qualitatively because of both practical and ethical considerations but also that you need to have thought your way to this method if you are to start learning it. Good qualitative research requires purpose, skill, and concentration, and unless you recognize this and your purpose is clear and committed, the task will quickly become onerous.

How Should You Be Working Qualitatively?

What we have described as a fit between research question and method is never a simple cause-and-effect relationship. As you decide on the focus and scope of your study, the firming up of research question will indicate the best method for you to use, and your reading on methods will suggest ways in which you can focus the study. In this and later chapters, we illustrate this fit by comparing just five of the qualitative methods commonly described in textbooks: ethnography, grounded theory, phenomenology, discourse analysis, and case study method.

These five methods answer quite different sorts of questions (see Table 2.1). Ethnography offers researchers tools to answer questions such as "What is happening here?" Researchers are directed to grounded theory by questions of interaction and process: "How does one

Table 2.1	The Fit of the Question to the Method
Type of Question	Method That Might Be Appropriate
Observational questions (e.g., What are the behavioral patterns of . . . ?) and descriptive questions (e.g., What is going on here?) about values, beliefs, and practices of a cultural group	Ethnography
Process questions about changing experience over time or its stages and phases (e.g., What is the process of becoming . . . ?) or understanding questions (e.g., What are the dimensions of this experience . . . ?)	Grounded theory
Questions about meaning (e.g., What is the meaning of . . . ?) and about the core or essence of phenomena or experiences	Phenomenology
Questions about the construction of social understanding (e.g., How is social reality formed through talk or writing?) or about the structure and content of discourse (e.g., How can we see power relationships by analyzing patterns of dominance in conversation?)	Discourse analysis
Focus and illustration questions (e.g., How do these problems appear in practice? How does one person/ department/industry encapsulate the bigger picture?) or comparative questions (e.g., How different can the experience of communities be in different settings?)	Case study

become a . . . ?" Usually (but not always), phenomenology best addresses a question about meaning: "What is the experience of . . . ?" But if your focus is on people's own accounts of their world, you may need discourse analysis. And if you want to understand that world through detailed comparison of particular examples, read up on case study method. The link between question and data is obvious when one contrasts these five "classic" methods.

From Selecting a Method to Making Data

As the purpose points to the research question and the research question informs the choice of method, so the method fits the type of data to be collected. (As shown in Table 2.2, the types of data required

Table 2.2	The Fit of Method and the Type of Data
Chosen Method	*Likely Data Sources*
Ethnography	Primary: participant observation; field notes; unstructured or structured interviews or focus groups (sometimes audio or video recorded) with people in the identified site
	Secondary: documents, records; photographs; video recordings; maps, genograms, sociograms
Grounded theory	Primary: interviews (usually audio recorded); participant and nonparticipant observations; conversations recorded in diaries and field notes with sample decided by research topic
	Secondary: comparative instances; personal experience
Phenomenology	Primary: audio recorded, in-depth interviews or conversations with usually a very small number of participants; phenomenological literature
	Secondary: poetry; art; films
Discourse analysis	Primary: interviews (usually audio recorded)
	Secondary: written sources such as documents, diaries, media accounts
Case study	Selection of a small number of particular cases (instances or settings) to address a question or issue
	Primary: participant observation; field notes; unstructured or structured interviews; focus groups (sometimes audio or video recorded)
	Secondary: documents, records; focus groups

by particular methods overlap a lot.) However, selecting a method and making data are not discrete events in the research process; rather, they are aspects linked by common ways of thinking.

The distinction between a method and a way of making data is not at all rigid. For example, both focus groups and participant observation are ways of making data, appropriate for several different methods. But many researchers would consider them methods in their own right: Each has a substantial literature, setting out goals that fit these ways of making data. And case studies can be conducted by several different methods (most commonly, ethnography and grounded theory); "case study method" is regarded as special because of the questions it asks and how they are answered.

In the chapters to come, we discuss types of data, ways of handling data, and analytic techniques that belong to no particular method and are used in many. For now, our goal is to suggest the ways some data fit some methods. This does not mean that a way of making data is a method or implies a method. The fact that you are interviewing people tells an observer nothing about why, or about what you will do with those data. But the content and form of interviews and what you see in them will be different for different methods. This is because *how you think about the data* differs from method to method.

From Choosing Sources and Sorts of Data to Managing and Analyzing Data

There is a further link in this methodological chain of research pur-pose, research question, choice of method, and the type of data needed. It is hardly surprising that the ways the researcher handles, manages, explores, and analyzes data are all part of the same chain. Consider, for example, that each of the methods sketched in Table 2.2 can use unstruc-tured interviews. Most transcribe them. But the *form* of the interview and what they do with the interview transcript may be very different. Ethnographers use description to seek patterns and categories; grounded theorists use narratives and aim to create theory from them; phenome-nologists initiate conversations and develop *themes* and seek *meaning*; discourse analysts dissect interviews in detail, and case study researchers compare them with those from other cases.

Thus, the difference is not in the technique per se but in the form of data and the way data are used. Different ways of approaching the research will mean the data are handled differently and the analytic techniques are used in different ways to produce different results. For example, research-ers using very different methods may all code and, while coding, use the same technique—selecting a portion of text and assigning it to a category. But the similarity ends there. For each of them, the *way of approaching and thinking* about the data means that codes are applied in a particular way, and this results in *a particular way of linking data to ideas*.

The differences show when we ask questions such as the following: What is a category? What data are coded there? Is the collection of data for a category the end or the beginning of analysis? How do you think about the category, and how do you use categories? The answers are very different from method to method. Although different qualitative methods may utilize similar strategies, *how you think* while using particular strategies differs. And how you think will be indicated by the method selected, which in turn is affected by *why you are doing this.* And, as shown in Table 2.1, the method will have been selected to best answer the question the researcher was to think about. The purpose of the research will also, therefore, influence whether a study is more descriptive or more theoretical. This is a distinction we will explore in later chapters.

We can expand Table 2.2, adding the mode of handling data and the analysis that fits; the results are displayed in Table 2.3.

Table 2.3	The Fit of Method, Data, and Analysis Techniques
Method	*Analysis Techniques*
Ethnography	• Thick description, rereading notes, storing information, storying; case analysis • Coding, diagramming to show patterns and processes
Grounded theory	• Theoretical sensitivity, developing concepts, coding into categories, open coding for theory generation • Focused memoing, diagramming, emphasis on search for core concepts and processes
Phenomenology	• Finding and exploring themes, phenomenological reflection • Memoing and reflective writing to identify meanings
Discourse analysis	• Finely grained study (often by a set of protocols) of very detailed transcripts of spoken or written words (including pauses, turn taking, etc.) to identify ways in which social processes are constructed through conversations, deconstructing texts, and studying their patterns and contexts, often with the goal of unveiling hidden meanings or social processes
Case study	• Data from a small number of cases selected to inform a particular issue or problem are thoroughly described • Coding and summarizing data are focused by prior questions of theory to inform detailed understanding and comparison by contextual analysis of factors, events, or condition of interest

☒ METHODOLOGICAL CONGRUENCE

In explaining the purposeful nature of qualitative inquiry, we arrive at our second principle of qualitative methods. Tables 2.1 through 2.3 show the way projects acquire *methodological congruence*—that is, fit between the research problem and the question; fit between the research question and the method; and, of course, fit among the method, the data, and the way of handling data. All these components of the research process mesh to help you provide the best possible answer to that question. Thus, each method is a distinctive way of approaching the world and data.

The concept of methodological congruence does not mean that data sources or analysis methods are predetermined once the researcher has chosen a method. It isn't that easy. Nor does it mean that a researcher has no flexibility once embarked on a particular path. Rather, it indicates that projects entail congruent ways of thinking. The researcher working with phenomenology must learn to think phenomenologically if the fit of purpose, method, and data is to work well. If you are working with grounded theory, it is important that you learn how to think as a grounded theorist. The same sorts of data (e.g., field notes) will be interpreted differently by researchers using different methods, and similar data analysis techniques (e.g., coding) employed by researchers using different methods will have quite different analytic results, *because each researcher is thinking a different way.*

Qualitative research is not just a matter of performing techniques on data; rather, each qualitative method has a specific way of thinking about data and using techniques as tools to manipulate data to achieve a goal. Each component of the research process is linked to the next, and the chosen method dictates combinations of strategies to be used in particular ways to ensure consistency throughout the research process.

Seeing Congruence by Doing It

The webs of methodological congruence are most easily illustrated by an exploration of the different ways a real research topic can be handled. In what follows, we present a fictitious project concerning human attachment. If you have data from a previous study or a growing sense of your research interest, you might try applying what you read below to your approaches to that topic.

What is "human attachment"? Which literature should we look to? We have many choices—we could look at the literature on bonding between mothers and infants, at the family studies literature on family relationships, or even at the social support literature. We could extend this to the relationship literature on interaction, the literature on marriage, or the literature on mothering. We could choose a situation in which we could observe the concept as well as obtain personal accounts of attachment. From our broad topic and scan of the literature, let's choose to study public displays of attachment behavior at the arrivals and departures gates at airports. There, we could observe attachment (and detachment) behaviors as passengers depart or as they greet family and friends on arrival. We could interview individuals (the passengers themselves or their relatives and friends) about the experience of greeting and leaving. Or we may consider interviewing "experts" who have observed many passengers greeting or leaving each other (porters, staff at car rental booths, security personnel waiting to check carry-on luggage, cleaning staff, and so on).

Given this topic (human attachment) and having identified a research context, our next step is to create a research question. Different questions will lead us to particular methods, and the method in turn will help us decide details of the research design, such as who the participants will be, what the sample size should be, how data will be created and analyzed, and, most important, what type of results we will obtain.

Let us explore the topic by conducting an *armchair walkthrough*—that is, by taking a mindful stroll through the topic and visualizing what it might look like when we anticipate doing the study using each of the five major methods sketched above. The first concern of all qualitative researchers is locating the project. The setting for the research must be one in which the phenomena of interest are likely to be seen—frequently and in an intense form. Those we choose to interview must be "expert participants," with much experience with the phenomena of interest. We must deliberately and purposefully select a setting or context where we will best see what we want to study. We do not usually choose a place or a sample randomly, for we would then have to rely on luck to see what we are interested in; we do not choose the "average" experience, as then the characteristics of the phenomena are diluted and less evident.

❈ THE ARMCHAIR WALKTHROUGH

How does one prepare to do a research study? Obviously, one may approach a particular problem in several different ways, developing several different questions, so that each one could be answered using a different method and could produce a slightly different result. Which one is best, and how is that determined?

One way to reduce the uncertainty is by conducting an armchair walkthrough (Morse, 1999)—that is, by mentally going through the process. If I ask *this* research question, then I will need to use *this* particular method, seek *this* type of data and involve *these* participants, ask *these* interview questions, and handle and analyze data *this* particular way, and the results will be in *this* form. On the other hand, if I do it using *that* method, then I will ask the questions *that* way, use *that* method, and involve *those* participants; data will look *that* way, and my results will be in *that* form.

By conducting an armchair walkthrough, we are trying to predict the research process and the outcome rather than going into research blindly. In this way, without losing flexibility or the ability to change some of our choices, we can focus on the data rather than on decisions about the administration of research. Although this type of conceptualizing will not detect every problem that may be encountered, it lets us get some sense of what we may learn by using each method. It allows for some level of informed choice about which method has the potential to provide the most suitable type of results, and it is helpful as we make preliminary preparation for writing the proposal. On the other hand, we need to be aware that such decisions are not carved in stone, and we should always be prepared to reevaluate and make changes if necessary. Table 2.4 displays the thinking that came out of the armchair walkthrough for our hypothetical project, "Arrivals and Departures: Patterns of Human Attachment."

❈ AND NOW—YOUR TOPIC?

"What are you studying?" is possibly the most common question asked of the researcher, and it is also quite often the most troublesome one. Interestingly, the issue of how to find a topic is not answered in any of the textbooks on qualitative research. This is because when you select a

Table 2.4 Comparison of Five Methods to Conduct a Hypothetical Project, "Arrivals and Departures: Patterns of Human Attachment"

Method	Research Question	Setting and Participants	Strategies	Types of Results
Ethnography	What are the patterns of human attachment displayed during arrivals and departures at the airport?	Airport departure and lounge arrival; passengers, friends, relatives, experts at the scene (porters, airport personnel); about 30 to 50 informants	Unstructured, audio recorded interviews and participant observation at the gate; field notes and other documents	Description of the patterns of greeting behaviors or styles of farewell
Grounded theory	What is the process of greeting or leaving your family?	Interviews anywhere; observations at the airport gate of passengers, family members; about 30 to 50 participants	Audio recorded interviews and observations; new data as theory directs research	Theory about leaving and reunion; focus on the social–psychological processes
Phenomenology	What is the meaning of separation from or rejoining your spouse?	Interviews at interviewees' convenience; person who has traveled recently; perhaps 6 to 10 in each group	In-depth audio recorded conversations; reflection on the phenomenological literature and other sources	In-depth reflective description of the experience of separating from or rejoining your spouse
Discourse analysis	What do messages displayed and words used show about attachment and its place in social structure?	The departures lounge as a source of meaning and the words people use there	Texts—those displayed in public places and (recorded) those written or spoken by people there	Critical account of the construction of "family" or "belonging" by the setting and the conversations
Case study	How do social attachments and the ways they are expressed differ by national location?	Cases of departure settings selected to show contrasts: airports in several very different countries	Observation and interviews with officials and with passengers and their families	Vivid accounts of the different sites, compared to give pictures of social differences

Source: Morse (1994a). Reprinted in part with permission from SAGE Publications, Inc.

topic, you still have not started the research project. Selecting a topic involves also seeing the *purposiveness* of the study and the *congruence* of question, method, and what your project will be like.

Selecting the topic also involves selecting where you will go to do the study—it is not the research question you ask when you get there, or the method you use to answer it. If you find yourself telling inquirers, "I'm *doing* classroom authority/nurses' experiences of chosen childlessness/inflicting pain . . ." listen to the words you are using. The researcher does not "do" a topic as the mindless tourist "does" Belgium, checking off museums between France and Scandinavia. The *topic* of a research project is where it is *located*, where you are going to place your study—not what you will ask, how you will ask it, or how your research will provide answers when you are there. (Incidentally, the term comes from Aristotle's *Topics*, which contains common*place* arguments, from the Greek *topikos*, "of a place.")

A topic may be any researchable area, subject, or experience (such as an organization, living in a community, or having a particular learning disability), a concept (such as corporate structure, classroom learning, social support, or coping), a setting (such as a boardroom, a school, a village, or a hospital ward), a group of persons (such as teachers, doctors, or teenagers), some aspect of their everyday activities (such as teachers' talk in the lounge), or activities that are unusual (case studies of teaching students with dyslexia). Those are all research locations or areas within which research questions can be defined. A topic may combine perspectives, so a researcher may be able to make an important argument for studying one of the above topics in a particular group by asserting that the experience of that group is sufficiently different from the experiences of other groups reported in the literature.

You may have several topics burning to be researched. The challenge, then, is to walk through each, asking how questions would be framed and what sorts of research they would require and, importantly, whether you could do this, given your skills and resources. Or you may have no topic but, instead, a requirement that you get a project up and running. It seems harder to start that way, because then research presents itself as the push of duty, not the pull of interest in a topic. Wanted: a good topic!

How to Find a Topic

Any attempt to summarize reasons for selecting a topic runs the risk of appearing to present the process as orderly. It usually is not. Insights about suitable topics occur to researchers as they stand on high hills, while they are in the shower, or when they are in the library; topics demand attention when you are trying to do something else. A sort of typology is possible, however. If you are stumped, try locating your research in each of the five ways listed below. But remember to locate the project to ask how your topic would be studied and what the outcome project would be like.

You Are Already There

"Already being there" is undoubtedly the most common reason for topic selection. It is also the most exciting and the most dangerous. Because you are there, you possibly have, or may be convinced that you have, intimate knowledge of the topic as a participant. It seems you can get going fast—the preparatory work has been done. You are familiar with the setting and comfortable with the people there. But be careful: You were there for reasons other than research (such as employment or group membership or shared experience). These required a different type of preparatory work for you to become a good participant observer or impartial interviewer in the setting. Being a researcher there may perhaps provide you with the opportunity to contribute new knowledge to an area you care about. And so you may, but you will have to ensure that your contribution represents valued research results and not merely what you wanted to prove or get done as a participant. If these ends are the same, you will have to be especially careful to establish that they were the same and that your study is rigorous. Being there means you already feel you know what matters—or who is a problem—the importance of particular people (including you), and the ways they are seen. How do you plan to deal with these preconceptions?

There Is a Gap in the Literature

Topics amenable to qualitative inquiry have often been relatively ignored in the literature. Of course, this may be because they are inaccessible to researchers or, worse, simply uninteresting. The fact that nobody has studied a particular topic is not a good reason for taking it up. On the other hand, such topics may be neglected because they are areas in need of qualitative inquiry, areas where framing clear questions is not easy, areas that are difficult to access, or areas obscured by received interpretations.

Of course, this is a double-edged sword. If a topic has not been investigated, you will have an explorer's challenge of discovering a new place, mapping the area, displaying it to an admiring world, maybe even getting your name on it. Classic qualitative research projects have opened up whole areas of investigation in this way. With the second wave of feminism, qualitative studies returned to topics in the hitherto taken-for-granted social lives of women, opening up research areas addressing motherhood, social support networks, and even housework.

However, undiscovered places are hard to sell. This is particularly important if you are a student applying for funding for research expenses. Research into topics that are "fashionable"—that is, topics that a number of other researchers are also investigating (or have investigated)—is generally easier to get funded, but there is usually a considerable amount of literature on those topics in the library already.

Another Way of Looking Is Needed

You might suspect that the literature is poorly focused or that there is something wrong, invalid, or inaccurate about the presentation and interpretation of the topic. Perhaps the received knowledge does not fit with the evidence, or results of the studies reported in the literature have been presented within the context of a theory that is invalid or inappropriate. It is time to take a fresh look at the phenomenon and reexamine the theory from within, taking into consideration the perceptions of those being studied. In recent decades, women's studies and studies of health and illness exemplify this approach, as qualitative studies challenged the functionalist paradigm, reopening questions of power and conflict.

What's Going on Here?

Qualitative methods are frequently used to discover the answers to quite pragmatic questions, such as "What is going on here?" or "How are we doing with this innovation?" Evaluation studies are of this type: The researchers are trying to understand and describe efficiently the processes or structures of particular phenomena. Much action research sets out to find out "what is going on here"—the topic is "here," this community, this fight, this local government organization, and so on.

Many such studies produce reports that are more descriptive than theoretical. Their goal is to do a really good job of describing what's going on, giving vivid illustrations so the problem or situation can be clearly seen by the reader. Thus, a researcher evaluating an educational innovation is not likely to divert to reflections on the meanings of education or try to create a new theory about the relation of teacher and pupil. The researcher's task is to do a good job of observing and reporting the evaluation and its effects. Case study method is often used in such studies to highlight different responses or important common experiences.

Supplementing Quantitative Inquiry

The topic may be an area where there is considerable knowledge of events or patterns from quantitative research, or where quantitative work needs prior backgrounding. The qualitative project may form the groundwork for subsequent quantitative inquiry or be used to supplement quantitative inquiry, or quantitative inquiry may be used to illustrate qualitative inquiry. The end result of a qualitative project may be insight into a problem, a rich description, a hypothesis, a theory to be tested further in quantitative research, or a qualitatively derived theory that is ready to use. You should consider the purpose of the qualitative project before commencing the project and selecting the method.

Now, Consider the Research Context

Once you have a topic—and maybe even a research question—there are many other considerations for selecting a method, and this section is intended to make you street-smart before you make your choice. While your choice comes from what you want to be the end results, constraints and benefits arise during the course of doing the research.

Considering What You Want to Know

First and foremost, think about the nature of your study. Do you want to describe what is there, exactly as it is presented, or to reveal what is there but not normally noticed? Or do you want to stand back and describe structures that are larger than normally viewed? Such *descriptive research* has its own set of standards, own methods, own data collection strategies, and own ways of ensuring validity and reliability. Think of it as looking at life, or slices of life, and recording as accurately as possible what is going on. Descriptive methods include ethnography, ethology, ethnology, video ethnography, and historical methods. They record: They may use photographs, videos, recorded dialogue, and documents such as maps, sociograms, and kinship charts. They document and evaluate. Because they have data in a form that can be verified, checked and rechecked, certain procedures for determining the rigor of the study are important—these often include interrater reliability checks. Data have been recorded in a permanent form (videos, recorded conversations, documents) that can be rechecked, reviewed, reexamined, and reanalyzed, or the researcher can return to the field and reexamine the evidence.

Or do you need to use more *interpretive methods*, methods that provide access to more subjective phenomena, or "softer" data—experience, perception, opinions, values, meanings, beliefs, dreams, things that are not directly accessible or sometimes not even evident on the surface? Access may be helped by the use of a theoretical perspective (for instance, feminist theory ties together observations about gender imbalances). Phenomenology and hermeneutics are examples of interpretive methods. For more on interpretive methods, see Smith, Flowers, and Larkin (2009) and Thorne (2008).

Or would you be best served by methods that use both description and interpretation? Grounded theory is in this category, commencing inquiry with descriptive method to identify the process but using interpretive methods later in the process to identify the core variables (Strauss, 1987) or the basic social process (Glaser, 1978), the theme that ties the process together and makes sense of the data. Most ethnographic methods both describe and interpret.

Considering What You Are Studying

Now, there are constraints depending on what you are planning to study. Is the phenomenon concrete, tangible, stable—will it always be there for you to see and photograph and touch? Or is it hidden, shadowed, internal experience? Is it a moving target? Do you have just one shot at seeing it? Is it unique, or will it reoccur? Is it patterned? Does it change over time or disappear in certain conditions? In other words, how will you see/record whatever you are studying? These questions will inform your research design. Will you have direct access to the people you want to understand or have to rely on others' observations of the phenomenon you are researching? Such "shadowed data" (Morse, 2001) will require a different design. For instance, when studying a bereaved family, we may interview other family members about the behaviors of the most bereft member. Another "indirect" method may be to use modeling (for instance, if lay births cannot be observed, you might ask the lay midwife to show you how she positions the laboring women and collect information that way).

Considering the Setting

Privacy legislation and the right of participants must always be considered when accessing populations. Is the setting in which you want to conduct your study private or public? Obviously, a person's home is private and you may not enter without permission or begin your study without consent. But privacy has other levels. Institutions, such as hospitals or schools, are protected environments, and many levels of permission are necessary before a researcher may enter. We consider ethics issues and processes in detail in Chapter 12.

Considering What You Want to Do

Researchers usually have a goal or agenda for conducting their research—and some of these reasons for doing a project are less problematic than others.

The best reason for doing a project may be "because it is fascinating" in itself. You can't stop thinking about, reading about, and talking about the topic. This is a great start because your fascination provides that impetus to keep you motivated through the months ahead, and gives you determination to complete your project when the going gets tough and the research tasks a little arduous.

Perhaps the most common reason for doing a project, however, is the researcher's personal experience. Perhaps they have recently divorced, experienced the death of a parent, or have some professional specialty and are convinced that nobody understands. Suddenly, doing a qualitative study seems to be a way to communicate their experience. One method—autoethnography—is designed for such reflection. Our advice is that qualitative research is not usually an effective way to work through your problems.

A third reason is perhaps the most risky—the researcher has an "axe to grind." You have noticed a problem at work or an injustice that needs to be explored—a fired coworker or some unfortunate caregiving experience or teaching incident. Investigating such issues seems a way to right the world. An inexperienced student may be accepted quickly in groups tackling such political issues. But this does not promise a good research design. As for all the examples above, the message is that you must be clear about why you are interested and want to tackle the topic you have selected, and how this will impact the research.

Considering Issues in Finding Participants

There are obvious constraints on finding and approaching participants for any research, and there are considerable specific constraints if your research is qualitative.

At the beginning of your project, you ask who you need to talk to for this project, and whether it will be possible. Whether it will be ethical is the next question (see below). Often, the answer to both is negative. Obviously, you cannot explore infant pain by interviewing the preverbal. Would it do to conduct behavioral coding and analyze the nature and patterns of crying? You cannot interview the elderly with advanced Alzheimer's disease, but is the alternative of some type of observational research satisfactory? Access to potential participants may be blocked, for instance in trauma care, because care is the first priority. In the case of family violence, the actual incident cannot be observed, so you must use retrospective data—interviews from participants about the experience.

Considering Ethical Constraints

At the earliest stage, the researcher must consider the ethical implications of what their topic and method seem to require. We consider these issues in detail in Chapter 12 when we return to the process of beginning your project.

Almost all the methods discussed above ensure invasion of privacy. Some seriously threaten a participant's rights. From the beginning of your project, these issues should be foremost in your concerns. Sensitivity about context and the participants' expectations is a necessary condition for good research design. Ethical as well as practical considerations must be explored. If you are planning to do research with vulnerable populations (such as groups in schools, prisons, hospitals, or some cultural groups), you must obtain special permission at the institutional level as well as from the guardian or parent, care provider, and individual. But "ordinary people" also require full protection of their privacy. Once you have obtained access, you must have in place strategies to protect the partici-pants' identities. Consider early who will have access to the raw data. How will it be stored? How will identities of participants or places be protected? Who will have access to the final report? And who will need to review it or approve it prior to publication?

Working with the appropriate bodies is essential to ensure acceptable practices. Attention to the impact of the proposed research, and to chang-ing conditions, allows researchers to negotiate access and allows ethics bodies to ensure that the access is appropriate. For instance, Morse was denied access for recording trauma care (audio and video) in the mid-1990s in Canada but was permitted access in the United States, where such video recording is a routine part of quality assurance. Video files were secured until consents were obtained, and if consent was not obtained the recording was destroyed. Once the Canadian ethics review committee considered how such procedures worked, on reapplication, they permitted the project to proceed.

From Topic to Researchable Question: Focusing Qualitative Inquiry

Deciding on a topic locates your research; this is where you are researching. Framing a qualitative question is harder because it requires that you think about what needs to be asked and of whom in this research location, as well as what you can practically and ethically ask and reason-ably expect to have answered given your resources and skills. A research question is a starting point only if it is researchable.

One of the most difficult tasks for the beginning researcher is to think qualitatively before the research begins. A researchable qualitative ques-tion is not the most obvious outcome of reflecting on a topic. The big first questions are as follows:

〰️ *What* needs to be asked?

〰️ *How* should it be asked? What data are required, and where will the researcher have to go to find answers to these questions?

〰️ *Can* it be asked? What access to the setting is necessary and what protection of the informants? What sort of a researcher or research stance is needed?

WHAT CAN YOU AIM FOR?

By now it should be clear that qualitative researchers are aiming for an outcome that is more than just a good story. It's the fit of method, data, and analysis that makes the difference between journalism and qualitative research. Good journalism and good qualitative research share goals of understanding people's situations, thoroughly researching and vividly illustrating what's found. But all qualitative methods aim for abstraction and analysis, a "higher" level of reporting that is not *only* description. (Robert Park, a founder of the Chicago School of Sociology and a journalist by training, called sociology "the Big News.")

And it will be a particular sort of analysis. In all the examples given above, the outcome is something *new*—a better, fuller account of the data or a discovery *from the data.* This goal explains much in the techniques for handling data throughout this book. Qualitative coding, for example, aims to retain the detail of the data so it can be explored and rethought. The researcher resists, or delays, reducing that detail to numbers, since doing so would prevent further discovery. Unlike much (though not all) quantitative research, the qualitative project is unlikely to be testing existing theories. Much more likely is that a new theory or a new explanation of the phenomenon studied will be created from the data.

These are not unreachable goals. Discovered theories may be very small and local. In Chapter 8, we discuss the task of abstraction and the ways it is done. Meanwhile, as you work toward a topic, ask what you could aim for. What would be a good outcome of this study? What would be good enough, and what would be excellent? (For discussion of possible study outcomes, see Richards, 2009, Chapter 7.)

SUMMARY

We see the principles we have discussed in this chapter—the purposiveness of qualitative inquiry and methodological congruence—as the hallmarks of good qualitative research. They mean that a project's goals and its methods cannot be considered separately or severed from the strategies of a research design. A research strategy is only a *tool,* and how one uses a tool depends on the purpose of inquiry, the method used, and the type of data. This is important: One may learn a strategy, but *the way one uses it depends on the method.*

In this chapter, we have emphasized the wholeness of methods—the fit of question, data, and analysis. In Chapter 3, we address the flip side of this wholeness: Although qualitative methods are congruent, they are not always complete, and they do not always fully direct each stage of the project. We compare the same five methods discussed above in terms of completeness, showing how some convey full instructions for the entire project whereas others leave the researcher to choose a methodological path.

❧ RE/OURCE/

Read different types of qualitative research studies to get a feel for the differing results.

Brizuela, D., Stewart, J. P., Carrillo, R. G., & Garbey, J. (2000). *Acts of inquiry and qualitative research.* Cambridge, MA: Harvard Educational Review.

Denzin, N. K., & Lincoln, Y. S. (Eds.). (2011). *The SAGE handbook of qualitative research* (4th ed.). Thousand Oaks, CA: Sage.

Ezzy, D., Liamputtong, P., & Hollis, D. B. (2005). *Qualitative research methods.* Oxford, UK: Oxford University Press.

Maxwell, J. A. (1998). Designing a qualitative study. In L. Bickman & D. J. Rog (Eds.), *Handbook of applied social research methods* (pp. 69–100). Thousand Oaks, CA: Sage.

Morse, J. M., & Field, P. A. (1995). *Qualitative research methods for health*

professionals (2nd ed.). Thousand Oaks, CA: Sage.

Richards, L. (2009). *Handling qualitative data: A practical guide* (2nd ed.). London: Sage.

Seale, C., Gobo, G., Gubrium, J., & Silverman, D. (Eds.). (2006). *Qualitative research practice.* London: Sage.

Wertz, F. J., Charmaz, K., McMullen, L. M., Josselson, R., Anderson, R., & McSpadden, E. (2011). *Five ways of doing qualitative analysis: Phenomenological psychology, grounded theory, discourse analysis, narrative research, and intuitive inquiry.* New York: Guilford.

Qualitative Research by Discipline

Not surprisingly, methods differ between disciplines. The following are suggested readings in different areas.

Daymon, C., Holloway, I., & Daymon, C. (2002). *Qualitative research methods*

and public relations and marketing communications. London: Routledge.

Eisner, E. W., & Peshkin, A. (Eds.). (1998). *Qualitative inquiry in education: The continuing debate.* New York: Teachers College Press.

Frost, N. (2011). *Qualitative research methods in psychology: Combining core approaches.* Berkshire, England: Open University Press.

Gilgun, J. F., & Sussman, M. B. (Eds.). (1996). *The methods and methodologies of qualitative family research.* New York: Haworth.

Golding, C. (2002). *Grounded theory: A practical guide for management, business, and market researchers.* Thousand Oaks, CA: Sage.

Holloway, I. (2005). *Qualitative research in health care.* Oxford, UK: Blackwell Science.

Latimer, J. (Ed.). (2003). *Advanced qualitative research for nursing.* Oxford, UK: Blackwell.

Mariampolski, H. (2001). *Qualitative market research: A comprehensive guide.* Thousand Oaks, CA: Sage.

Merriman, N. B. (1997). *Qualitative research and case study applications in education.* Toronto: John Wiley.

Munhall, P. L. (2012). *Nursing research: A qualitative perspective* (5th ed.). Boston: Jones & Bartlett.

Padgett, D. (2008). *Qualitative methods in social work research* (2nd ed.). Thousand Oaks, CA: Sage.

Patton, M. Q. (2002). *Qualitative research and evaluation methods* (3rd ed.). Thousand Oaks, CA: Sage.

Seale, C., Silverman, D., Gubrium, J., & Gobo, G. (Eds.). (2007). *Qualitative research practice.* London: Sage.

Shaw, I. S., & Gould, N. (2001). *Qualitative research and social work.* Thousand Oaks, CA: Sage.

Ulin, P. R., Robinson, E. T., & Tolley, E. E. (2005). *Qualitative methods in public health: A field guide for applied research.* San Francisco: Jossey-Bass.

Journals

Ethnography Field Methods Forum: Qualitative Social Research (http://qualitative-research.net/fqs/fqs-eng.html)

International Journal of Qualitative Methods (http://ejournals.library.ualberta.ca/index.php/IJQM/index)

International Journal of Qualitative Studies in Education

International Journal of Qualitative Studies on Health & Well-Being

Journal of Contemporary Ethnography

Qualitative Health Research

Qualitative Inquiry

Qualitative Report (http://www.nova.edu/ssss/QR/)

Qualitative Research (http://qrj.sagepub.com/)

Qualitative Research Journal (http://www.informit.com.au/products/ProductDetails.aspx?id=L_QRJ&container=qualitative-research-journal-link)

3

Choosing a Method

To those new to qualitative inquiry, the choice of research methods can appear overwhelming. But it has to be made, since the key to doing qualitative research is selecting the "best" method to answer your research question. How can you prepare to understand the choice and select the best?

It helps to start with commonalities. These are all called "qualitative" methods, and they do have a lot in common. All qualitative research seeks understanding of data that are complex and can be approached only in context. The methods we sketch in this book differ widely in how they do this and what the results look like, but all aim at constructing a new understanding using analytic processes that do justice to the data.

Some analytic strategies may appear common to several methods, and the ways they are applied within each method make those methods different from one another. The key to their differences is in the *way the researcher thinks about the data* and subsequently *conceptualizes*— that is, "thinks up" from data. In later chapters, we address some of the generic processes of coding, categorizing, and theme-ing and reintroduce the strategies that make methods distinct from one another. But here, our focus is on differences and choice.

The best method for your project will be the one that best helps you think about your data and work with data in the way best suited to your research goals. It may not be the one with the most unpronounceable name or the most scholarly aura. It is also unlikely to be the one your friend is using or the one you attended a workshop about or happen to have a book on or, as mentioned in the previous chapter, the method taught in your school. Rather, the best method is the one that promises to address *your* sort of research question, and to provide the results *your* project requires, as efficiently, effectively, and "on target" as possible. It will be the method that best enables you to access the slice of life you need to study, and best report and reveal it to others. It is most likely to provide you with a new and exciting understanding of your topic—and might even earn you a degree, a publication, a chance to assist people in the studied situation, or another desired outcome.

In this chapter we will briefly sketch the five methods introduced in the previous chapter, according to the sorts of questions they ask, how they are asked, and what the outcomes look like. This overview is to offer you a map of methods so you may start thinking about matching your topic with a method. In the next sections we will address how to use research strategies and discuss how these strategies are used in each of the most commonly used methods.

※ DESCRIPTION AND INTERPRETATION

To the new researcher, many of these methods appear similar or overlapping. Two methods may seem the same because they have certain procedures in common (such as a type of coding) or share some features with other methods (such as categorizing or "theme-ing"). Yet each method has an underlying logic that provides a distinct and different perspective on reality, and each method has its own particular approach to the strategies involved. While methods may share some of these strategies (or techniques), their analytic perspective gives each a unique and distinct way of *thinking about the data and reflecting on these data*.

How to distinguish them? To help you find your way with this map of various methods, we start with the distinction made in our previous chapter between description and interpretation. All methods describe and interpret, but they vary in the emphases they put on these tasks. The differences in research goals drive the emphases on description and interpretation, resulting in very different outcomes.

The more *descriptive methods* are those whose primary goal is to describe a situation or phenomenon vividly and in detail, to give a clear picture of "what is going on." They are used when the researcher aims to reveal what is there, or link processes. The results may clarify problem situations, highlight differences in lifestyles, or make our lives richer by expanding our horizons or increasing our awareness of what we already know. Descriptive methods are used extensively to evaluate a program or organization, or to determine, detect, or monitor change. They are varied and often combined—and few stop at description.

The traditional descriptive method is ethnography. Originating in anthropology, its central approach to studying reality is a focus on the cultural context of behavior. Ethnography always uses the sometimes long-term and demanding technique of participant observation, often treated as a method in itself. Now used across disciplines, ethnography takes many forms, most interpretive and many aiming at critical reflection. Action research is often done by ethnographic techniques, and the researcher aims not just to describe but to involve participants in rigorous research and, through it, to change the situation over time.

Is any qualitative research entirely descriptive? Of the methods we compare in this chapter, the answer is no. For example, case study method, like ethnography, aims at very good description (often using ethnographic techniques). But any research starts with a goal, and for case studies, there is a prior reason why these cases were selected. So the project design should reach beyond description, usually to comparison of cases and elucidation of the issue or problem *of which they are cases.*

Across disciplines, possibly the most common source of descriptive research is the sometimes short-term, rapid technique of conducting focus groups. Like participant observation, it is often treated as a method in itself and has its own considerable literature. Focus groups provide a way of gathering sometimes complex data rapidly (which we explore in Chapter 6). Those data may be quickly and descriptively reported, as, for example, in short-term market research. (If the focus groups are conducted to gauge reactions to a new product label, the client wants a description of those reactions and will not be pleased by a subtle analysis of the ideological meanings of product labeling.) But focus groups are used in many methods for many different research purposes, some aimed at describing and others theorizing.

Most qualitative research is done with more *interpretive methods* that move "up" from descriptions to theories about processes and experiences discovered. These are for projects aiming to see both "what is going on" and also what it *means,* or how it could be *explained.* Some may use theory from previous studies or literature to guide the perspective, and some construct or contribute new "midrange" theory as an explanatory tool, aiming for insights that would not otherwise be accessible or available if they stopped at description. In very different ways, such a combination of description and interpretation is offered by grounded theory and discourse analysis. Studies using either may draw on existing higher-level theory or may use their own data to discover and build new theory.

Some methods, however, are primarily interpretive. They place much less emphasis on description; rather, they focus on interpretations of the discovered world, what is experienced by those studied, and how their perceptions might be understood. Phenomenology is the classic example, often regarded as a philosophical perspective as well as a social research method. It is used in many disciplines and takes very many forms. Phenomenological research may produce studies full of feeling, reflectively describing meaning, emotions, and experience, pulling and using similar emotional responses from the reader. Their role is to identify the essence of the phenomenon and perhaps to construct and explore concepts. But note, there is description behind these outcomes.

Now, consult your research goal. It will indicate the relative need for description and interpretation. When researchers are thinking about their topic, they usually decide at what level of analysis the main phenomenon of interest *needs* to be accessed. They will usually also have a practical or political agenda, which often is the reason they are doing the research. Thus, in a study to improve patient care, an action research approach might be used to expose problems, an evaluation framework to report performance, and a phenomenological approach to explore the patients' experiences. Each purpose has suggested a different method, which will focus and frame the research differently. Each of these studies may use some form of ethnography, but different data will be gathered and handled differently in the analysis. For instance, what the researcher ignores as "irrelevant" or attends to as pertinent, significant, and interesting differs according to the focus of the research question. And, of course, while all the ethnographies in these examples may be based on the same broad assumptions about culture, they will be differently led by theories and literature used to inform the research, and by the researcher's perspective and stance. These differences within and among methods give each method—and every study—a unique purpose or function and lead to different types of results.

❧ STARTING SIMPLE

We offer this map of methods to assist you in starting out toward your own project with one method. Once you can recognize each method's approach and way of looking, and the sort of study it can produce, you will be able to locate the approach most appropriate to ask and answer your question and most likely to provide the needed outcome. Once familiar with and able to recognize the different kinds of qualitative research, you will be able to learn more about the appropriate method and, from there, to start designing your project. Locating your project in one method, you can get to know it well and start thinking that way. Remember, all methods have integrity—there is a fit of question, data, and analysis. So in selecting the method that best enables you to achieve your goals and best answers your research question, it is wise to understand the method as a whole. As you read texts and explore real examples of studies using this method, you will discover what your selected method does to data.

Why just one method? Experienced researchers often mix and match approaches from many methods, even melding them into a new research approach. But for a new researcher, it is too easy to create methodological messes, violate assumptions, and create a weakened design and fragmented study that will not answer the question or be publishable. If you are just starting out, we strongly advise that you find the appropriate method for your project and work within it, rather than taking techniques from several.

For novice researchers, we also advise against starting in what is often termed mixed- or multiple-methods design, where studies are built from a combination of segments conducted by different methods. Such designs can be most useful when a single method does not adequately answer the question but may be answered by combining the results of more than one data set in the analysis of one project. But method combinations require very careful research design, and the workload amounts to two (or more!) studies. We strongly recommend, for your first project, that you start simple and small.

The same advice applies to research designs that combine a number of studies on a topic (sometimes termed *metasynthesis*). Here, the researcher "pools" the results from the findings of many studies to compare and contrast, to combine or synthesize the concepts and theory to produce results of great scope or certainty. By examining the similarities and differences, by "smoothing" or merging them into a "mega model," the findings may move the area forward more quickly than would conducting yet another context-bound study. But the task of bringing multiple studies together can be daunting. (Studies combining multiple projects in these ways are discussed in Chapter 4.)

☖ FIVE METHOD*

In the following sections, we sketch each of the five very different qualitative methods already introduced. Each is explored under five headings. What sorts of questions are asked? What is the researcher's stance? What sorts of data are needed? What do the results look like? And, finally, what are some of the different approaches to working in this method?

These sketches aim to help you identify relevant methods to explore for your own work, to find a fit of your question with a method. When that fit is found, follow the suggested reading to get a fuller understanding of the method and its varieties, and to make an informed choice about the approach. A resources section ends each method's sketch, and more resources at the end of the chapter will direct you into the literature. Your goal is to assess methods for their usefulness to your research and, within those methods, assess approaches. Keep assessing, even when the claims for a method or approach are apparently authoritative (or dogmatic)—and especially then.

We return in Chapter 9 to these five methods, to suggest how it would feel to work in each, their different ways of making data, and different analysis strategies.

☖ ETHNOGRAPHY

What Sorts of Questions Are Asked?

Ethnography traditionally involved the researcher, usually an anthropologist, traveling to some "primitive" tribe and asking how they lived and what their culture was like. The goal would be to live with them for several years, thereby learning (and recording) their language and documenting their culture—their kinship system, work patterns, ways of life, beliefs and values—as comprehensively as possible. It is often termed *field research* because the goal is for the researcher to enter the "field" of the setting to be studied and ask what is going on there.

Since that time, the role and function of ethnography has changed considerably: Ethnography is now used far more widely and usually topic focused. Researchers are now using ethnographic methods to explore smaller *subcultural* units, such as institutions—in particular closed institutions (e.g., prisons, hospitals, and nursing homes)—and to study loosely connected groups of people (e.g., hockey teams or motorcycle gangs), those with particular occupations (e.g., university professors or politicians), and persons with particular characteristics, such as a shared difficulty or illness (e.g., earthquake victims or stroke patients).

An ethnographer may go into a setting with a particular research question or with the more open goal of describing the culture. Davis (1983, 1986/1992), for instance, describes the meaning menopause holds for women of Grey Rock Harbour, "taking into account both the collective and idiosyncratic elements of village life which help explicate the emic perspective of menopause. These include (1) the semantics of menopause, (2) lay semantics and (3) local institutions and the moral order" (Davis, 1986/1992, p. 151). Cassell (1987/1992) used ethnographic methods to explore the work of surgeons, as well as the ethos and "the set of traits distinctive of that profession." She also examined some of "the dynamics and the personal cost and benefits of maintaining the ethos and the set of traits" (pp. 170–171).

The Researcher's Stance

The ethnographer is always a "participant observer." This is a role with its own literature and its own challenges. If you are considering working with ethnography, you must understand the requirements for good participant observation. A useful early indication of the challenge is to try seriously observing, and recording your observations, in a situation where you want to be a genuine participant (Richards, 2009, pp. 40–42).

How much will you expect to participate, and what will be the challenges? Participant observation can vary from a situation in which the researcher is a *complete observer,* outside looking in, to one in which the researcher is a *complete participant,* fully participating in all that is observed. More common are the situations between, where the researcher is *mainly participant* or *mainly observer.* It is important to be "up front" about these roles—especially if you are entering a situation (such as a community or family setting or work environment) in which you could well be expected to assist. What you are told and allowed to see will be affected by the degree of trust and acceptance you achieve, thus affecting the quality of the data and the study itself. Establishing good relationships takes time, so you cannot expect excellent data to be gathered immediately. Critical to the success of participant observation is the relationship between those observed and the researcher. As the field experience is being negotiated, the researcher must reflect on and negotiate their role with the group whilst obtaining permissions and consents.

Traditionally, ethnographic research explores phenomena within cultural contexts from the *emic* perspective—that is, from the perspective of the members of the cultural groups involved. The perspective used in data analysis is from the participants themselves. Compare this with the *etic* perspective, or the perspective of the outsider/researcher, which is usually the perspective used in quantitative inquiry. But there is always a tension between these perspectives. Because cultural assumptions, beliefs, and behaviors are embedded within a cultural group, they are not always evident to those who are a part of the group. If a researcher shares the participants' culture (so can take the *emic*, or insider, perspective), they will find it difficult to "see" the beliefs, values, practices, and behaviors embedded in everyday life. The research will be easier, and the differences more evident, if the researcher is an outsider to both of the cultures being compared and contrasted.

Ethnography is always conducted in the natural setting, or the *field*, so that the researcher can study the lives of members of the cultural group directly, in their everyday setting. Ethnographers work to become participants, as integrated as possible into the lives of the people they are studying. Recall that the researcher's stance is outside the group being studied, yet the data collection procedures are designed to elicit emic data (i.e., data reflecting the "native" point of view). The researcher is a "student" of the group under study, learning and being taught by, yet not truly one of the group—a role Agar (1996) termed a "professional stranger."

An ethnography usually has distinct *stages* and *phases*, during which different types of data are collected and the researcher's effectiveness as an analyst varies (Morse & Field, 1995, pp. 71–73). The *first phase* is "getting in," during which the researcher is a stranger to the setting and the primary task is *negotiating entry*, finding a role and fitting in. The researcher feels awkward and self-conscious. Wax (1971) notes that one should not become an ethnographer unless one can tolerate feeling "out of place" and "making a fool of one's self" (p. 370). Usually, during this phase the researcher does not understand the setting or the participants, so interpretation is premature. Thus, data making at this stage should focus on relatively concrete tasks, such as making maps of the setting or becoming acquainted with who's who in the community under study. The researcher keeps a diary of initial impressions and uses field notes to record observations.

During the *second phase,* the researcher becomes better acquainted with the routines in the setting, and the participants become more comfortable with the researcher. Data making now consists of nonparticipant observations and informal conversations. Key informants are identified, and initial participants are selected and perhaps interviewed. With acceptance into the setting come initial analytic hunches about the situation studied.

Trust has developed between the participants and the researcher by the *third phase,* which is marked by *cooperation and acceptance.* Data making is most productive in this phase. The researcher now understands what is happening in the setting, and the data become more focused; the researcher also uses the data to verify hunches and to develop theoretical formulations.

At the end of the third phase, the researcher may feel relaxed and integrated into the setting, to the extent of becoming acculturated. This may introduce a problem if they identify more with the cultural norms of the group than with their own research agenda, losing objectivity in conducting observations and analysis. The *fourth phase* is, therefore, one of *withdrawal.* The research focus at this stage is primarily on data analysis, with any further data collection focused on gathering data to resolve ambiguities, fill in thin areas, and verify previous data. The task of the *last phase* is analysis; the research is completed and the ethnography written.

Awareness of self during data collection is vital. Crucial to good ethnography is the researcher's awareness of his or her own cultural values, beliefs, and biases and the way they influence what data are collected. The researcher must also be aware of roles and relationships with others in the field, what data are collected, and why, and must record all these self-observations in a research diary. A good research diary can have a profound impact on how the researcher moves through the process of making sense of the data, affecting whether they see the obvious and the less obvious. Relationships established between the researcher and those in the field, the development of trust, and the degree of the researcher's inclusion as a member of the group—all these factors have some influence on the type and quality of data that are collected and available for analysis.

What Sorts of Data Are Needed?

Ethnography provides many strategies for obtaining data that will enable the researcher to describe cultural norms, perspectives, characteristics, behavior, and patterns. But within this variety, the primary data of ethnographic studies will always be *field notes* and other documentary or visual records of what is seen and experienced or learned by observation or through conversation. Good field researchers take very thorough and detailed field notes and also keep a diary, recording not only the detail of what is discovered but also the researcher's experience and responses.

Data are not usually of a single type. The research purpose and question dictate the types and forms of data collected. *Observational data* (recorded as field notes or in the form of photographs, video recordings, and so forth) may be supplemented by *interviews* (recorded as field notes or audio recorded and transcribed), the researcher's ongoing theoretical notes in a *diary*, plus historical records or other documentary data that may be relevant. In turn, these data may take various forms. For instance, interviews may be unstructured, semistructured, or structured; they may include questionnaires, surveys, or special techniques such as sentence frames and card sorts to elicit particular kinds of responses that fall within the parameters of whatever is being studied. Quantitative data may also be included.

When an ethnographic researcher is gathering data, the fact that culture is shared among all group members theoretically means that any member of the group may serve as a participant in the study. However, the researcher must consider the characteristics of *good informants* (i.e., having the ability to reflect on and describe the culture, being articulate and patient) and the type of data required. Participants who work most closely with and interpret the culture for the researcher are known as *key informants*. They serve to inform and instruct the researcher about the culture, although the researcher compiles these data and may verify them with data from other participants. During data collection and analysis, the researcher must consistently reflect on the results in the context of the cultural values, beliefs, and behaviors of the group being studied.

Where ethnography is used in more limited settings, in organizations or social groups where much of the information sought is documented, the ethnographer seeks and sorts this information, learning from the differences, for example, between formal accounts of institutional rules and observation of what in fact goes on.

What Do the Results Look Like?

The main goal of most ethnographic research is what has been classically termed *thick description* (Geertz, 1973): an account that describes richly and in detail all features of the culture.

Cognitive ethnography (Spradley, 1979) may include presenting data as *taxonomies* or *classification systems,* whose function is to identify objects that are culturally significant, but implicit in the culture, and to display the relationships among them, thus creating a framework for unique insights into the culture. A taxonomy permits the researcher to display classes of objects according to common characteristics as well as the sub-categories of related objects within a particular class, but it does not account for processes.

Ethnography, perhaps more than any of the other methods sketched here, has undergone major changes in recent years. You will find that the literature contains a lively debate about the rival goals of description and theorizing. The results may look like theoretical monographs or like documentary films and articles on some aspect of daily life (e.g., eating, dance, health beliefs), special circumstances (e.g., childbirth, funeral ceremonies), or representation (e.g., use of media such as art, drama, dance).

Different Approaches Within Ethnography

Ethnography may take several forms, depending on the type of research question, its scope, and the researcher's perspective or location.

Focused ethnography is a term created to deal with departures from the traditional image of ethnography. "Only long-term field studies, it seems, epitomise what may rightly be called ethnography. With this ideal derived from anthropology, many of the ethnographies done in sociology and other fields frequently appear to fall short or to be 'deficient'" (Knoblauch, 2005). It recognizes the increasing trend for ethnography to be used where, as Muecke (1994) notes, the topic is specific and may be identified before the researcher commences the study. Focused ethnography might be conducted with a subcultural group rather than with a cultural group completely different from that of the researcher. It may also be used to study *institutions,* focusing on how the lives of those in institutions are "embedded in social relations, both those of ruling and economy" (Smith, 2005, p. 31). For example, Gubrium (1975) studied a nursing home, and Germain (1979) studied a cancer ward. Ethnographic studies may focus on groups of participants who share some feature or features, such as a particular disability. In such studies, participants may not know one another, but the researcher focuses on their common behaviors and experiences resulting from their shared features, such as being treated the same way by care providers. This enables the researcher to apply the assumptions from a shared culture. In focused ethnography, data making may include only some of the strategies that define ethnography. For instance, fieldwork may be less important than interviews.

Autoethnography is, as the name suggests, ethnography of the researcher's own experience. Rather than study "others," these writers analyze personal narratives in the light of sociological literature (see Ellis & Bochner, 1996, 2000). The field raises complex questions of the researcher's role and reflexivity. Autoethnography uses the methods of ethnography, but with very different purposes and results. The researcher records and writes narrative, reflects and makes field notes, and may use a diary and other forms of documentation to refresh their recollection of the event and add details. But the researcher is also the subject, and the purpose is usually to research experiences they consider unique, important, and unforgettable. They are usually "milestone" events that have significance for their own lives—uncommon, extraordinary events. Auto-ethnographers sometimes feel that the sharing of and reflections on their own experiences will somehow assist others, make them feel less alone or in the same despair they felt, or will support and encourage them. Sharing their experiences will enable others to seek therapy, to persevere, or at least to understand what has happened to them and that they are not alone.

Critical ethnography emerged, with broader "critical theory," in the 1960s and '70s, challenging established social values and power relations. Feminist and postmodern approaches insisted on "ethical responsibility to address processes of unfairness or injustice within a particular *lived domain*" (Madison, 2005, p. 5). Thomas (1993) gives a wide definition: "Critical ethnographers describe, analyze, and open to scrutiny otherwise hidden agendas, power centers, and assumptions that inhibit, repress, and constrain. Critical scholarship requires that commonsense assumptions be questioned" (pp. 2–3). Critical ethnography assumes that the researcher cannot be value-free and should direct efforts toward positive social change (Carspecken, 1996, p. 3). Criticism of fieldwork conducted mainly by male anthropologists was extended to the ethnographic methods themselves, from the focus of the research question to data collection and the presentation of the results, revealing how the contribution of women had been silenced by omission.

Participatory action research (PAR) follows the ethnographic methods of conducting field research using strategies of interviews and observations, but it challenges the researcher–participant relationship. Rather than conducting research *on* people, practitioners of PAR conduct research *with* the people being studied (Reason & Bradbury, 2008). They believe that such *cooperative inquiry* is less likely to "undermine the self-determination of their participants" (p. 4). Participants discuss and agree on what they want to research, the nature of the questions, modes of data collection and analysis, the way data are written up, and how the findings are distributed.

Action research (AR) is research also conducted by a team of professional action researchers and stakeholders—members of the organization or community being studied—with the goal of *seeking to improve their situation*. As in PAR, they jointly define the research problem, cogenerate relevant background knowledge, identify and learn research methods, and interpret and implement the findings. Thus, "AR democratizes the relationship between the professional researcher and the local interested parties" (Greenwood & Levin, 2007, p. 4).

Film, and now primarily video, has been an important medium for ethnography since Bates and Mead (1942) used film to document fieldwork. In *visual ethnography*, video or film is used to record the scene, the daily lives of participants, interviews, and those events that cannot accurately (or with detail) be stored as field notes. Researchers may use video recording in two ways: to record, catalog, and gather data to supplement participant observation or as a stand-alone strategy for interpretation (for example, researchers may manipulate video recorded data, slowing down or speeding up the recording, to explore interactions or nonverbal gestures in microanalytic detail). In addition, video enables researchers to examine dialogue, along with its accompanying gestures, in detail (see Goldman-Segall, 1998).

░ GROUNDED THEORY

What Sorts of Questions Are Asked?

Grounded theory has its origins in symbolic interactionism, taking the perspective that reality is negotiated between people, always changing, and constantly evolving (Blumer, 1969/1986). Research questions in grounded theory are about process and change over time, and the methods of making and analyzing data reflect a commitment to understanding the ways in which reality is socially constructed. The assumption is that through detailed exploration, with theoretical sensitivity, the researcher can construct theory *grounded in* data.

Grounded theory studies usually begin with questions about "what's going on here." This is an appropriate method for the researcher wishing to learn *from* the participants how to understand a process or a situation. The questions themselves suggest the examination of a process. Thus, grounded theory studies are usually situated in experiences in which change is expected, and the method has become dominant in research areas where the understanding of change and process is central, such as in health and business studies. For instance, Lorencz (1988/1992) explored the experiences of predischarge schizophrenics with at least 2 years of illness. Morse and Bottorff (1988/1992) studied mothers who were breast feeding to find attitudes to breast milk expression. Turner (1994) gives a detailed account of his techniques for discovery of a grounded theory in his description of the organizational processes that led to a ferry disaster.

The method was originally developed by Glaser and Strauss (1967), with equal attribution; as we show below, the idea of theoretical sensitivity (Glaser, 1978) and the techniques for creating theory grounded in data (Strauss, 1987; Strauss & Corbin, 1990) were developed separately by the two authors. In their works, Glaser and Strauss presented researchers with what at the time was a radical proposal—that theory should be developed "in intimate relationship with data, with researchers fully aware of themselves as instruments for developing that grounded theory" (Strauss, 1987, p. 6).

Such theory will usually be small-scale, midrange, and focused, and techniques will emphasize the "continuous interplay between analysis and data collection" (Strauss & Corbin, 1994, p. 273) until a theory fitting the data is created. The process involves a data-driven design (theoretical sampling). The key goal is the creation of new theoretical concepts *from* the data and the seeking of *core concepts* (Strauss, 1987), or the pursuit of what Glaser (1978) terms the *basic social process* or the *basic social psychological process*.

The Researcher's Stance

The concept of *theoretical sensitivity* is crucial in grounded theory. The researcher *seeks* theory, constantly working with data records and records of ideas to tease from them the concepts and the linkages that might generate theoretical insight. Those emerging concepts are also in constant interplay with the data as the researcher seeks integration and synthesis.

The perspective that reality is constantly changing and being negotiated leads the researcher to active inquiry into the event over time. There is an emphasis on detailed knowledge, constant comparison, and the trajectory of the event. The researcher consistently asks not only "What is going on here?" but "How is it different?" The method of grounded theory promotes a stance of refusal to accept a report at face value, a sort of methodological restlessness that leads the researcher to seek characteristics, conditions, causes, antecedents, and consequences of events or responses as ways of drawing them together in an integrated theory.

What Sorts of Data Are Needed?

Grounded theory research does not require any particular data source, but it does require data within which theory can be grounded. The goal of discovering theory from data sets high standards for the data, both in depth of detail and in coverage of process. However the data are made, the records must support the probing and friction of constant comparison and reflection. A study may commence with an observational phase in the field or with interviews—narratives about the event, told sequentially from beginning to end. Such interviews are much more able to support the method than are semistructured interviews or brief accounts.

Researchers should beware of attempting grounded theory research with structured data records, which preemptively limit what they will hear in response to their preconceived questions. In such data, it is difficult to identify the process or discover categories derived from the meanings held by others.

What Do the Results Look Like?

Grounded theory is undoubtedly the label most popularly applied to qualitative research, and undoubtedly the most misapplied, often being taken as synonymous with *qualitative* (Lee & Fielding, 1996). We share a concern that researchers should understand the true nature of grounded theory; it is a unique and highly demanding method, with strong congruence. If you don't know what method you are using, it is highly unlikely to be grounded theory.

The explicit goal of grounded theory studies is to develop theory. So reports will feature theory that is limited and *local*—theory derived from, and grounded in, the data. A study using grounded theory will usually have a single story line, offering a core concept and its attendant theory as a way of making sense of the data. These are *new* theoretical offerings, not seen before that particular study because they are the product of it. Often, the core concepts are also new, not everyday, concepts.

A grounded theory study is densely argued; the researcher identifies the concepts involved and develops theory by exploring the relationships between these concepts in the stages or phases of the process and the core category or variable (or *basic social process*). This one category is the theme that runs through the data and accounts for most of the variance. A grounded theory study attempts to account for the centrality of the core concept by telling the story of its emergence. Reports may include diagrams of the process, or summary typologies, indicating the presence or absence of selected factors.

Different Approaches Within Grounded Theory

The founders of grounded theory came from contrasting backgrounds and worked as co-investigators on high-profile projects. For two decades, based on the original work of Glaser and Strauss (1967), grounded theory was presented as a coherent and complete method—but as one method. Over the next two decades, as each author worked independently, the method evolved and diverged, with Glaser (1978) and Strauss (1987) separately writing significant and very different methodological texts. At that time, most researchers using the techniques assumed there was a single set of methodological procedures for grounded theory research.

Divisions between Glaser and Strauss appeared in the early 1990s with a publication by Glaser (1992) in which he rejected Strauss's book coauthored with Corbin (1990). Instead of generating a methodological debate, this created in some locations two "schools" of grounded theory, termed *Glaserian* and *Straussian* grounded theory (Stern, 1994, p. 219). Researchers in these areas are increasingly (and, arguably, regrettably) expected to choose between two distinct sets of procedures, using as their primary source either Glaser's (1978) or Strauss's (1987) text, which was in turn developed and, arguably, greatly changed in joint publication by Strauss and Corbin (1994, 1998) and after Strauss's death (Corbin & Strauss, 2008).

All methods evolve, and should do so. Below we outline four variants. We share a hope that the various strands of grounded theory will be used to fit projects as appropriate, and we encourage you to explore and, if appropriate, draw on both these groups of techniques. But you should be aware that the following distinctions are commonly made.

〰 ***Glaserian grounded theory:*** Glaserian grounded theory takes the more objectivist perspective: Data are both separate and distant from both the participants and the analyst (Charmaz, 2006). Glaser focuses his attention *on* the data to allow the data to tell their own story (Stern, 2009; Stern & Porr, 2011). The Glaserian analyst attends to the data and asks, "What do we have here?" (Stern, 1994, p. 220). As in the original documents on grounded theory, analysis focuses on components of the theory—on the processes, categories, dimensions, and properties—and the development of, and interaction between, these components allows the theory to emerge. In Glaserian approaches, the theory is more often diagrammed to illustrate the relationships between concepts and categories.

〰 ***Straussian grounded theory:*** Straussian grounded theorists examine the data and stop at each word or phrase to ask, "What if?" Thus, the analyst "brings to bear every possible contingency that could relate to the data, whether it appears in the data or not" (Stern, 1994, p. 220). Straussian grounded theorists are concerned with striving to rise above the data to develop more abstract concepts and their descriptions (Corbin & Strauss, 2008). Theories are created in interaction with the data and (as in Glaserian approaches) retain the emphasis on categories, dimensions, and properties. There is a strong emphasis on "open coding," best exemplified in the recorded research conversations in Strauss's (1987) book. Theories are the product of reflection, discussion, and detailed examination of text, constructed from memos and dense coding (Corbin, 2009). Straussian researchers rely less on diagrams than do Glaserian grounded theorists.

☙ *Dimensional analysis:* A third early version of grounded theory (and one very different from the other two) is dimensional analysis, developed by Schatzman (1991), a colleague of Glaser and Strauss. Dimensional analysis allows for the "explicit articulation of the analytic process" and provides "an overarching structure to guide analysis" (Kools, McCarthy, Durham, & Robrecht, 1996, p. 314). Based on comparative analysis, dimensional analysis was presented as providing a fuller approach to social life than could grounded theory (Bowers & Schatzman, 2009).

☙ *Constructivist grounded theory:* In contrast to the Glaserian method and Strauss and Corbin's "objectivist" method, constructivist grounded theory is presented as more interpretive—both the data and the analysis are created from shared experiences and relationships with participants.

> Constructivist inquiry starts with the experience and asks how members [i.e., participants] construct it. To the best of their ability, constructivists enter the phenomenon, gain multiple views of it, and locate it in its web of connections and constraints. Constructivists acknowledge that their interpretation of the studied phenomenon is itself a construction. (Charmaz, 2006, p. 187)

☙ *Situational analysis:* Recently developed by Adele Clarke (2005, 2009), situational analysis focuses on the situation—context and people, and their relations, actions, and interactions. It uses interview, observational, and other sources. Situational analysis "allows researchers to draw together studies of discourse and agency, action and structure, image, text and context, history and the present moment—to analyze complex situations of inquiry broadly conceived" (Clarke, 2005, p. xxii). Thus, it differs dramatically from process-oriented grounded theory in that the theory is not constructed around a basic social process. Rather, it is organized by a situation-centered framework developed by Anselm Strauss, using three types of mapping data, to organize "key elements, materialities, discourses, structures, and conditions that characterize the situation of the inquiry" (Clarke, 2005, p. xxii). In this way, "the *situation becomes the unit of analysis,* and understanding its elements and their relations is the primary goal" (Clarke, 2005, p. xxii; italics in original). More closely aligned with ethnography than is traditional grounded theory, it enables the analysis of "highly complex situations of actions and positionality, of heterogeneous discourses . . . and situated knowledges and positionality, of the heterogenous discourses . . . and of the situated knowledges of life itself" (Clarke, 2005, p. xxiii).

We urge you to discover the differences in these approaches and evaluate their significance, avoiding the abyss created by claims that there is only one way to achieve grounded theory. Such claims ossify methods and prevent researchers from modifying recommended procedures or developing new ways of combining them. Our advice is that you return to the earlier works of the founders and note the tone of those writings. Strauss wrote in 1987 that the methods he describes "are by no means to be regarded as hard and fixed rules for converting data into effective theory" (p. 7). Rigid rules, after all, are particularly inimical to grounded theory approaches.

Researchers need to be alert not only to the constraints and challenges of research settings and research aims but to the nature of their data. They must also be aware of the temporal aspects or phasing of their researches, the open-ended character of the "best research" in any discipline, the immense significance of their own experiences as researchers, and the local contexts in which the researches are conducted (Strauss, 1987, pp. 7–8).

☄ PHENOMENOLOGY

Phenomenology is an important philosophical movement of the 20th century. Founded by Edmund Husserl (1859–1938), it is used to refer to both a philosophy and a research approach. As a method, it has undergone many shifts in orientations and approaches.

Here we describe the *hermeneutical phenomenology*, as a method. From this perspective, phenomenology offers a descriptive, reflective, interpretive, and engaging mode of inquiry from which the essence of an experience may be elicited. Experience is considered to be an individual's perceptions of his or her presence in the world at the moment when things, truths, or values are constituted (van Manen, 1990).

Four existentialisms guide phenomenological reflection: *temporality* (lived time), *spatiality* (lived space), *corporeality* (lived body), and *relationality* or *communality* (lived human relation) (van Manen, 1990). People are considered to be tied to their worlds—embodied—and are understandable only in their contexts. Existence in this sense is meaningful (*being in the world*), and the focus is on the lived experience. Human behavior occurs in the context of relationships to things, people, events, and situations.

Two major assumptions underlie phenomenology. The first is that perceptions present us with evidence of the world—not as it is thought to be but as it is lived. The lived world, or the *lived experience,* is critical to phenomenology. The second assumption is that human existence is meaningful and of interest in the sense that we are always conscious of something. Existence as *being in the world* is a phenomenological phrase acknowledging that people are in their worlds and are understandable only in their contexts. Human behavior occurs in the context of the four existentialisms introduced above: relationships to things, people, events, and situations.

What Sorts of Questions Are Asked?

Phenomenological inquiry may not be formalized as a question per se. The researcher may have an interest targeted toward simply understanding the meaning of the lived experience in a particular phenomenon, with questions arising as inquiry proceeds. Therefore, these questions are what sensitize inquiry in the study. For instance, in considering his experiences as a parent of a child undergoing a heart transplant, Smith (1989/1992) describes his frustration with the delays in obtaining postoperative analgesic for his child:

> The interviewer does not simply ask a question of whose interests are being served—the parents' or the child's? But rather, he asks, how can a medical decision be made in presumably the best interests of the child by ignoring those of us who have been responsible by now for the welfare of the child? If we, the parents of a particular child, want to remain close to our child, what might we be up against when a crucial medical decision is made as to what should be done for our child? What sort of logic would deny fundamental responsibility we feel for our child? (p. 106)

In published reports, the research questions are often embedded in the introductory remarks that set the context of the study. For instance, Kelpin (1984/1992), in her study of birthing pain, notes that the pain of childbirth has a particular "centrality" for women's relationships as mothers and as human beings. The way Kelpin considers her research topic provides us with an excellent example of the way phenomenologists consider their research questions:

> What do the pains of birth tell us about ourselves, about our sufferings and our joys? Is there something in the pangs of childbirth which holds true for all women: those who pleasure and ride above the pain? Those who endure it? And those who suffer? Some birthings are short and intense, some are long and exhausting, and some in need of medical intervention and treatment with forceps, medication and Caesarian delivery. Is it possible that viewing pain-as-lived may reveal sublimity and joy as well as the agony, the hurtfulness of the pain of childbirth? Our immediate appraisal of pain-as-experienced may bring light to inner meanings that go beyond theoretical and practical approaches. By coming to an understanding of the pain as experienced by women we may be able to come to grips with the significance or essence of the pain. (pp. 93–94; reprinted with permission from the University of Alberta and SAGE)

Van Manen (1990) notes that stating a question directly often simplifies the problem, so in phenomenology, the actual research question may be left implicit. Clarke (1990/1992), for instance, explores her child's experience of asthma in light of her own reflections on her child's experience. She does not state the question explicitly but introduces it in the phenomenological way, using voices of her daughter's essay ("Memories of Breathing"), voices of poets as illustrators, and voices from the phenomenological literature, while her own voice guides our insights into the experience.

The Researcher's Stance

When thinking phenomenologically, the researcher attempts to understand, or grasp, the essence of how people attend to the world (using the four existentialisms), remembering that a person's description

is a _perception_, a form of interpretation (Boyd, 1993; van Manen, 1990).
Every day, we consciously experience concrete objects through intuition.
Giorgi (1997), on the other hand, notes that _presences_ are the experience
of many phenomena that are not "realistic" but are vital to the understanding of the lived experience. These are such things as dreams and
delusions. _Intentionality_ is the essential feature of consciousness. Consciousness is always "directed to an object that is not in itself conscious,
although it could be, as in reflected acts" (p. 236).

What Sorts of Data Are Needed?

Phenomenological researchers aim to _bracket_ all a priori knowledge
about the topic; by writing their assumptions, knowledge, and expectations, they hope to enter the conversation with no presuppositions.
These early writings are themselves data. They most frequently gather
new data by using audio recorded "conversations" without predetermined
questions, following a "clue-and-clue-taking process" as the conversations proceed (Ray, 1994, p. 129). They then transcribe these recorded
conversations and use them as a basis for reflection. During analysis,
phenomenologists also reflect on personal experiences, observations, and
the experiences of others—even those expressed in poetry, literature, and
film.

What Do the Results Look Like?

Phenomenology gives us insights into the meanings or the essences of
experiences we may previously have been unaware of but can recognize.
This experience of confirmation is known as the _phenomenological nod._
The essence may be presented in an essay as several segments or perspectives, each describing a different dimension of the experience. Phenomenological researchers may share the results of their studies in essays or in
book-length works.

Different Approaches Within Phenomenology

All phenomenologists subscribe to the belief that being human is a
unique way of being, in that human experiences and actions follow from

their self-interpretation (Benner, 1994, p. ix). But phenomenological methods have evolved in more than one direction and take several forms that have some commonalities. Van Manen (2011) has classified the following orientations:

⋙ **Transcendental phenomenology** (Husserl and his collaborators: Eugen Fink, Tymieniecka, Van Breda, and Giorgi): This interpretation is presuppositionless and based on "intentionality" ("all conscious awarenesses are intentional awarenesses") and "eidetic reduction" (vivid and detailed attentiveness to description). Transcendental phenomenology explores the way knowledge comes into being, and knowledge is based on insights rather than objective characteristics, which "constitutes meaning."

⋙ **Existential phenomenology** (Heidegger, Sartre, de Beauvoir, Merleau-Ponty, Marcel, and others): According to this perspective, the observer cannot separate him-/herself from the lived world. "Being-in-the-world" is reality as it is perceived, and a reciprocal relationship exists between the observer and the phenomenon that includes all thoughts, moods, efforts, and actions within the lifeworld that is man situated. Pre-reflected experiences, the lifeworld, and phenomena constitute *existence*, or human reality.

⋙ **Hermeneutical phenomenology** (Heidegger, Gadamer, Ricoeur, and van Manen): In this orientation, knowledge comes into being through language and understanding. Understanding and interpretation are intertwined, and interpretation is an evolving process. Hermeneutic phenomenologists use culture (symbols, myth, religion, art, and language), poetry, and art in their interpretations. Van Manen's (1990) method starts with the exploration of a pedagogically grounded concept within the everyday lived experience. Through processes of reflection, writing and rewriting, and thematic analysis, the researcher may describe and interpret the essence or meaning of the lived experience.

⋙ **Linguistical phenomenology** (Blanchot, Derrida, and Foucault): This orientation takes the perspective that language and discourse reveal the relations between "understanding, culture, historicality, identity, and human life." Meaning "resides in language and the text, rather than in the subject, in consciousness, or even in lived experience."

Researchers use *heuristic phenomenology* (Moustakas, 1994) when they seek to understand themselves and their lived worlds. Although such research is autobiographical, the questions it answers may have social, and even universal, significance. Heuristic research "unfolds" through initial engagement, immersion into the topic and the question, incubation, explication, and culmination of the research in "creative synthesis" (Moustakas, 1990).

＊ DISCOURSE ANALYSIS

Briefly, discourse analysis is the study of "language in use"—not just the study of language to say things but to "do things. People use language to communicate, co-operate, help others, and build things like marriages, reputations, and institutions. They also use it to lie, advantage themselves, to harm people, and destroy things like marriages, reputations, and institutions" (Gee, 2011, p. ix).

At first glance, there could hardly be greater contrast than that between phenomenology and discourse analysis. They seem to represent the extremes of interpretive flight and disciplined description. Where the phenomenological researcher is positing meanings and essences of a phenomenon, the discourse analyst is intent on interpreting what is said and written.

But there is a strong link between this method and the others considered so far. All are based in the conviction that social reality is socially constructed. The ethnographer watches that reality unfold, the grounded theorist examines the processes of acceptance or challenge, and the phenomenologist directs attention to the meanings "reality" gives to our lives and their parts.

For the discourse analyst, the focus is on speech and written communication. Speech includes the speaker's nonverbal cues (such as gaze, gesture, and action), the listener, and relevant context. By examining these, we can, it is argued, gain insight into the social construction of our lives.

What Sorts of Questions Are Asked?

The questions asked by all sorts of discourse analysis concern the meanings and implications of words spoken or recorded, and how the taken-for-granted messages behind these words have social implications. But different approaches will pursue these questions in different ways and, thus, have different emphases on interpretation and description.

Phillips and Hardy (2002, pp. 34–38) provide a useful tabulation of selected examples of studies. They include studies from political, business, organizational, media, and cultural enquiries, which have tackled small and huge questions. In a later chapter, they outline in detail how they framed the research question in their own study of refugee politics. "In this study, we examined the way in which organizations used power to discursively shape the conceptualization of a refugee in ways that protected their interests" (p. 61).

For some discourse analysts, the questions cover wide enquiry about discourse as a creator and reflector of social reality. "Whereas other qualitative methodologies work to understand or interpret social reality as it exists, discourse analysis endeavors to uncover the way in which it is produced" (Phillips & Hardy, 2002, p. 6). Discourse for these researchers is "an interrelated set of texts, and the practices of their production, dissemination, and reception, that brings an object into being" (p. 3). Importantly, the questions may come from the texts. Crawford (1995, p. 126), in her analysis of a talk show discussion of date rape, offers an extended example of questions raised by texts, using the show transcripts and researcher's reflections on them.

As mentioned in Chapter 2, such questions are tackled also by the method of conversation analysis. The contrast is so sharp that you will find conversation analysis sometimes discussed as a separate method. Discourse analysis is interpretive, focuses on language use, prepares the text differently, uses different analytic methods, and answers different types of questions than does conversation analysis (Morse considers them to be different). On the other hand, because its focus is on analysis of speech and texts, Richards sees conversation analysis as a variant of discourse analysis, considering the main aim of conversation analysis to be elucidating the structures of talk. Here the questions may be about repetitions, hesitations, or turn taking in conversation. "They study talk because they want to know about talk" (Cameron, 2001, p. 1).

The questions asked, not surprisingly, vary widely. Discourse may be studied to elicit differences in gendered experience (see Wodak, 1997) or the ways one political approach is made to seem "natural." Or, for the conversation analysis, the recording of speech enables talk and interaction to be explored "at a site where intersubjective understanding about the participants' intentions is created and maintained. It therefore gives access to the construction of meaning in real time" (Peräkylä, 2004, p. 168). The questions asked are detailed, about "the architecture of interaction, and the attendant expectations" (Wooffitt, 2005, p. 7).

The Researcher's Stance

Since the emphasis is on discourse as part of the social construction of everyday life, it is not surprising to find that discourse analysis strongly argues for "reflexivity." This is a demand common across qualitative methods, where attention is increasingly paid to the researchers' ability to reflect on and acknowledge their place in and impact on what is studied. Discourse analysts argue that their methodology unusually directs researchers, who are investigating their own social worlds and languages, to reflect on their part in what is studied, their selection of the voices to be heard, and their ability to challenge or question the texts studied. Phillips and Hardy (2002, p. 85) provide a table of aspects of reflexivity.

A strong tradition in discourse analysis is "critical"; here the researcher stands in defiance against taken-for-granted assumptions and justifications.

What Sorts of Data Are Needed?

Usually, the discourse analyst will examine many episodes of texts or talk and their interrelationships. Transcription is required and is usually "broad" (that is, accurate text including expressions such as "laughs, or coughs" and pauses, and line numbers). This type of transcription may be contrasted with narrow transcription conventions used in conversation analysis (see Titscher, Meyer, Wodak, & Vetter, 2000, p. 58). There is usually also a preference to use bodies of text, "because it is the interrelations between texts, changes in texts, new textual forms, and new systems of distributing texts that constitute a discourse over time" (Phillips & Hardy, 2002, p. 5). Depending on the research question, these data are supplemented with data about the society and current context.

Conversation analysis has a different, "data-centered" emphasis. Sampling of texts is done carefully to represent aspects of the problem studied (see Titscher et al., 2000, p. 58). Because all accounts of the situation are problematized by the method, there is "a principled reluctance to draw on ethnographic characterizations of the setting and its participants in the analysis" (Wooffitt, 2005, p. 63). Focus on the text means that other "external" issues such as power or gender relations become relevant only if made so by that text. Moreover, issues about the text may become the entire focus of the study, as the researcher observes turn taking or hesitations.

What Do the Results Look Like?

Such studies always surprise. The goal of the discourse analyst is to get behind taken-for-granted meanings of language or text. So reports will challenge assumptions, deconstruct apparently straightforward accounts, and display hidden meanings. For a reader unfamiliar with such research, articles in discourse analysis are often startling. Taking a few passages of text, these methods expand analysis to sometimes extraordinary complexity, since any particular phrase or repetition may lead to a reflection on its significance. Thus, most studies start very focused, on a text or a conversation, and work in great detail through its parts and possibilities. From the minutiae of conversation, they move to often high-level social or political claims.

Different Approaches Within Discourse Analysis

There are many forms of discourse analysis, the main one being critical discourse analysis. *Critical discourse analysis* (Fairclough, 2010) focuses on power and "hidden agendas," on what is "*wrong* with a society (institution, an organization, etc.) and how the 'wrongs' might be 'righted' or mitigated, for a particular normative standpoint" (p. 7). Fairclough emphasizes that this approach is more than the analysis of discourse but "some form of systematic transdisciplinary analysis of relations between discourse and other elements of the social process" (p. 10).

※ CAJE JTUDY METHOD

We have sketched four very different qualitative methods, each challenging for the newcomer. These ways of approaching social questions are not immediately familiar. Each has its origin in a wider theoretical tradition.

Each has its own fit of question, data, and outcome, and to achieve that fit, the researcher will have to learn a new way of thinking about reality and new skills to design and conduct research.

By contrast, our fifth method, case studies, seems much more approachable. Everyone knows what a case study is; descriptions of "case studies" adorn website marketing and brochures for products from investment portfolios to governmental programs. These case studies offer cheery thumbnail sketches of the (always positive) experience of a small number of people who have used the product or tried the program, usually studded with quotations of their own enthusiastic words. As a quick way to a deadline, this sounds easy. But be warned: As for all qualitative research, what works for the marketing manager can spell disaster for the PhD student!

In the introduction to his classic text, Yin (2009) comments that "using case studies for research purposes remains one of the most challenging of all social science endeavors" (p. 3). Why should this be so?

What Sorts of Questions Are Asked?

Case study is usually seen as a study of a particular social unit or system. Most writers emphasize that a case is "bounded" and studied in its natural setting as a whole. Usually, the larger question is to understand the wider social phenomenon of which it is a case. Stake (1995) explains,

> Custom has it that not everything is a case. A child may be a case. A teacher may be a case. But her teaching lacks the specificity, the boundedness, to be called a case. An innovative program may be a case. All the schools in Sweden can be a case. But a relationship among schools, the reasons for innovative teaching, or the policies of school reform are less commonly considered a case. These topics are generalities rather than specifics. The case is a specific, a complex, functioning thing. (p. 2)

This is a method, then, that seeks understanding of a social situation or process by focusing on how it is played out in one or more cases. In other words, the cases studied are always cases *of* something. The researcher has started with a question and moved to locating it in a microcosm, one or a few bounded cases.

The Researcher's Stance

Case studies have long been used in social research, traditionally by researchers wishing to give voice to less-prominent social groups or types. The relevant tradition in British sociology is "community studies," and in the United States, the work of the Chicago School, picturing the lives and contexts of slum neighborhoods and their occupants.

"Case study *method*" is a more recent arrival—and still a highly controversial one—with very different meanings across disciplines. You will find some collections of case studies designed simply to assist a reader in gaining a vivid picture of examples of an innovation or sites of a problem, whereas others aim more at meta-analysis (see Chapter 4), bringing together conclusions from many research sites.

Almost always, there is a commitment to qualitative techniques, to methods seeking to understand how those under study experience their world. In some texts, including Yin's (2009), case study method is treated as the alternative to experiment, survey, archival, or historical analysis; here "case study" appears sometimes to encompass any qualitative research. In others, a "case study" is a particular way of pursuing qualitative inquiry, distinguished from other qualitative research by its own design rules (for two recent examples, see Swanborn, 2010, and Thomas, 2011; see also the collection edited by Gomm, Hammersley, & Foster, 2000). Many authors, particularly in educational and business studies, write "with some sense of advocacy" (Stake, 1995, p. xii)—not for those they are studying but for the method itself, promoting case studies as the most desirable and convincing way of conducting and presenting research.

What Sorts of Data Are Needed?

Case study research, ideally, will need detailed data on that case, thoroughly analyzed, to provide "a rich picture—with boundaries" (Thomas, 2011, p. 21). The goal is to understand the case or cases as completely as possible. Most case study texts offer the full palette of qualitative data-making methods, with a particular emphasis on field research by participant observation and interviewing. Some include, and a few emphasize, quantitative methods.

So case study research is unlike the other methods sketched in this chapter in that it is defined by the location and focus of the study, not by an intellectual and methodological tradition. It may use methods from many traditions. Stake (1995) says his view of case studies "draws from naturalistic, holistic, ethnographic, phenomenological and biographic research methods" (p. xi).

Studies are conducted within a limited geographical scope (in a single institution, unit, family, village), are located within a single program or incident, or may even be bounded by a single person's experience. The researcher gathers in-depth data, focusing on the particular problem and analyzing all data obtained from that particular case in context, within the identified boundaries.

What Do the Results Look Like?

A good case study is usually a good read. This is because it is focused, offering a powerful representation of the situation or person studied. It may look like a story or a journalistic account, as did the classic studies of the Chicago School vividly conveying city lives and their contexts (Platt, 1992). Or it may look like a thorough dissection of all the factors and forces affecting a program or site. Whatever its presentation, it will offer intensive, detailed descriptions of the case and a sense that the case is thoroughly understood.

It will usually not claim generalization beyond the case or offer external comparison.

> The real business of case study is particularization, not generalization. We take a particular case and come to know it well, not primarily as to how it is different from others but what it is, what it does. There is emphasis on uniqueness, and that implies knowledge of others that the case is different from, but the first emphasis is on understanding the case itself. (Stake, 1995, p. 8)

Note that this mode of handling data is very different from the synthesis of grounded theory or ethnography, in which data for each category from each participant are merged and analyzed as a category, separate from the participant. Herein lies the challenge of case study research. The study will stand or fall on the quality of the analysis of one or a few cases. It is all too easy for such a study to become simply richly descriptive.

Different Approaches Within Case Study Method

Given the variety of purposes and approaches, it is not surprising that studies using "case study method" are highly diverse, recommending different procedures, research techniques, and rules. But unlike the other methods discussed in this chapter, there are, as yet, no clearly defined methodological "schools" with their own approaches.

Several texts do offer typologies of case studies. Stake (2005) suggests three types of case studies—not as different approaches to the method but as different research designs for different questions. *Intrinsic* case studies are basically about the case—there is an intrinsic interest in it. *Instrumental* case studies, by comparison, are for a wider purpose, to answer a question through study of a particular case. And *collective* case studies are designed where it is necessary to compare cases, identifying patterns.

For the newcomer, Thomas offers a summary of several typologies of case study research, based on their goals, the researcher's stance, or their methods, and suggests the ways these can be used to chart an "investigative path" (Thomas, 2011, pp. 91–95).

The uses of case studies vary considerably between disciplines. Go to readings in your research area to find the methodological standards applied.

〴 SUMMARY

We have illustrated methodological congruence with sketches of only five methods. Myriad other methods exist in qualitative research, and more are being proposed at any time.

The appropriate method for your study may not be one of the five discussed here. Working from your research question, you may be led to another qualitative approach, which you will recognize as better able to ask your question or more likely to produce the outcome you seek. When you meet a new method, ask of it the questions we posed above—what questions will it answer, how is the researcher positioned, what data are needed, and how will this study look when finished? Keep looking until you find a fit with your project, and resist pressures to fit the project to a method.

Working this way, from question to method, you will not be tempted to approach qualitative research as though it were done by one generic method. A researcher who does so can get far into a study, even all the way through it, with a result that invites the question, "So what?" That outcome will be descriptive rather than analytic, the researcher going through the motions of identifying a question, conducting interviews, and then sorting data by identifying themes or categories. The report will locate patterns but will rarely produce a theoretical outcome. "Sorted data" as an end result are only as interesting as the data themselves. Such a study may be very interesting, but if conducted without the benefit of a coherent method, it will usually end at this descriptive level.

You will encounter many examples of such work. Our aim is not to condemn descriptive work but, rather, to show how it differs crucially from research within a congruent qualitative method and why such descriptive work is often not regarded as qualitative or accepted for publication in qualitative journals (Morse, 1996). Concerned with the problems of researchers' attempting to retrofit a congruent qualitative method to data-sorting and pattern-finding tasks, Richards (2000) has labeled such descriptive work "pattern analysis." In short-term pragmatic studies especially, researchers may have no goals beyond seeking and reporting patterns in data—for example, by demographic variables such as gender or structural factors such as socioeconomic settings of schools studied. If the task is to find out whether the responses to an idea addressed in focus groups vary by gender, or to establish whether the level of acceptance of an initiative in schools is different in lower- and upper-class areas, unstructured data may be necessary and relevant, and analysis may not require abstraction. Often, such studies combine qualitative and quantitative data skillfully and usefully, with the discovery of patterns in the unstructured data illuminating the statistical analysis. If your goal is pattern analysis, many of the techniques discussed in this book may assist you in discovering and reporting patterns. But don't represent your study as grounded theory.

The lens provided by a method is what enables abstraction from data, the emergence and construction of theory about the data, and the linking of the results to the literature and other theories. In this chapter, we have tried to convey that each method will have a different fit of question to research process and outcome. That fit will set the researcher's perspective. To do a phenomenological study, you must think as a phenomenologist; to do an ethnography, you must think as an ethnographer; to discover a grounded theory, you must think as a grounded theorist; and so forth. This is so important that Morse says she has "different tracks" in her brain for thinking in the various ways demanded by individual methods. Within the perspective of each method, the researcher manipulates data by using *analytic techniques.* Although these analytic techniques appear similar for all methods, *how they are used with the data* is what makes a method a particular method. Different methods may use similar techniques, but the individual method's strategy (the way the techniques are used) gives it a unique application and produces a unique result.

The goal of all qualitative inquiry is not to reproduce reality descriptively but to add insight and understanding and to create theory that provides explanation and even prediction. The best way to gain an appreciation for these differences is to read completed studies that provide examples of the various methods. Ask yourself: How do these studies differ? What contributions do each offer? What level of abstraction or theory development has each reached? Can you begin to identify how each of the authors has obtained abstraction and has, at the same time, come to understand the phenomenon in context?

⫸ RE*J*OURCE*J*

Ethnography: Methodological Resources

Agar, M. H. (1986). *Speaking of ethnography.* Beverly Hills, CA: Sage.

Agar, M. H. (1996). *The professional stranger: An informal introduction to ethnography* (2nd ed.). San Diego, CA: Academic Press.

Atkinson, P., Coffey, A., Delamont, S., Lofland, J., & Lofland, L. (2001). *Handbook of ethnography.* Thousand Oaks, CA: Sage.

Bernard, R. H. (1988). *Research methods in cultural anthropology.* Newbury Park, CA: Sage.

Boyle, J. S. (1994). Styles of ethnography. In J. M. Morse (Ed.), *Critical issues in qualitative research methods* (pp. 159–185). Thousand Oaks, CA: Sage.

Carspecken, P. F. (1996). *Critical ethnography in educational research.* New York: Routledge.

Ellis, C., & Bochner, A. P. (Eds.). (1996). *Composing ethnography: Alternative forms of qualitative writing.* Walnut Creek, CA: AltaMira.

Ellis, C., & Bochner, A. P. (2000). Autoethnography, personal narrative, reflexivity: Researcher as subject. In N. K. Denzin & Y. S. Lincoln (Eds.), *The SAGE handbook of qualitative research* (2nd ed., pp. 733–768). Thousand Oaks, CA: Sage.

Fetterman, D. M. (2010). *Ethnography: Step-by-step* (3rd ed.). Newbury Park, CA: Sage.

Goldman-Segall, R. (1998). *Points of viewing children's thinking: A digital ethnographer's journey.* Mahwah, NJ: Lawrence Erlbaum. (See also website at http://www.pointsofviewing.com)

Greenwood, D. J., & Levin, M. (1998). *Introduction to action research: Social research for social change.* Thousand Oaks, CA: Sage.

Hammersley, M., & Atkinson, P. (1983). *Ethnography: Principles in practice.* London: Tavistock.

Knoblauch, H. (2005). Focused ethnography. *Forum Qualitative Sozialforschung/ Forum: Qualitative Social Research,* 6(3), Art. 44. Retrieved from http://nbn-resolving.de/urn:nbn:de:0114-fqs 0503440

LeCompte, M. D., & Preissle, J. (1993). *Ethnography and qualitative design in educational research.* San Diego, CA: Academic Press.

Madison, D. S. (2005). *Critical ethnography: Method, ethics, and performance.* Thousand Oaks, CA: Sage.

Muecke, M. (1994). On the evaluation of ethnographies. In J. Morse (Ed.), *Critical issues in qualitative research methods* (pp. 187–209). Thousand Oaks, CA: Sage.

Reason, P., & Bradbury, H. (2008). *The SAGE handbook of action research: Participative inquiry and practice* (2nd ed.). London: Sage.

Schensul, J. J., & LeCompte, M. D. (Series Eds.). (1999). *Ethnographer's toolkit* (7 vols.). Walnut Creek, CA: AltaMira.

Smith, D. E. (2005). *Institutional ethnography: A sociology for the people.* Toronto, Canada: AltaMira.

Spradley, J. P. (1979). *The ethnographic interview.* New York: Holt, Rinehart & Winston.

Spradley, J. P. (1980). *Participant observation.* New York: Holt, Rinehart & Winston.

Tedlock, B. (2000). Ethnography and ethnographic representation. In N. K. Denzin & Y. S. Lincoln (Eds.), *The SAGE handbook of qualitative research* (2nd ed., pp. 455–486). Thousand Oaks, CA: Sage.

Thomas, J. (1993). *Doing critical ethnography.* Newbury Park, CA: Sage.

Van Maanen, J. (Ed.). (1995). *Representation in ethnography.* Thousand Oaks, CA: Sage.

van Manen, M. (2011). Orientations in phenomenology. Retrieved January 17, 2012, from http://www.phenomenology online.com/inquiry/orientations-in-phenomenology/

Wolcott, H. F. (1999). *Ethnography: A way of seeing.* Walnut Creek, CA: AltaMira.

Reading Ethnography

Applegate, M., & Morse, J. M. (1994). Personal privacy and interaction patterns in a nursing home. *Journal of Aging Studies, 8,* 413–434.

Cassell, J. (1992). On control, certitude and the "paranoia" of surgeons. In J. M. Morse (Ed.), *Qualitative health research* (pp. 170–191). Newbury Park, CA: Sage. (Original work published 1987)

Davis, D. L. (1992). The meaning of menopause in a Newfoundland fishing village. In J. M. Morse (Ed.), *Qualitative health research* (pp. 145–169). Newbury Park, CA: Sage. (Original work published 1986)

Germain, C. (1979). *The cancer unit: An ethnography.* Wakefield, MA: Nursing Resources.

Morse, J. M. (1989). Cultural variation in behavioral response to parturition: Childbirth in Fiji. *Medical Anthropology, 12*(1), 35–44.

Spradley, J. P. (1970). *You owe yourself a drunk: An ethnography of urban nomads*. Boston: Little, Brown.

Grounded Theory: Methodological Resources

Bowers, B., & Schatzman, L. (2009). Dimensional analysis. In J. M. Morse, P. N. Stern, J. Corbin, B. Bowers, K. Charmaz, & A. E. Clarke (Eds.), *Developing grounded theory: The second generation* (pp. 86–124). Walnut Creek, CA: Left Coast Press.

Charmaz, K. (2000). Grounded theory: Objectivist and constructivist methods. In N. K. Denzin & Y. S. Lincoln (Eds.), *The SAGE handbook of qualitative research* (2nd ed., pp. 509–535). Thousand Oaks, CA: Sage.

Charmaz, K. (2006). *Constructing grounded theory: A practical guide through qualitative analysis*. Thousand Oaks, CA: Sage.

Charmaz, K. (2009). Shifting the grounds: Constructivist grounded theory. In J. M. Morse, P. N. Stern, J. Corbin, B. Bowers, K. Charmaz, & A. E. Clarke (Eds.), *Developing grounded theory: The second generation* (pp. 127–154). Walnut Creek, CA: Left Coast Press.

Chenitz, W. C., & Swanson, J. M. (1986). *From practice to grounded theory*. Reading, MA: Addison-Wesley.

Clarke, A. (2005). *Situational analysis: Grounded theory after the postmodern turn*. Thousand Oaks, CA: Sage.

Clarke, A. (2009). From grounded theory to situational analysis: What's new? Why? How? In J. M. Morse, P. N. Stern, J. Corbin, B. Bowers, K. Charmaz, & A. E. Clarke (Eds.), *Developing grounded theory: The second generation*

(pp. 194–234). Walnut Creek, CA: Left Coast Press.

Corbin, J. (2009). Taking an analytic journey. In J. M. Morse, P. N. Stern, J. Corbin, B. Bowers, K. Charmaz, & A. E. Clarke (Eds.), *Developing grounded theory: The second generation* (pp. 35–53). Walnut Creek, CA: Left Coast Press.

Corbin, J., & Strauss, A. (2008). *Basics of qualitative research: Techniques and procedures for developing grounded theory* (3rd ed.). Thousand Oaks, CA: Sage.

Glaser, B. G. (1978). *Theoretical sensitivity: Advances in the methodology of grounded theory*. Mill Valley, CA: Sociology Press.

Glaser, B. G. (1992). *Basics of grounded theory analysis: Emergence vs. forcing*. Mill Valley, CA: Sociology Press.

Glaser, B. G., & Strauss, A. L. (1967). *The discovery of grounded theory: Strategies for qualitative research*. Chicago: Aldine.

Morse, J. M., Stern, P. N., Corbin, J., Bowers, B., Charmaz, K., & Clarke, A. E. (Eds.). (2009). *Developing grounded theory: The second generation*. Walnut Creek, CA: Left Coast Press.

Schreiber, R. S., & Stern, P. N. (Eds.). (2001). *Using grounded theory in nursing*. New York: Springer.

Stern, P. N. (1994). Eroding grounded theory. In J. M. Morse (Ed.), *Critical issues in qualitative research methods* (pp. 212–223). Thousand Oaks, CA: Sage.

Stern, P. N. (2009). Glaserian grounded theory. In J. M. Morse, P. N. Stern, J. Corbin, B. Bowers, K. Charmaz, & A. E. Clarke (Eds.), *Developing grounded theory: The second generation* (pp. 55–84). Walnut Creek, CA: Left Coast Press.

Stern, P. N., & Porr, C. (2011). *Essentials of accessible grounded theory*. Walnut Creek, CA: Left Coast Press.

Strauss, A. L. (1987). *Qualitative analysis for social scientists*. New York: Cambridge University Press.

Strauss, A. L., & Corbin, J. (1994). Grounded theory methodology: An overview. In N. K. Denzin & Y. S. Lincoln (Eds.), *The SAGE handbook of qualitative research* (pp. 273–285). Thousand Oaks, CA: Sage.

Strauss, A. L., & Corbin, J. (1998). *Basics of qualitative research: Techniques and procedures for developing grounded theory* (2nd ed.). Thousand Oaks, CA: Sage.

Reading Grounded Theory

Corbin, J., & Strauss, A. L. (1992). A nursing model for chronic illness management based on the trajectory framework. In P. Woog (Ed.), *The chronic illness trajectory framework: The Corbin and Strauss nursing model* (pp. 9–28). New York: Springer.

Glaser, B. G. (Ed.). (1993). *Examples of grounded theory: A reader*. Mill Valley, CA: Sociology Press.

Lorencz, B. J. (1992). Becoming ordinary: Leaving the psychiatric hospital. In J. M. Morse (Ed.), *Qualitative health research* (pp. 259–318). Newbury Park, CA: Sage. (Original work published 1988)

Morse, J. M., & Bottorff, J. L. (1992). The emotional experience of breast expression. In J. M. Morse (Ed.), *Qualitative health research* (pp. 319–332). Newbury Park, CA: Sage. (Original work published 1988)

Stern, P. N., & Kerry, J. (1996). Restructuring life after home loss by fire. *Image: Journal of Nursing Scholarship, 28*, 9–14.

Turner, B. A. (1994). Patterns of crisis behaviour: A qualitative inquiry. In A. Bryman & R. G. Burgess (Eds.), *Analyzing qualitative data* (pp. 195–216). London: Routledge.

Phenomenology: Methodological Resources

Benner, P. (Ed.). (1994). *Interpretive phenomenology: Embodiment, caring, and ethics in health and illness*. Thousand Oaks, CA: Sage.

Boyd, C. O. (1993). Phenomenology: The method. In P. L. Munhall & C. O. Boyd (Eds.), *Nursing research: A qualitative perspective* (2nd ed., pp. 99–132). New York: National League for Nursing.

Giorgi, A. (1997). The theory, practice, and evaluation of the phenomenological methods as a qualitative research procedure. *Journal of Phenomenological Psychology, 28*, 235–281.

Moustakas, C. (1990). *Heuristic research: Design, methodology, and applications*. Newbury Park, CA: Sage.

Moustakas, C. (1994). *Phenomenological research methods*. Thousand Oaks, CA: Sage.

Ray, M. A. (1994). The richness of phenomenology: Philosophic, theoretic, and methodologic concerns. In J. M. Morse (Ed.), *Critical issues in qualitative research methods* (pp. 117–133). Thousand Oaks, CA: Sage.

van Manen, M. (1990). *Researching lived experience: Human science for an action sensitive pedagogy*. London, Ontario: Althouse.

van Manen, M. (2011). Orientations in phenomenology. Retrieved January 17, 2012, from http://www.phenomenology online.com/inquiry/orientations-in-phenomenology/

Reading Phenomenology

Clarke, M. (1992). Memories of breathing: Asthma as a way of becoming. In J. M. Morse (Ed.), *Qualitative health research* (pp. 123–140). Newbury Park, CA: Sage. (Original work published 1990)

Kelpin, V. (1992). Birthing pain. In J. M. Morse (Ed.), *Qualitative health research* (pp. 93–103). Newbury Park, CA: Sage. (Original work published 1984)

Smith, S. J. (1992). Operating on a child's heart: A pedagogical view of hospitalization. In J. M. Morse (Ed.), *Qualitative health research* (pp. 104–122). Newbury Park, CA: Sage. (Original work published 1989)

van Manen, M. (1991). *The tact of teaching: The meaning of pedagogical thoughtfulness*. London, Ontario: Althouse.

van Manen, M. (Ed.). (2011). Textorium. Retrieved January 17, 2012, from http://www.phenomenologyonline.com/sources/textorium/

Discourse Analysis: Methodological Resources

Cameron, D. (2001). *Working with spoken discourse*. London: Sage.

Crawford, M. (1995). *Talking difference: On gender and language*. London: Sage.

Fairclough, N. (2003). *Analysing discourse: Textual analysis for social research*. New York: Routledge.

Gee, P. J. (2011). *How to do discourse analysis: A toolkit*. New York: Routledge.

Peräkylä, A. (2004). Conversational analysis. In C. Seale, G. Gobo, J. F. Gubrium, & D. Silverman (Eds.), *Qualitative research practice* (pp. 165–179). London: Sage.

Ten Have, P. (1999). *Doing conversation analysis: A practical guide*. London: Sage.

Titscher, S., Meyer, M., Wodak, R., & Vetter, E. (2000). *Methods of text and discourse analysis*. London: Sage.

van Leeuwen, T. (2008). *Discourse and practice: New tools for critical discourse analysis*. New York: Oxford University Press.

Wodak, R., & Meyer, M. (2009). *Methods for critical discourse analysis*. London: Sage.

Wooffitt, R. (2005). *Conversation analysis and discourse analysis: A comparative and critical introduction*. London: Sage.

Reading Discourse Analysis

Antaki, C., Finlay, W. M. L., & Walton, C. (2007). Conversational shaping: Staff members, solicitation of talk from people with intellectual impairment. *Qualitative Health Research, 17,* 1403–1414.

Barnard, R., Cruice, M. N., & Playford, E. D. (2010). Strategies used in the pursuit of achievability during goal setting in rehabilitation. *Qualitative Health Research, 20,* 239–250.

Caldas-Coulthard, C., & Coulthard, M. (1996). *Texts and practices: Readings in critical discourse analysis.* London: Routledge.

Crawford, M. (1995). *Talking difference: On gender and language.* London: Sage.

Fairclough, N. (2010). *Critical discourse analysis: The critical study of language.* Harlow, UK: Longman.

Gee, J. P. (2011). *Hope to do discourse analysis: A toolkit.* New York: Routledge.

van Leeuwen, T. (2008). *Discourse and practice: New tools for critical discourse analysis.* New York: Oxford University Press.

Wodak, R. (Ed.). (1997). *Gender and discourse.* London: Sage.

Case Study Method: Methodological Resources

Gagnon, Y.-C. (2010). *The case study as research method.* Boisbriand, Quebec, Canada: Presses de l'Université du Quebec.

Gomm, R., Hammersley, M., & Foster, P. (Eds.). (2000). *Case study method.* London: Sage.

Platt, J. (1992). Cases of cases . . . of cases. In C. C. Ragin & H. S. Becker (Eds.), *What is a case? Exploring the foundations of social inquiry* (pp. 21–52). New York: Cambridge University Press.

Stake, R. E. (2005). *The art of case study research.* Thousand Oaks, CA: Sage.

Swanborn, P. (2011). *Case study research: What, why and how?* London: Sage.

Thomas, G. (2011). *How to do your case study: A guide for students and researchers.* London: Sage.

Yin, R. K. (2009). *Case study research: Design and methods* (4th ed.). Thousand Oaks, CA: Sage.

Reading Case Study Method

Aldinger, C., & Whitman, C. V. (2009). *Case studies in global school health promotion: From research to practice.* New York: Springer.

Kinuthia, W., & Marshall, S. (2010). *Educational technology in practice research* *and practical case studies from the field.* Charlotte, NC: Information Age.

McNabb, D. (2010). *Case research in public management.* New York: M. E. Sharpe.

Yin, R. K. (2003). *Applications of case study research.* Thousand Oaks, CA: Sage.

4

Qualitative Research Design

A common feature of qualitative projects is that they aim to create understanding from data as the analysis proceeds. This means that the research design of a qualitative study differs from that of a study that starts with an understanding to be tested, where often the hypothesis literally dictates the form, quantity, and scope of required data. This sort of design preempts other ways of looking at the research question.

Qualitative research is usually not preemptive. Whatever the study and whatever the method, the indications of form, quantity, and scope must be obtained from the question, from the chosen method, from the selected topic and goals, and also, in an ongoing process, from the data. Thus, research design is both challenging and essential, yet it is the least discussed and least adequately critiqued component of many qualitative projects.

Freedom from a preemptive research design should never be seen as release from a requirement to have a research design. In Chapter 2, we established how a research purpose points to a research question and how the question informs the choice of method. But these choices do not remove the task of designing a qualitative project. Therefore, we start this chapter by looking first at the levels of design and then at the goals of designing to specify the ultimate *scope* of a project and the *type* of data required. We end with practical advice on how you can tackle the ongoing tasks of designing your project so that you develop a research topic into a researchable question; we discuss the different levels and ways of planning, and the pacing of the project as a whole.

※ THE LEVELS OF DESIGN

Research design is created by the researcher, is molded (rather than dictated) by the method, and is responsive to the context and the participants. Creating research design involves seeing the project at different levels. Once you have located your project methodologically, you need to design the *pacing* of processes and *strategies* to be used, and at the same time you need to see the project as a *whole*.

The *pacing* of the project involves planning the sequencing of its components and the movement between data gathering and data analysis. This requires ongoing decisions during the project: When should you stop interviewing? When do you return to observing—as processes of analysis show that more data are needed to verify, or when thin areas in analysis are revealed? The selection of method informs selection of research strategies, but these are also chosen in the context of the research question (i.e., what you want to find out) and the research context. For example, because she was interested in emotions and private behavior, studying the experience of menopause in a Newfoundland village, Davis (1983) relied on interviews rather than observational data. On the other hand, Richards, Seibold, and Davis (1997) were investigating the social construction of menopause, so they used observation of women's support groups and information centers as well as many forms of interview.

The overall design of the project must be aimed at answering your research question, and we look at detailed examples of design below. You need to design a project that both fits and is obtained from the question, the chosen method, the selected topic, and the research goals. You should treat research design as a problem to be considered carefully at the beginning of the study and reconsidered throughout—it is never a given.

※ PLANNING DESIGN

Where to start? If the questions, problem, and method are to guide design, then this becomes a highly conceptual and complex process. It is helpful to start with two questions: What is the *scope* of this project, and what is the *nature* of the data required?

The Scope of the Project

By *scope*, we refer to the domain of inquiry, the coverage and reach of the project. Scope involves both the substantive area of inquiry (the limits of the research topic) and the areas to be researched (the setting[s] and the sample).

Definitions of the topic and the relevant concepts and theories as perceived by other investigators in part delimit the area of inquiry. Consideration of the scope of the study continues in the process of gathering and analyzing data. You must work carefully and in depth, without losing sight of the research goals; remain flexible, self-critical, and, at all times, analytical; and use the literature as a comparative template. Coding decisions demand that you constantly ask: "Is this an instance of this category, or is it something different?" During the project, you must continually revisit the substantive scope of inquiry. If the data do not fit the question, analysis is likely to lack clear focus; the project may take too long to saturate and conceptualize and so, frustratingly, may achieve very little. On the other hand, if the scope is set too rigidly too early, the study will be severely limited. Avoid preemptively committing your study to definitions of the phenomenon of interest and concepts from the literature, thereby predetermining meanings of concepts; avoid making decisions too early in the study and drawing conclusions too quickly. Such preemptive scoping will result in premature closure.

The *scope of the sample* and the selection of the setting are driven by two principles. One is that setting and sample are purposively selected. This may involve choosing the "best," most optimal example of the phenomenon and the setting in which you are most likely to see whatever it is you are interested in. It may involve observing or interviewing experts on that particular topic or experience. Alternatively, you may select a setting because it allows you to obtain examples of each of several stances or experiences. The study may proceed by snowball sampling (seeking further participants by using the recommendations of those participants already in the study).

The second principle of sampling is that once you have begun to understand whatever it is you are studying, your sampling strategies normally are extended through *theoretical sampling* (Glaser, 1978). This means that your selection of participants is directed by the emerging analysis, and the theory being developed from data is subsequently modified by data obtained from the next participants. The scope of a study is never just a question of how many but always includes who, where, and which settings will be studied; in what ways, by whom, and for how long they will be studied; and what can be asked and answered. All these questions must be asked repeatedly as the project progresses. The research question may require that you seek out *negative cases* (examples of experiences that are contrary to cases that support the emerging theory and that provide new dimensions, perhaps as indicated by the theory but not yet encountered) or *thin areas* from participants who have experienced special conditions that have been identified as significant. The scope of a project is bigger than its sample, for participants provide information about others *like them* or *unlike them*. Such "shadowed data" (Morse, 2001) provide you with further direction for your theoretical sampling. When sampling, you must be aware of when you are working inductively and discovering and when you are working deductively and verifying.

The interrelationship of the two components of scope becomes clear during the processes of data gathering and analysis. You need to ask constantly, "What scale of data and what range of settings and sources of data will give the strands required for *this* question, *this* topic, *this* method, *this* audience, *this* disciplinary or political context?" Asking and answering these questions about the project will help you locate it and establish the bounds of the question to be addressed and the goals to be rethought and realistically revised.

Designing the Scope

Scoping is an ongoing process in a project. It is rare for a qualitative researcher to set a scope and stick to it. Adjustments to the mode of making data are frequently required so that the project can be data driven. But this does not mean that such changes can "just happen." Changes ideally build on the researcher's growing understanding of the situation.

We recommend that you always keep in mind the following issues regarding scoping:

- The *substantive scope* of a project involves issues of comparison ("Will I understand the wider situation if I stay in this group?") and intervention ("Before I influence policy, how would I know if I were wrong?"). How many perspectives are needed? It is hard, for example, to study relationships only by observing interaction. If your question is about the relations between management and staff, you need to observe, if possible, but you must interpret your observations strictly in terms of your presence. You will also need other data sources; you need to talk to the managers and the staff, and you should examine relevant documents. These data sources will provide conflicting information—and you as the researcher have to make sense of the contradictions.

〰️ *Scoping for change* involves asking if this is a study of a process (most qualitative studies are) and, if so, what time period it involves. Beware of studying a process with static data. One-off interviews, for example, will give interviewees' accounts, or the versions they see as appropriate in the interview situation, of what happened in the past. Is this the process and are these the perceptions you need?

〰️ *Scoping for diversity* involves examining the sample, asking questions such as "Is the research question comparative? If so, how do I achieve an adequate comparative base?" As you come to understand gender, race, or class divisions, new issues of scope will emerge ("If I observe only those folks, I will not be accepted over there"). Scoping for diversity involves considering the scale of the research question ("Whose experience will I not hear?"). It requires attention to representation ("What is it that I want to make statements about? Does what I won't see matter?"). It also requires attention to the areas to be covered ("Is there more than one perspective on this issue?").

As you reevaluate each of these issues, the answers will shift in response to your discovering, theorizing, and constructing theory. Scoping the project almost always shifts the question in the interplay between what can realistically be asked and what can properly be discovered. The process moves the question from a research question to a *researchable* one.

The Nature of the Data

How will you create data, and how will you ensure a fit of data to the research task? These are different questions. They require you to explore the possible ways of constructing data within a setting and to select methods that will combine to ensure that the data will be sufficiently rich, complex, and contextual to address the question and support the required analysis.

Thus, rather than preparing a research instrument for use throughout the project, in undertaking the design of a qualitative study, you need to consider carefully the variety of approaches available and the sorts of data they generate. Predesigned research instruments may be useful for some tasks (e.g., a survey form may be used to record basic demographic data about participants). But because the goals of the project include learning inductively from the data, instruments designed entirely in advance will rarely support an entire project.

You should expect that an interesting research question will usually require several strategies for making data. Relying on one technique may produce homogeneous data, which are highly unlikely to provide enough sources of understanding and ways of looking at a situation or a problem. Commitment to one sort of data makes the techniques of theoretical sampling very difficult to follow, so you need to resist the easy route of selecting one technique and building in the assumption that you will "do focus groups" or "do in-depth interviews." Keep asking, "Why would this one way of making data suffice to answer my question?" We share a concern with other scholars that data in qualitative projects are becoming increasingly homogeneous, as "in-depth" interviews take over from the previous speckled diversity of qualitative records. Our advice is to avoid reaching for a technique of making data with which you are familiar or in which you have been trained. Rather, ask how, in this situation, you can best access the accounts of behavior and experience required by your topic, best weigh the different versions of "reality," and best interpret them.

You should expect that the nature of the data will change during your project. The importance of having a budget and timeline can easily overtake the requirement of growing a project informed by the data. Starting with the assumption that they are "doing interviews," researchers are easily led to see as the only relevant question the issue of how many respondents they should "do." (We recommend reflection on discourse here—both about what you are proposing and how you are expressing it!) Even the most expert researchers cannot answer the sample size question without involvement in the project. What constitutes a large enough sample will be determined in the future by the topic, the situation studied, and the quality of data. But the fact that the question is asked should alert you to its corollary: "What else could or should I be doing to create a strong and rich data set?"

Focus on the end, not only on the beginning, of the project, and particularly on the claims to be made ("What am I asking of these data?" "What types and combinations of data do I need to create?"). Try to foresee the adequacy of likely results ("What will I not see if I rely on these sources?").

Ask yourself about your own ability to create the data ("Will I be able to do this, to be accepted in this situation, to conduct these sessions, to find participants?"). Try also to foresee limitations ("If I seek nuances of meaning in people's language, how can I ensure that my records contain these and that they are not determined by my intervention?"). At this earliest stage, it is helpful to *think backward* from possible outcomes. What sort of a study of this issue would be convincing? What ground do you want to be able to claim? Who do you want to persuade, and how would they be persuaded? How will you know, at that wonderful final stage of reporting, if you were wrong?

◊◊ DOING DE/IGN

We have emphasized the importance of allowing the questions, problem, and method to inform the scope of the project and nature of the data, and also the importance of the researcher's actively designing and controlling the project. How do you do both?

A good place to start is to read other studies critically. What is it about particular studies and their designs that convinces you (or that is convincing to you)? Do those authors persuade you that they were not wrong? The qualitative studies that you find exciting are likely to be convincing because the projects had the scope of design and the nature of data necessary to answer the research questions with the methods chosen. Unconvincing projects are those in which the researchers try to make claims where there is no justification or try to stretch thin data beyond their capacity to hold an argument.

If the task of starting is daunting, we recommend that you approach it by taking the five steps outlined below. As you prepare your proposal, you will find it helpful to keep an account of these steps and your thinking as you proceed and of the puzzles that confront you and the ideas that occur. Many researchers commence their projects with proposals that avoid critical questions, which also often means that they avoid design—a problematic stance.

◊◊ *Step 1: Establishing purpose.* What are you asking? Why are you asking it? Who has asked it or something like it before, and how and why did those studies not satisfy your curiosity? (Treat your literature review as qualitative research.) What are you doing that adds to what they did? What is your intent? What do you want to come out of this? What do you know, and what advantage and disadvantage is this? Revisit the discussion of topic selection in Chapter 2. (Particularly, at this stage, do not assume that being "one of them" gives you enough knowledge to research "them." Treat being one of them as a problem, not an advantage.)

※ *Step 2: Methodological location.* What is the appropriate fit of qualitative method to this question and topic? Never start with the method and then seek a topic. Does the method point you in the direction of research design? Particular methods usually require certain sorts of data—what sorts of data are you going to need to do your project this way? Revisit the discussion in Chapter 2 of the armchair walkthrough technique.

※ *Step 3: Scoping.* Now move on to the task of defining the scope of your project. What is it that you want to make statements about? Do you know enough about the field to determine who you should sample? If not, build in preparatory fieldwork—this is *not a pilot* but a stage in itself. Do you know enough about the issues? If not, build in preparatory identification of them. Are you comparing anything? If so, design for comparison. Are you intervening? If so, how, and are you planning for this?

※ *Step 4: Planning the nature of your data.* What *sorts* of data will be relevant? What sorts are available? How, and in what order, will they be combined? Are you able to handle those sorts of data? The design should include your data-handling methods and the ways you will use software. (Note that one of the classic howlers of research is to say of any software program that it "will analyze" the data!)

※ *Step 5: Thinking ahead.* How satisfying will this study be? How robust? Why should it be believed? How will you know if you were wrong? Present your proposal to skeptical audiences, and become a skeptic yourself. The goal is to start your study knowing that it will be convincing at the end.

※ DESIGNING FOR VALIDITY

Validity is a term too often avoided in qualitative research because it is mistakenly seen as an indicator of attitudes toward analysis or interpretation that do not fit with qualitative methods. In the literature of every method you will find debate about the term's possible meanings in qualitative research, and sometimes alerts about "the crisis of legitimation" (Denzin & Lincoln, 2005) or complex suggestions about especially "qualitative" terminology. As you prepare your research design, it is important to be aware of how the issues are considered in your chosen method.

However, it is also important to ensure that you are designing a project whose outcome will be appropriate and fully justifiable, as properly based in the data. This is the commonsense and dictionary meaning of *validity*: a valid assertion is "well founded and applicable; sound and to the point; against which no objection can fairly be brought" (*Shorter Oxford English Dictionary*, as quoted in Richards, 2005, p. 139).

Two general rules guide research design for validity in all qualitative projects. The first is the theme of this book: Pay attention always to the fit of question, data, and method. This will ensure that the data are appropriate and appropriately handled and the question addressed fully and responsibly. From this requirement, it may follow that you should set up specific ways of checking how the data and method are performing. For example, checking the reliability of coding may assist a team project. However, those checks should always be designed and carried out consistently with the method (Richards, 2009, pp. 108–109).

The second general rule is to ensure that you can properly account for each step in your analysis. All qualitative projects get their claim to trustworthiness from the researcher's ability to account for the outcome (Maxwell, 1992). From this requirement, it follows that from the design stage, you should set up processes by which you can log each significant decision and the interpretation of each discovery. Doing this as you work will be very important. Remember that qualitative analysis builds theory out of the data, one interpretation providing the platform for another inquiry. Your log of that journey will be the prime source of your justification of where you arrived and what you discovered (Richards, 2009, pp. 25–27, 193–195).

At the research design stage, consider what your project design needs now to ensure that your conclusions will be regarded as sound and well founded. The steps outlined in this chapter take you through stages of design, with warnings about how they can go wrong. For more detail on the ways you can check the soundness of your analysis, go to Chapter 9, where we return to the challenges of "getting it right."

⟨⟨ PROJECT PACING

What does a good design look like? The sort of evolving design described above will be less tidy than one for a survey research project, where properly collecting data is the first stage, followed in turn by coding and analyzing. A qualitative research design is more like a journey in which each of the stages builds on previous experiences. Planning flexibly for these stages helps you confront the work often not factored into a design, helps you budget time and money, and helps you distribute workloads and manage relationships with your significant others. One of the interesting results of planning this way is that you discover that no stage ends neatly so another can begin. Whether or not you are required to make a formal proposal with timelines, it is worthwhile to draw up a schedule that includes the five stages described below. (If you are required to write a proposal, see the details provided in Chapter 11.)

Conceptualizing Stage

Plan and budget for careful thinking through of the project, the literature review, and critiques of other studies. Plan to do this early—and keep doing it. You will need to continue to read and critique the literature throughout the study as new relevant research appears and new studies emerge. Handle the literature review data as data—using the data-handling method you intend to use later for the interviews or field notes. (If you are using a computer program, now is the time to get to know it well. Aim to learn ways to use your software for the basic techniques of storing the materials acquired—before you acquire them.)

Entering the Field

Treat entering the field as research work: Prepare and budget for it. Your field may be a location (such as a school), or it may be entering a topic (the people who have the disease you are studying or who share an experience of discrimination). In many disciplines, the emphasis is on making data through direct, obtrusive methods such as interviews or focus groups, where researchers are deprived of the insights of ethnography. If you do not know the literature on field research, explore it now. It will alert you to the observer's task of preparing for, gaining entry to, and becoming accepted in a setting.

If you are working in a familiar area, be especially careful. A useful mind-set is to regard yourself as *reentering* the field as an observer. Assume that the advantage of understanding problems and perspectives is at least partly balanced by the disadvantage of the insider's taken-for-granted assumptions, commitments, labels, and ways of seeing. If you are studying a familiar topic (a problem or group you know) by more obtrusive methods, such as interviews, be particularly cautious on entering the field. When you spend only a couple of hours with an interviewee, your assumptions can go unchallenged.

Setting Up and Managing a Data Management System

For obvious reasons, any research design must include the ways in which you intend to handle data. We hope that by now it is clear that establishing a data-handling system must be done very carefully: The system you choose must be tailored to the task and adequate to the scope of the project and the varieties of data and analysis expected. (The literature is often silent on this essential stage, but for exceptions, see Lofland & Lofland, 1995, and Richards, 2009.) You need to plan for the data-handling system you will use from the beginning of the project; you must be sure that you are familiar with it and that it is working from the start. Note that this advice is especially important for team projects (Richards, 1999, 2009). Your research design should allow for the time you will need to develop a system that works for you and for the time it will take for you to learn any skills, particularly computer skills, that the project will require.

Now is the time to learn the software skills that you will need throughout the project. You should at this stage make decisions about the software you will use, learn to use it competently, and become familiar with the range of processes it will support. Then, as soon as possible, you should start using it. To delay working with your software is to risk serious disadvantage. If material piles up on paper, waiting to be entered on your computer, the workload of managing your data will grow, as will your anxiety about being able to handle your data. Bringing the early material immediately into the computer will give you confidence, time to learn software techniques, and the ability to integrate research design materials with the data records you will soon start to create. This chapter, and each of the next three, concludes with a section on software tools relevant to the chapter's content.

Sampling and Theoretical Sampling

Allow time in your design for the process of locating and evaluating the ways you can sample the studied area. This can be very demanding; never assume a sample is waiting for you like an apple waiting to be plucked from a tree.

Treat theoretical sampling (i.e., the selection of participants according to the needs of your emerging analysis) as a necessity and build time and budget for it into your design. In a grant application, state areas where further sampling is likely, and budget time and other resources accordingly.

Analysis

Any project design must allow for the cognitive processes of research. Build *thinking* into your timeline and your budget. In a grant application, allow time for coding of data, for recoding of exploratory categories, and for management and exploration of category systems, as well as for coding validation and reliability exploration. Allow time for asking questions and incorporating the answers into your analysis. And, above all, allow time for writing, rewriting, revisiting the data, and verifying your conclusions.

⁂ DESIGNS USING MORE THAN ONE STUDY

We argued in Chapter 3 that for novices it is unwise to attempt research designs that fit two or more methods into the same study. But you will meet research projects that clearly require more than one study, possibly using more than one method. So you need to understand how good designs can combine methods to increase the scope of the project, either by obtaining new dimensions of the topic or by expanding it theoretically. They may aim to

⧼⧽ increase the scope of the study by addressing questions that require *a method and at least one additional strategy* from a different method to be adequately answered (a *mixed method design*);

⧼⧽ increase the scope of the study by addressing questions that require more than one study using *different methods* (a *multiple method design*); or

⧼⧽ increase the scope of an area of inquiry by evaluating and combining a set of completed studies addressing a similar topic (sometimes termed *metasynthesis*).

Mixed Method Designs

We have emphasized that particular methods are better than others at obtaining certain types of data, by accessing dimensions of the phenomena more easily than other methods can. An ethnography, for instance, may access structure but poorly describe emotions (Beatty, 2010), and a phenomenological study may access meaning and emotion but offer little about context and structure. A mixed method design may access more than one dimension within the same project, thereby making the results broader and more comprehensive.

Combining Qualitative Studies

Sometimes a single qualitative method cannot access data adequately to answer the research question completely. The core method—that is, the main, complete method—may be supplemented by another project, *paced* either simultaneously with the core project or sequentially. Different data will be needed for this strategy and should be kept separate from the main project data, even though the participants may be the same and it may seem to them that they are participating in the same project. When the analysis is completed, the results of the supplementary component may be incorporated into the results narrative, contributing comparative accounts or adding description that the first core methods could not access. Usually such a supplementary component continues until the researcher is *certain enough* that the component's subquestion is answered. For example:

- Building an assessment guide: The core component may be a grounded theory exploring the process and stages of recovering; from this theory, the researcher subsequently develops indicators that may be used in surveys.
- Qualitative evaluation research: The core component consists of ethnography, based on nonparticipant observations of workers. Once this is analyzed, a supplemental component is semistructured interviews developed from these observations.

Combining Qualitative and Quantitative Studies

Undoubtedly, the most common mixed method design is one that combines a qualitative study with a quantitative one. You will find a wide range of such studies and growing literature about them (Tashakkori & Teddlie, 2010). There is a strong emphasis on the ways such combinations can be rigorously done using computer software (Bazeley, 2010). In designing such a study, consider always that it has two parts, with different methods. Whether the primary study is qualitative or quantitative, the validity of its partner study must not be compromised by inadequate design and data.

Frequently, in mixed method designs the qualitative component is the minor supplementary component. A subsequent qualitative project may take analysis further than statistical analysis could do. For example, a case study project may be designed to explore in depth the experiences of a minority group whose problems are identified by the main project, a quantitative survey.

When the main project (i.e., the core component) is qualitative, it may have a simultaneous or sequential supplemental quantitative component (Morse & Niehaus, 2009). This usually employs a standardized instrument to measure quantifiable aspects of the sample characteristics and/or their responses. The primary role of a supplementary component is to measure responses, or, with a sequential component, to test conjectures or hypotheses by using quantification.

Different procedures will be required to ensure validity of both studies. For example, because the core component requires a small, purposeful sample, rather than the larger, random sample required in quantitative methods, any instrument used with the qualitative sample must either have standardized norms against which the researcher can compare the obtained scores. The quantitative supplementary data may be used in two ways. Each individual's score may be used in the descriptive profiling of each participant. Alternatively, if a separate sample is drawn, data sets are analyzed separately and the results of the quantitative supplementary strategy used to enhance description of the findings of the primary qualitative study. For instance, a researcher may note, "The participants in the study were so anxious that their scores on the anxiety scale were 2 standard deviations above the mean of the standardized population."

Multiple Method Designs

Researchers may conduct simultaneously or sequentially two complete projects that address the same research question. In contrast to mixed method design, this is comparatively easy. The two projects are self-contained and could be published separately. But, because each project addresses a different dimension of the research question and may differ in scope or level of abstraction about the same phenomenon, the two projects are complementary and together enhance our understanding of the phenomenon under study. (Often researchers get three publications from a two-project multiple methods study: one from each method and one combined.)

The two projects may be at different levels of abstraction (for instance, a microanalytic study of touch and one of gross motor movement). Or they could be studies using different data types (for instance, a qualitative and a quantitative study) or conducted on different populations (but perhaps linked by context). Because both studies are complete in themselves, multiple method design does not have any of the complexities we find in mixed methods studies regarding incompatibilities with sampling, inductive/deductive incompatibilities, or difficulties defending inadequate, unsaturated data.

Synthesizing Multiple Studies

Finally, researchers may conduct systematic review of a number of studies pertaining to a common topic and formally integrate the findings to create a new "metasynthesis" (Sandelowski & Barroso, 2007). Through integration and analysis of the categories and themes, the concepts and theories of a set of completed studies—by different researchers—are melded into new findings. The challenges of this work are considerable, since researchers may have focused on slightly different questions, used a different theoretical stance, had a different political purpose for conducting the study, held a different disciplinary perspective, or worked with different populations. The synthesis might focus on a problem within a particular group, such as Hispanics and obesity in adolescents (Jean, Bondy, Wilkinson, & Forman, 2009) or Hispanics and obesity in children with diabetes (Clark, Bunik, & Johnson, 2010). Or the synthesis might center on a theory—for instance, body image and obesity in Hispanics (Hughes, Sherman, & Whitaker, 2010)—or on the outcomes of the research—for instance, the effects of quality improvement and health information technology on diabetes outcomes in African American and Hispanic patients (Baig et al., 2010).

Using Different Ways of Looking

Variety of data and focus can be built into a research design without its involving multiple projects. We conclude this discussion with two ways of using different data sources within the same project—comparative research and triangulated research design.

Comparative Design

If your question demands that you determine what is special about a group or identify particular conditions or circumstances, you may need a two-group design. Ideally, you will keep data from the two groups separate, as well as theoretical sampling driven by each group, and saturate the data separately. Later in the research process, you will compare and contrast these data sets to determine similarities and differences between the two groups. Sampling and data collection will continue beyond this phase so that the emerging analysis may be expanded and verified.

Comparative qualitative research is important, for example, in evaluation. Qualitative inquiry alone will not answer "how much" or "how many" or, therefore, how great a difference has resulted from an intervention. But a researcher can look at such questions by using a two-group design in which both groups have had similar experiences but only one group received the intervention, or by examining a single group before, during, and after intervention. Such studies, conducted outside of the laboratory, are called naturalistic experiments.

Triangulated Design

A text search of grant applications in many countries would return a high count for the odd word *triangulation*—so would a vote among researchers for the most misused term. Originally coined to describe a specific sort of research design, *triangulation* is now widely used to mean vaguely "three sorts of something." But exactly what is triangulation?

Triangulation refers to the gaining of multiple perspectives through completed studies that have been conducted on the same topic and directly address one another's findings. To be considered triangulated, studies must "meet"—that is, one must encounter another in order to challenge it (for clarification), illuminate it (add to it conceptually or theoretically), or verify it (provide the same conclusions). Goffman (1989) coined the term, drawing on the metaphor of the surveyor's practice of making sightings from two known points to a third.

Like the surveyor, the qualitative researcher may be aided by drawing from different perspectives on the same question or topic. Triangulation requires careful research designs to ensure the same question will be addressed, and answered, by each of the proposed approaches (Richards, 2009, p. 20). A researcher may do this by juxtaposing analysis of different data *types* and *methods* to illuminate the same *question* (e.g., field note records of participant observation in a school are examined for the picture they give of authority behavior, and authority is "sighted" differently via a study that used interviews in private with students and teachers). More ambitiously, researchers may address the same question in *separate studies* designed for direct comparison and using different methods and data. If they reach the same conclusion, they will use triangulation to verify or challenge alternative interpretations. Or, in a third form of triangulation, a researcher may address the same topic as that addressed by another but through a different *question, method, setting,* and *data* to gain a different perspective (e.g., in a study of prejudice in a community, a study using a survey method gathers precoded results to feed statistical analysis while observation in various community organizations reaps a record of how people from the same community, who may or may not have participated in the survey study, behave in public).

These are all useful techniques—as long as the question is being properly sighted from the different angles. Such multiple sightings on an understanding can be extraordinarily revealing; a new interpretation of the sources of teachers' apparent authority may come to light or new information concerning the ways in which prejudice is concealed.

The necessary condition of such good results is, of course, a good research design. If you elect to use a triangulated design, it is essential that, from the start, you are clear about your purpose in using such a design and that you make explicit in each stage of the research design what you are claiming you can do with it and what it will add.

Avoid misusing the term *triangulation*. One does *not* do triangulation by interpreting the same data using different theories or by gathering a multidisciplinary team of investigators or coders. And although you may have complicated data—for example, in the form of a couple of data sets, neither of which can be a complete study in itself, or a few interviews conducted from a different perspective—they do not necessarily offer different sightings on the same question. The following research designs, all of which may be constructive and successful, are *not* examples of triangulation:

- \\\\ Multiple data sources used in a single study to build a single picture (such as ethnography consisting of interviews, observations, and so forth)

- \\\\ A second study added on to the first (six case studies more! Increasing your sample size is not triangulation.)

- \\\\ Two studies that do not reflect on the same phenomenon or the same question (Studies that are not designed to give sightings on the same question are highly unlikely to meet in their conclusions.)

- \\\\ Juxtaposition of quantitative and qualitative inquiry (For example, a study of step-parenting that uses in-depth interviews of step-parents may be informed by a study using census data on the distribution of step-parenting across California. The survey provides context for the qualitative study, but it does not address the same question or strengthen, add to, or potentially challenge the results of the other.)

\\\\ TAKING AN OVERVIEW

As you design your project, step back frequently to view it from afar. Talk about it to skeptical colleagues. Write about it to distant friends. Being able to see it as a whole is important. What will it uncover, and what are you aiming for (Richards, 2009, Chapter 7)?

Seeing your project overall will prevent you from going into a situation with the conviction that understanding will just happen, or from collecting the data first and then thinking about them. It will help you avoid narrow designs, homogeneous data projects, and making data (often volumes of data) without knowing why or that you have the skills and resources to handle the resulting richness. It will warn you against writing a proposal that gives a vague direction—to "get in there and find out what's going on." It will push you to sharpen your reflection on the appropriate *ways* to get in, on where or what *there* is, and how one *would* find out. The vaguer the research question and the less located the context, the more the project is at risk of wandering aimlessly—and the more you need a research design. Good studies rarely, if ever, just happen (and studies are not often funded on the basis of a promise that they will be good).

When detail threatens to cloud your bigger picture, return to looking at your project overall. Unfunded research requires focus on a question and a design to answer it, perhaps more urgently than does funded research because the constraints may be greater. Just as the funding body needs to understand your research design, so do you need to know that your project is likely to contribute to understanding of your topic, that it is within your capability and resources, and that it has a shape and a likely outcome. Like the funding body, you will also want to know for ethical reasons that the possibly invasive processes of data making are designed to contribute an answer to something worth asking. During this process, you will be asking yourself constantly how to scope the project to maximize the chances of achieving an adequate answer and how to design the data so they contribute to an understanding that is not just good enough but convincing.

〰 CHOOSING YOUR SOFTWARE

Researchers who have not previously used specialist qualitative software will face an obvious early task, to choose from the available software types and products. If the choice is not made for you, by institutional licensing or availability of skilled assistance, you will need to research the range of software functions and then their appropriateness to your research design.

If you are planning to combine qualitative and quantitative modes of analysis, this means you are choosing *two* software packages. Making that choice requires a good knowledge not only of how each works but also of their compatibility and appropriateness to your project.

Note from Tables 4.2 and 4.3 that qualitative programs differ greatly in the ways they can link with quantitative programs.

Think of this choice process as another step in the pursuit of methodological congruence. Just as research purposes and questions fit with data types and analysis strategies, so do software tools fit, for better or worse, with all these aspects of research design. Start there, setting out what you are asking, what data you expect to be handling, and by what methods of analysis, and then ask which of the tools available in software would best assist you.

The task is less daunting now than it was in earlier stages of software development. When computer tools were first designed for qualitative research, very different types could be identified (Tesch, 1990; Weitzman & Miles, 1995). Two decades later, there is a substantial common ground for basic functions, summarized in the regularly updated comparisons at the CAQDAS Networking Project website (http://www.surrey.ac.uk/sociology/research/researchcentres/caqdas/index.htm).

The main commonalities and differences at the time of writing are summarized in Tables 4.1 through 4.4.

Table 4.1 Your Project and Your First Data		
Expect This of All Qualitative Software	*Look for These Differences*	*When Will This Matter?*
Provision for storage and managing of data and interpretations in a single unit or project	Programs differ in how a project is saved, stored, and transported.	Researchers nervous about security, ease of backup, and sharing of team projects should check for software help.
Ways of combining and comparing projects	Most programs support merging of projects, but they differ in flexibility of merging parts of projects.	This will matter if you have multiple researchers or sites or a good reason for combining your own projects.
Ways of backing up and safely storing projects	Programs differ in whether the source data is imported to the software or remains external to the software.	Mode of storage, if not understood, can imperil a project—be very clear about what should be backed up!
Ways of interfacing with other software	Programs differ greatly in whether they are designed to import from and export to statistical or database software.	This will be critical if you plan mixed methods research.

Table 4.2 Your Data Documents, Ideas, and Links

Expect This of All Qualitative Software	Look for These Differences	When Will This Matter?
Handling of text data for the project	Programs differ in permitted file formats (plain text, rich text, or specialized formats, including pictures, tables, etc.).	Text formatting matters most for projects with "rich" records.
Ability to create and edit text within the project; ability to type memos	Programs differ in whether data documents can be freely edited once "in" and in the flexibility of editing memos.	Typing up in the project matters most for records you want to code or annotate as you create them.
Inclusion of text data files in the project	Programs differ in whether they import the documents or link to files kept externally.	Where the data are stored may matter for security and convenience.
Handling nontext data—photos, videos, etc. (either importing and coding directly or ways of representing nontext records)	Some but not all will import nontext (pictures, video, or audio). Others vary in terms of what can be done with multimedia data.	This is a central concern if your design requires detailed analysis of nontext data.
Storing information (such as demographics) about people or places, etc.	Most will import such information from spreadsheets or statistics software but differ in options and display and in the flexibility with which you can use this information.	This is critical if you are doing mixed methods research or have a large sample.
Creation and editing of documents and memos from within the program	Programs differ in flexibility to edit and in ways memos are created and whether and how they are searched. Check whether the program is designed for extensive editing or just for corrections.	This is important if your method requires constant reflective records as theories are built (e.g., grounded theory).
Annotating or commenting on text	Programs differ in ways of annotating particular passages of your data, how annotations can be viewed, and how they are reported.	This is important if your method requires fine-detail commenting on discourse in texts (e.g., discourse analysis).
Support for linking to data within and outside of project	Programs have very different approaches and methods of linking: Look for what can be linked and how.	This matters if your method requires you to bring data together in ways other than coding.

Table 4.3 Coding and Text Search

Expect This of All Qualitative Software	Look for These Differences	When Will This Matter?
Coding of selected data into categories created by the researcher (called "codes" or "nodes") and retrieving all data coded into a category	Programs differ in mode of selection of data and procedure of coding. Some programs allow the researcher to record weighting of coding.	Coding style and facility are important to most researchers—try out software to see if you like the way it codes!
Ability to view all the data you have coded at a category	Programs differ in how you view coded data and whether and how the context can be retrieved. They also differ in how you can work with coded data to revise coding and optionally code further from it.	This matters most for methods where coding is just a first step toward interpretation, especially if it is important to explore the dimensions of a category.
Ability to see on the screen what coding you've done (usually in margin, sometimes by highlighting or reporting)	Programs differ in whether all coding can be seen at once and how the markings can be used to explore that code.	It will matter if you rely on (and are concerned about) coding or if in teams you want to compare coding.
Autocoding of data (mechanical finding and coding of words or segments)	Programs differ in how easily this is done and how much formatting is required, as well as whether you can set the context you want coded.	This is particularly important to projects with a lot of very structured data or requiring immediate retrieval (e.g., everything said by a particular speaker).
Text search of words in data and sometimes coding of the findings	Programs differ in the ways they conduct searches and store results, and whether you can save searches and results.	This is important if your method requires the mechanical processes of word search and/or further exploration of results.
Counting of codes or occurrences of words; quantitative content analysis	Some offer word frequency counts and quantitative reporting of searches, and some the ability to create your own dictionary.	This is important if your method requires counts. If so, check out "text retriever" and "content analysis" programs.

Table 4.4 Abstracting, Modeling, Questioning, and Reporting

Expect This of All Qualitative Software	Look for These Differences	When Will This Matter?
Management and viewing of coding categories	Most programs support hierarchical cataloguing of categories for review and access.	This is important if your coding categories will be numerous and/or if you are sharing coding schema.
Asking questions (with "search" or "query" tools) about patterns in the coding of data	Programs differ in ability to search combinations (e.g., Boolean, proximity) of coding, text, and the characteristics associated with people or places. Some allow multiple searches producing matrices for pattern exploration.	Some methods require sophisticated searches (e.g., matrices to show patterns). Do a "walkthrough" of the project to check how you want to query your data.
Saving of search results	Some save them as reports only, while others allow the possibility for the search results to be incorporated in the database.	This matters if you want to build inquiries on your coding patterns.
Ability to run repetitive searches	Only some programs provide for the researcher to write scripts to set up analysis processes.	This is important for projects where computer searching must be adapted to the design.
Visual displays	Most provide some tool for modeling. These vary greatly from simple diagrams to live data representations of theories and networks.	If visual representation of what is happening in your project is important, check what you need the software to display.
Ways of seeing connections you have recorded in the data	Some packages have tools to get you "up" from the text and display connections in a model view.	This is important for analyzing a case in depth instead of across cases and for getting the big picture of a project.
Making reports of data, codes, coding, etc.	Programs vary in the way reports are created and presented.	If you have particular report needs, check that these are supported.

⫸ U∫ING YOUR ∫OFTWARE FOR RE∫EARCH DE∫IGN

We end this chapter, and each of the next three, with a brief discussion of what specialized qualitative software offers for the tasks discussed and how it changes what the researcher can do. These sections describe and discuss the ways of doing qualitative research using computer software under three headings—approaches, advances, and alerts. They advise on what you can ask of your software, then on the ways software enables doing things that could not be done by manual methods, and, finally, on how to avoid temptations and pitfalls.

All qualitative researchers now use software of some sort. Their interviews are typed on computers, their sample characteristics entered in spreadsheets. But most will also use specialist software designed to help with the challenges of managing complex qualitative data records without losing their context, and with storing and exploring the growing ideas about those data records.

What does software offer the researcher approaching the issues discussed in this chapter? At this early stage of a project, what approaches are supported by software? What advances in method does software offer? And what are the traps and temptations to which you should be alerted?

Approaches

Early in a project, important tasks are organizational. Taking the steps to a good research design as described in this chapter, you will make a lot of records of your thinking, reading, scoping of the project, and planning. Research proposals, grant applications, and literature reviews are the intended outputs. The inputs can be messy and confusing.

Qualitative software is designed to help you handle messy inputs, so it will assist with these early records. Novice researchers often are misled into thinking they have to have "real" data before they can start using software. But there is no need to start by storing research design records separately from later records of interviews or field research. If you do so, it will be much harder to access these together throughout the project.

Start by learning how your software will store records and allow you to see them separately—in folders, sets, or groups. If you set up a project carefully, you will be able to access your plans and reviews alongside the other data records you will create when you commence interviewing or field research. So the contribution of software at the research design stage is as a reliable (but not rigid) container for plans, early considerations, and topics.

You need to learn now

〰 what your software can do and how to do it,

〰 how to start a project, and

〰 how to manage it—saving, backing up, and transporting it.

If you are planning to combine qualitative and quantitative modes of analysis, it is important to build into your research design consideration of the ways you will "mix" these. This will involve moving data between software packages. While it is still common for a "mixed method" study to be designed simply as two studies (Bryman, 2006), good mixed method research does not merely juxtapose two projects but also integrates them. To do this, you will need to plan, from the start of your research design, for the appropriate data and staging of analysis. Bazeley (2010) distinguishes between two major strategies for integration: using software to *combine* numeric and text data and using software to *convert* coding from qualitative data for statistical analysis. For more resources on this topic, visit www.researchsupport .com.au.

Advances

Computer software cannot design your project, but it can assist greatly in the data management tasks at this stage. Once you learn software skills, you will find that starting early in software has great advantages. And more important, starting early in software does not disadvantage you. Software tools are now far more fluid than those first developed for qualitative research. A good software package will allow you to create a project and then later change practically all aspects of it as your ideas about the data and analysis grow.

At the early stage of design, you can store drafts and estimates of project stages, and using the tools taught in later tutorials, you will be able to link them and shape the ideas that inform your design. As you work with the ideas and issues, you will be able to see more clearly what design decisions must be made or how, for example, you can design the sample of your study to encounter the range of discovered issues.

In the early stages of research design, the computer offers storage for documents and ideas—and the ability to link them by coding the relevant passages of documents and the relevant ideas so that all the relevant material can be retrieved later. The research design can be informed and directed by systematic storage of early explorations of the topic, serious reflection on the range of options for approaching it, and informed decision making.

Alerts

1. Software is not a method. Having chosen the software you will use, ensure that all your research moves are directed by your design and your method. Always be concerned if you are doing something just because your software can do it.

2. Starting in software gives great advantages later—as long as you remain flexible. Where you start will not be where you go: This is built into the method. If you start your project with software, start flexibly. Use software tools for storing your *changing* definitions of concepts, finely coding data about them, ordering them, and exploring their relationships. Any qualitative software package will allow the memos or coding categories to be changed at any time, reordered at any time, combined, or deleted as the data direct your understanding of them.

3. Avoid computer-assisted preemptive analysis. Software invites detailed elaboration of ideas and concepts from early data.

4. Setting up a project is not analysis. You must also start and continue reflecting on what you do. Making and designing a project should involve processes of recording and logging your thinking about your research design. The computer is not necessary to do this, of course, but it will help you clarify the choices you have and

the decisions to be made. As you prepare designs and time estimates, edit them to reflect on, change, and manage them. As you store your early ideas, describe and write about them.

5. Beware of flexibility as well as rigidity! Don't allow the fun of setting up a project and moving parts of it around distract you from the tasks of creating a research design (at least not for too long).

〰 ſUMMΛRY

Before beginning your project, you must carefully consider design, including how research strategies will be paced and how the method you choose will answer your research question. Consider how you will find participants and what scope your sample will obtain for the project. Does your design account for the purpose of the study? How will you locate your study methodologically? What data will you gather, and how will you handle these data? Which software will you use? Finally, consider *how* you will use the computer for management and analysis of data.

In this chapter, we have explained the need for careful design of a qualitative project and the special requirements of qualitative research design. Qualitative projects usually involve ongoing processes of design as the researcher designs and reviews the scope of the project and the nature of the data required. We have suggested the questions you should ask and the issues you should consider as you prepare a design, as well as the ways in which you can revisit and revise it as you commence your project. We have described the five steps of establishing your purpose, locating the study methodologically, deciding the scope of your inquiry, planning the nature of your data, and then thinking ahead to the goals you wish to achieve. As you plan, anticipate that your study will involve different stages, and allow time for each—conceptualizing, entering the field, creating a data management system, sampling and theoretical sampling, and final analysis.

Throughout this chapter, we emphasized that you need to see your project in terms of its overall design. We discussed combinations of designs. In addition, we introduced the first of a series of sections on qualitative computing. If you wish to learn software skills, Appendix 1 provides some places to start.

RESOURCES

Beginning Design

Hart, C. (1998). *Doing a literature review: Releasing the social science research imagination*. London: Sage.

Piantanida, M., & Garman, N. B. (2009). *The qualitative dissertation: A guide for students and faculty* (2nd ed.). Thousand Oaks, CA: Corwin Press.

Richards, L. (2005). *Handling qualitative data: A practical guide*. London: Sage.

Yin, R. K. (2011). *Qualitative research from start to finish*. New York: Guilford.

Doing Design

Bernard, H. R. (2000). *Social research methods: Qualitative and quantitative approaches*. Thousand Oaks, CA: Sage.

Creswell, J. W. (2009). Qualitative inquiry and research design: Choosing among five approaches (2nd ed.). Thousand Oaks, CA: Sage.

Goffman, E. (1989). On fieldwork. *Journal of Contemporary Ethnography, 18*, 123–132.

Lofland, J., & Lofland, L. H. (1995). *Analyzing social settings* (3rd ed.). Belmont, CA: Wadsworth.

Marshall, C., & Rossman, G. B. (1999). *Designing qualitative research* (3rd ed.). Thousand Oaks, CA: Sage.

Mason, J. (1996). *Qualitative researching*. London: Sage.

Maxwell, J. A. (1996). *Qualitative research design: An interactive approach*. Thousand Oaks, CA: Sage.

May, T. (Ed.). (2002). *Qualitative research in action*. Thousand Oaks, CA: Sage.

Morse, J. M. (2002). Principles of mixed and multimethod design. In A. Tashakkori & C. Teddlie (Eds.), *Mixed methodology: Combining qualitative and quantitative approaches*. Thousand Oaks, CA: Sage.

Morse, J. M., & Niehaus, L. (2009). *Mixed-method design: Principles and procedures*. Walnut Creek, CA: Left Coast Press.

Patton, M. Q. (2002). *Qualitative research and evaluation methods* (3rd ed.). Thousand Oaks, CA: Sage.

Richards, L. (1999). Qualitative teamwork: Making it work. *Qualitative Health Research, 9*, 7–10.

Richards, L. (2005). *Handling qualitative data: A practical guide*. London: Sage.

On Analysis

Bernard, H. R., & Ryan, G. W. (2010). *Analyzing qualitative data*. Thousand Oaks, CA: Sage.

Coffey, A., & Atkinson, P. (1996). *Making sense of qualitative data*. Thousand Oaks, CA: Sage.

Miles, M. B., & Huberman, A. M. (1994). *Qualitative data analysis: An expanded sourcebook* (2nd ed.). Thousand Oaks, CA: Sage.

Wolcott, H. F. (1994). *Transforming qualitative data: Description, analysis, and interpretation.* Thousand Oaks, CA: Sage.

Mixed Methods

Bazeley, P. (2009). Integrating analyses in mixed methods research [Editorial]. *Journal of Mixed Methods Research,* 3(3), 203–207.

Bazeley, P. (2009). Mixed methods data analysis. In S. Andrew & E. Halcomb (Eds.), *Mixed methods research for nursing and the health sciences* (pp. 84–118). Chichester, UK: Wiley-Blackwell.

Bazeley, P. (2010). Computer assisted integration of mixed methods data sources and analyses. In A. Tashakkori & C. Teddlie (Eds.), *Handbook of mixed methods research for the social and behavioral sciences* (2nd ed., pp. 431–467). Thousand Oaks, CA: Sage.

Creswell, J., & Plano-Clark, V. L. (2007). *Designing and conducting mixed methods research.* Thousand Oaks, CA: Sage.

Greene, J. C. (2007). *Mixed methods in social inquiry.* San Francisco: Jossey-Bass. Halcomb, E., & Andrew, S. (Eds.). (2010). *Mixed methods research for nursing and the health sciences.* Chichester, UK: Wiley-Blackwell.

Hesse-Biber, S. (2010). *Mixed methods research: Merging theory with practice.* New York: Guilford.

Morse, J. M., & Niehaus, L. (2009). *Mixed methods design: Principles and procedures.* Walnut Creek, CA: Left Coast Press.

Tashakkori, A., & Teddlie, C. (Eds.). (2010). *Handbook of mixed methods research for the social and behavioral sciences* (2nd ed.). Thousand Oaks, CA: Sage.

Multiple Method Designs

Darbyshire, P., Macdougall, C., & Schiller, W. (2005). Multiple methods in qualitative research with children: More insight or just more? *Qualitative Research,* 5(4), 417–436.

Morse, J. M., & Niehaus, L. (2009). *Mixed-method design: Principles and procedures.* Walnut Creek, CA: Left Coast Press.

Taber, N. (2010). Institutional ethnography, autoethnography, and narrative: An argument for incorporating multiple methodologies. *Qualitative Research,* 10(5), 5–25.

Metasynthesis

Morse, J. M., & Johnson, J. L. (Eds.). (1991). *The illness experience: Dimensions of suffering.* Newbury Park, CA: Sage.

Paterson, B. L., Dubouloz, C.-J., Chevrier, J., Ashe, B., King, J., & Moldoveanu, M. (2009). Conducting qualitative metasynthesis research: Insights from a metasynthesis project. *International Journal of Qualitative Methods, 8*(3), 22–33.

Sandelowski, M., & Barroso, J. (2007). *Handbook for synthesizing qualitative research.* New York: Springer.

Schrieber, R., Crooks, D., & Stern, P. N. (1997). Qualitative meta-analysis. In J. M. Morse (Ed.), *Completing a qualitative project: Details and dialogue.* Thousand Oaks: CA: Sage.

Thorne, S., Paterson, B., Acorn, S., Canam, C., Joachim, G., & Jillings, C. (2002). Chronic illness experience: Insights from a metastudy. *Qualitative Health Research, 2*(4), 437–452.

Zhao, S. (1991). Meta-theory, meta-method, meta-data analysis: What, why, and how? *Sociological Perspectives, 34,* 377–390.

Software and Design

Bazeley, P. (2008). Software tools and the development of multiple and mixed methods research. *International Journal of Multiple Research Approaches, 2*(1), 127–132.

Lewins, A., & Silver, C. (2007). *Using qualitative software: A step-by-step guide.* London: Sage.

Richards, L. (1998). Closeness to data: The changing goals of qualitative data handling. *Qualitative Health Research, 8,* 319–328.

Tesch, R. (1990). *Qualitative research: Analysis types and software tools.* London: Falmer.

Thompson, P. R. (1998). Sharing and reshaping life stories: Problems and potential in archiving research narratives. In M. Chamberlain & P. R. Thompson (Eds.), *Narrative and genre* (pp. 167–181). London: Routledge.

Weitzman, E., & Miles, M. B. (1995). *Computer programs for qualitative data analysis.* Thousand Oaks, CA: Sage.

Part II

INSIDE ANALYSIS

Chapter 5. Making Data

Chapter 6. Coding

Chapter 7. Abstracting

Chapter 8. From Method to Analysis: Revisiting
Methodological Congruence

5

Making Data

One of our goals in the preceding chapters has been to demystify the process of getting started on a qualitative research project. We aim to show it as a process of informed choice, reflection, flexible planning, and decision making, in which each step follows from the earlier ones and each choice fits with the others. In this chapter, we move to the tasks of asking what sorts of data you will need for the project on which you have embarked. As you are preparing to start a project, it is important to have a sense of the kinds of data you need to "make" in order to ask the questions you have posited, using the methodological approach you think is most relevant, to attain the kinds of outcomes you seek.

It helps to think of qualitative data as *made* rather than merely "collected." To speak of data as being "gathered" or "collected" is to imply that data preexist, ready to be picked like apples from a tree. Gathering apples from a tree changes the context of the apples (they are in a basket instead of on a branch) but makes no inherent change in the apples themselves. This is not so with data. Qualitative researchers collect not actual events but representations, usually reports or accounts of events. Talking of "collecting" data denies the agency of the researcher. Try challenging this convention by referring to data as being "made." *Making data* is a collaborative, ongoing process in which data are interactively negotiated by the researcher and participants; the data are rarely fixed and unchanging, never exactly replicating what is being studied. And of course, like any collaborative process, making data is complex and, in the laboratory/experimental sense, impossible to control.

All these observations are true of research employing questionnaires as well as observation or unstructured interviews. The stereotypical pollster with a foot in the door and a clipboard-mounted checklist instrument is probably more active than the participant observer in defining a situation in which certain answers are more or less likely, but all qualitative data have particularly intriguing relationships with their researchers, the participants, and the realities they represent.

〽 WHAT DATA WILL YOUR STUDY NEED?

On the path from selecting a topic and refining a question, investigating the appropriateness of different methods and considering research design, you will often have considered what data such a study would require. The topic and question indicate not only what you need answers to but also *whose* answers and what sorts of answers. The method selected suggests what you will want to *do with* your data, what you will need to *ask of* your data records, and what sorts of inquiry they must support. If tackling your research question with a grounded theory study, you will need people's own rich accounts of their experiences. So your method of gathering these accounts will have to allow them to talk on, unimpeded by your questions. If your task is to analyze cultural practices, you may need rich records over time, of closely observed behavior.

This fit of question, method, and data may not be immediately obvious, and the data indicated may not be easily obtained. Most projects at this stage require thinking through what would be ideal data, and then thinking of what chances *this* researcher has of providing such data, given their resources, position, and skills. Don't despair if you clearly cannot access the ideal participants or travel to the perfect site. But when you are faced with your inability to provide the required data, always revisit the fit of question, method, and data. It is essential not to cling to a research question and method for which you cannot provide adequate data. Rather, return from such discoveries to rethink the topic, respecify the question as researchable, and revisit the method in the light of your understanding of what data you can realistically expect to bring to the project.

〽 WHAT WILL BE DATA (AND WHAT WILL NOT)?

All researchers, in many ways, select from everything they have seen or heard and decide what elements, from all this input, are and are not data. When observing a setting, for example, a researcher will focus on some things and pay less attention to others—things that seem not to relate to the research question or seem to be irrelevant "noise"—excluding them from data collections or from analysis. Those things that the researcher considers interesting and relevant to the research topic or question are recorded, usually in field notes or on audio or video recordings. This focusing is simply the way fieldwork progresses; not everything is relevant, and directing one's gaze toward significant events permits one to move along without getting bogged down in everyday trivia. But, of course, this judgment is selective, and you must always be aware of what you are selecting and why.

The process of recording compartmentalizes individual incidents. A researcher views a scene *interpretively*, responding from personal beliefs and values and filtering what is seen or recorded. Some details will simply be taken for granted, and the researcher will not even record them. Other things will jar or appear surprising, and the researcher will give them greater weight in the data, perhaps to the point that they overshadow other activities. Some things will distract or bore the researcher; others will excite or surprise. Thus, from what is experienced and observed, the researcher makes data.

It is a mistake to assume that technology removes interpretation. Video recording, for example, delimits an incident to what the researcher chooses to record and to whatever can be captured within the frame itself, giving each recorded incident a beginning and an end. Writing, with the limitations of language, memory, and the slow speed at which one can write, makes a summary representation of the actual scene.

The Researcher in the Data

Data are created in a particular form according to the method used. The research question determines the nature or type of research context the researcher must select and also indicates the type of participants and the form of the data (e.g., observational, verbal, or visual). These requirements delimit the choice of a research site and also indicate the nature of the resulting data.

Within this context, researchers make data in collaboration with their participants. The same technique—interviewing, for example—can make very different data records given different settings, research goals, and relationships between the researcher and those studied. The researcher may have no other relationship with participants than that of this fleeting encounter. At the other extreme, the researcher may see participants as equals, considering them to be co-researchers.

The increasing use of online data sources further complicates these relationships. Chat rooms, blogs, websites, and e-mail lists offer ethically challenging opportunities for anonymity, and the interaction of researcher and participant is far harder to assess and control than in face-to-face encounters.

It is obvious, then, that the nature of your relationship with those you study will dramatically affect all aspects of your project—the data, the analysis process, the ways you report and to whom. We return to these relationships, and the challenges of accounting for them, in later chapters. (For advice on logging your participation in the research, see Richards, 1990.) Making data is not a passive process; rather, it is an active, cognitive process that requires tremendous investment on the part of the researcher and requires extraordinary concentration. The nature of the questions asked and the attention the researcher gives to the participants and to detail will determine the quality of the data. For example, when the researcher is assuming the listening role in an interview, the participant is constantly observing the researcher and picking up nonverbal cues that implicitly guide the interview. Thus, the researcher must actively explore and unravel all aspects of the research questions and the interview context.

Good Data/Bad Data

Given the variety of processes involved in making data, the interaction between the researcher and the participant, and the collaboration necessary in data collection, data inevitably vary in quality. What constitutes "good" data for a project also varies, of course, with the research goals and opportunities. The collection of good data requires the best possible appropriate collaboration with participants—not only for ethical reasons but also so the participants will trust and help the researcher.

Within this variety, experienced researchers have a sense of what constitutes good data. The records are rich, thick, and dense, offering enough detail to allow someone to comprehend the situation or understand the setting without asking additional questions. Good data are relevant and focused, but not focused so tightly that the context is omitted from or restricted within the description. Good data have density. For example, in an interview project, questions asked of participants are usually consistent so that one interview, at least in part, confirms or builds on other interviews. Good data are developed in careful recognition of participants' perspectives. An interviewer, for example, guides interviews without "leading" the participants. The participants must always have enough space to present their own perspectives and have their say.

From this description of good data, we can learn what constitutes bad or unhelpful data. Again, generalizations are dangerous: What has no use for one research purpose may be valuable for another. Some data may disappoint, for example, because the researcher is too "present" in the data. In an interview project, if the interviewer asks leading questions or interrupts the participant, the data will explain things out of order, in a disjointed manner, rather than presenting the participant's story sequentially. In observational research, a researcher can easily become an artificial presence in a setting. Ideally, researchers have to maintain a delicate balance in which they are both in (a part of the scene) and out (not dominant). Researchers develop the skill of building this "in-but-not-in" relationship over time as they develop the ability to create appropriate relationships with participants.

It is important to note that most projects will include some data that are off topic or that prove irrelevant, but this does not mean they are bad data. Although a research question focuses the research study, the researcher may not always be aware of all the factors that are important or unimportant at the beginning of the study. It is prudent to keep the data broadly focused at the beginning of the study to ensure that the project retains all the necessary contextual data. Later, when the research becomes more focused, the researcher will find that some of the data from the beginning of the study are not pertinent. Researchers usually retain such data (sometimes called *dross*), as they may later prove relevant to emerging theoretical schemes or may be used for secondary analysis.

﷽ WAYſ OF MAKING DATA

How do you know what ways of making data are appropriate to your study? Data in qualitative research take many forms, and these do not belong to any particular methods (see Table 5.1). Almost all forms of qualitative inquiry may at some stage use some type of interview strategy, and most other ways of making data are also shared across methods. These include recording dialogues as they occur in the setting, making recordings or photographs as one observes the setting, writing field notes,

Table 5.1   Techniques for Making Qualitative Data

Technique	Characteristics	Used Commonly In
Unstructured, interactive interviews	Relatively few prepared questions are asked; there may be only one or more grand tour questions. Researcher listens to and learns from participant. Unplanned, unanticipated questions may be used, along with probes for clarification.	Ethnography, discourse analysis, grounded theory, narrative inquiry, life history, case study
Informal conversations	Researcher assumes a more active role than in interactive interviews.	Phenomenology, ethnography, grounded theory
Semistructured interviews	Open-ended questions are developed in advance, along with prepared probes. Unplanned, unanticipated probes may also be used.	May be used in ethnography and grounded theory, or as a "stand-alone method."
Group interviews	These are audio or video recorded, and six to eight open-ended questions are asked. Facilitator stimulates dialogue among participants.	Focus groups (a particular type of group interview) used across methods; informal groups may be used in ethnography.
Observations	Field notes may be recorded as notes (and later expanded) or spoken into an audio recorder and later transcribed. Participant or nonparticipant observation (dependent on the extent to which the researcher participates) may be used.	Ethnography, grounded theory, supplement to interviews in all methods

Technique	Characteristics	Used Commonly In
Online sources	Discussions and contributions are input online by participants in blogs or chat rooms. Researcher is known to be listening and using this data but may not be an active participant.	All methods
Videos	May be retained whole for replaying and reviewing or summarized or transcribed (optionally with single frames retained for illustration).	Ethnography, ethology
Photographs	May be used to illustrate and facilitate recall.	Many methods, especially ethnography
Maps	May be stored and referenced.	All methods where understanding a site is important
Documents	May be collected during project and used to give background or detail.	All methods
Diaries, letters	May be retained and studied in detail or summarized.	Many methods, especially life history
Indirect methods of representing	Researcher finds ways of simulating or representing the phenomenon studied.	All methods

recording descriptions of the setting, and collecting documents or diaries about the setting. Other indirect modes of learning about what goes on in the setting studied include simulated observation through exploration of literature and other media, such as movies.

Our advice is that you read widely about the skills each technique requires, the ways they can be combined, and choices between types of interviews and other strategies. Below, we briefly sketch some ways of making data. For each, we discuss where it is appropriate (or not) and what issues you need to consider in its application.

Interviews

Most researchers approaching qualitative research expect that they will conduct interviews. But interviews may not be the most appropriate way of making data and often will not be the easiest. The types of interview used and the ways in which the interviews are conducted depend on the research question and method (see, e.g., Holstein & Gubrium, 2003; Kvale, 1996; Mason, 2002; Olson, 2011).

Interactive Interviews

The most common type of qualitative interview is "unstructured" and interactive. Conducted well, this type of interview offers a participant an opportunity to tell his or her story with minimal interruption by the researcher. Unstructured interviews are most appropriately used in studies where the researcher seeks to learn primarily from respondents what matters or how procedures are understood.

No situation, of course, is truly unstructured: The setting, the questions you ask, and the relationship you have with the participants will set the stage. The goal is to reduce these effects on the data. A quiet, comfortable, and private setting is needed, ideally with the television, radio, and phone switched off, to avoid distractions and interruptions. Unless the participant needs a companion, or the research design demands that interviews be conducted jointly by co-researchers, it is preferable to be alone with the participant while you conduct the interview.

How much preparation should you do prior to conducting an interview? Some researchers prepare broad, open-ended questions as a guide to topics they want to cover. However, as the purpose of the interview is to elicit the participant's story, asking such questions initially may preemptively determine what is discussed. It is better if you simply let the participants tell their stories, and then, if you have not learned about all aspects of whatever it is you want to know, you can ask questions when the participants finish speaking or at a second interview. You might prepare only an opening question (sometimes called a "grand tour" question; Spradley, 1979). The grand tour question is intended to focus the participant on the topic, and the researcher, in essence, assumes a listening stance.

Beware of the assumption that any good listener can interview. Skill is required to guide the needed narrative without interrupting or skewing the respondent's story. This is not an easy task. Like any good listener, a skilled interviewer is responsive and interested, helping maintain the conversation rather than interrupting the participant's flow of thought. Probes or questions designed to elicit further information may sometimes be developed ahead of time; they may also be unplanned, arising from the context of the interview. But you need to take care that you offer such input only as appropriate during the interview; often, it is best left until the end.

Before the interview, the participant already knows the general subject of the research, as the researcher must provide this information during the process of obtaining consent for the interview. During some interviews, the researcher may ask an occasional question for clarification or to redirect or focus the account, but the goal is to permit the participants to tell their stories with little interruption.

Semistructured Questionnaires

Sometimes, the researcher knows enough about the domain of inquiry to develop questions about the topic in advance of interviewing but not enough to anticipate the answers. A semistructured interview is appropriate here. The researcher designs open-ended questions, arranged in a reasonably logical order, to cover the ground required. Usually, the interviewer will ask the same questions of all the participants, although not necessarily in the same order, supplementing the main questions with either planned or unplanned probes. The interviews are normally audio recorded and transcribed in preparation for analysis.

The use of semistructured interviews is appropriate when the researcher knows enough about the study topic to frame the needed discussion in advance, as long as there is no danger that structuring will limit the discovery of significant aspects not previously recognized.

Such interviews offer the researcher the organization and comfort of preplanned questions and confidence that data will be reliably retained from all participants on these questions. Where the design requires linking with quantitative data, this may be essential. But note the challenges: The prestructured questions must be worded so as not to exclude answers that would usefully widen the topic. And there is work to be done in wording and presenting these questions to participants in ways that invite detailed, complex answers.

Sometimes, if participants cannot be interviewed face-to-face or if the topic is sensitive or embarrassing, the researcher may provide participants with a paper or electronic copy of the questionnaire so they can write their open-ended responses. This way of gathering responses is no less "qualitative" but is, of course, very different from face-to-face interviewing, and the context, like all contexts, will be relevant to the analysis.

Conversations

Researchers who are interested in linguistic or discourse analysis often record dialogue and analyze it as it occurs (for instance, the dialogue between a doctor and a patient). There is normally little or no interjection from the researcher in these data, and the data are usually audio recorded. If dialogue is your focus, this strategy is, of course, necessary and relatively straightforward. But beware of recording dialogue that may not address your topic. If you are using conversation analysis techniques, there will be specific rules for what should be recorded and how (see, for example, Cameron, 2001; Wooffitt, 2005).

Group Interviews

Group discussions and more-guided group interviews can take many forms. These include unguided conversations, formal meeting interactions, social gatherings, and multiple-respondent interviews. Anthropologists encounter or construct such opportunities throughout their studies, recording what they learn in field notes.

Such group interview situations are to be distinguished from focus groups, which consist of individuals brought together by the researcher to focus specifically on one, usually narrow, topic. Often researchers use focus groups to gain understanding of the research domain relatively quickly. They may also employ focus groups to scope a project early in its design; such groups can provide researchers with information about a topic's dimensions or people's attitudes on an issue.

Focus group research has become very popular in many areas; it has its own literature, some of which narrowly specifies rules and requirements (see the list of resources at the end of this chapter). Most authors who offer advice about conducting focus groups assert that a group should normally consist of 6 to 10 participants and that a typical group session should last from 1½ to 2 hours. The group facilitator is responsible for the interaction of the group, the way topics are introduced, and, thus, the quality of the data. The facilitator introduces the questions and attempts to ensure that the conversation is balanced (e.g., not dominated by one or two participants) and that the dialogue stays more or less on topic and does not get stuck on one point for too long.

Because the strategies are so specifically detailed in the literature, conducting focus groups may sound easy. They are also frequently welcomed as a way of rapidly collecting comments from a large number of participants. But the context and the limitations of those comments ensure the data will be very different from individual interview data, and analysis will require very different techniques. If you are considering using focus groups in your research, we advise you to think carefully about the sort of information likely to be obtained through this method, as well as the context of that information. And don't underestimate the skills required of a focus group facilitator.

Observations

Observing is the most natural of all the ways of making data, but observing unobtrusively is extremely difficult. Some behaviors may be accessible for research only through observation. It may not be possible to interview some participants (due to language differences or other reasons for an inability to communicate), or participants themselves may not be aware of some of their behaviors. The observer's perspective may be different from that of the participants, or there may be a weak link between reported behavior and actual behavior.

But observation is a primary strategy for making data, even in situations where interviewing would be easy. The assumption behind most observational strategies is that they enable the researcher to learn what is taken for granted in a situation and to discover best what is going on by watching and listening.

Observational techniques differ in the researcher's level of visibility and involvement in the setting. The usual distinction between *participant observation* and *nonparticipant observation* hides the fact that there are myriad ways of watching and listening. No observer is entirely a participant, and observing without some participation is impossible in almost every nonexperimental situation. If you plan to undertake observation, we advise you to read not only texts about it but also monograph accounts of the experience and the resulting data (for many relevant references, see Atkinson & Hammersley, 1994; Mason, 2002).

Traditionally, researchers have recorded their observational data, along with their own interpretations, in the form of field notes. The researcher observes a setting for a short period of time and retreats to a quiet place to record and reflect on the observations. Often, researchers supplement their field notes with maps or diagrams that they use to record interaction patterns or to clarify the positions of features within the setting. Occasionally, they include in their observations records of the actual words of participants' conversations in the setting. Researchers also commonly use photographs to support their observational data, analyzing them to gain additional insights into the setting.

Online Sources

Chat rooms, blogs, websites, and e-mail lists are attractive, indeed seductive, sources of data for the qualitative researcher, not least because they appear to provide "instant" data. The text record is available immediately—there is no need to transcribe audio recordings or write up notes! These online settings, very different from the more structured setting of an interview, also encourage relaxed and open discussion among virtual friends.

The same aspects that make these sources attractive also make them risky. The researcher in such a setting can easily "lurk," fading into the background even when ethical requirements are duly met. For such studies, stringent ethical requirements should ensure disclosure of the purpose of participation and seeking of permission to use the material published online. Even when these requirements are satisfied, there is a danger that the researcher can retain relative anonymity, and the interaction of researcher and participant is far harder to assess and control than in face-to-face encounters.

Video Recording

As video recording became more widely used in observational settings and interviewing, handling of video recorded data was integrated into qualitative software. Video cameras are now common (and smaller, with advanced technology), so the presence of these cameras seems less intrusive to participants, and fears among researchers that they invade privacy or change behavior are now diminishing. The attractions of a video record are obvious: retaining as much data as possible for the researcher to revisit and review the visual as well as audible record. But such confidence makes two warnings even more relevant. First, special practical and ethical considerations for video recording must be addressed. Will video recording invade privacy, capturing images or information that participants would not want strangers to see—and that may be unnecessary to the project? Will it inflict stress or embarrassment? What is the representation of the research situation being recorded? Did the video recording change participants' behavior?

Second, if you use video recording, it is important that you avoid the trap of assuming that by having filmed an event you have fully recorded it, let alone interpreted it. Video recording does not replace the process of compiling field notes—data assessment and interpretation. Beware of the study design that produces hours of uninterrupted recordings with no provision for how and when they will be observed and analyzed.

Photography

Researchers may use photography as an independent way of making data to record a setting or scene, to record directly "how much" or "how many," or to provide illustrations. Researchers' photographs may serve as data in historical studies or in life history studies, or they may provide background as a part of the ongoing data collection scene. Sometimes, researchers retrieve photographs from other collections, with the aim of providing a means for comparison to illustrate change. With the availability of computer storage, photographs have become more easily accessible, and researchers are increasingly integrating photography into their data in innovative ways. For example, Westphal (2000), in her study of the use of urban space, gave local children disposable cameras and asked them to take photos of places significant to them. Westphal's interviews with these young respondents, who had little education, were facilitated by discussion of their photos.

Documents

Data often consist of documents that exist independently of the research process. These may be institutional records, such as school or management records, minutes of business meetings, policy statements, home records, or the website texts by which institutions declare their goals and structures. Maps may be used to locate research sites and identify their features. Some qualitative software now links with online maps for this purpose.

Diaries and Letters

Participants' diaries or letters may be the sole source of data where the research concerns the past. And for projects in the present, diaries or letters can provide more direct insight into participants' lives and experiences than can be obtained in interviews asking them to recall the events. One approach is to ask participants to keep diaries for the researchers during the research period. This may be helpful to participant as well as researcher. Rolfe and Richards (1993) gave young mothers diaries to fill in during the first months of using day care for their firstborn children, a process and record that pleased participants as well as providing detailed, vivid data.

A diary can be recorded visually: Researchers may provide participants with video cameras (e.g., Rich & Patashnick, 2002) or disposable cameras (e.g., Drew, Duncan, & Sawyer, 2010) to record their daily lives or experiences relevant to the research topic.

Indirect Strategies

"Indirect" prompts and probes can be used in many different methods to generate interpretations and responses to hypothetical situations. Finch (1984) used *vignettes* to discuss the highly emotional topic of family obligation for caring and found that participants could respond firmly about the duties or problems of vignette characters even when they were unwilling to discuss their own. *Simulated observation* involves using participants as actors to show the researcher what they normally do. For example, in her study of traditional birth attendants in Fiji, Morse (1989a) asked the participants to show her the positions that the women they attended normally used while giving birth. Robertson (2008) gave kits of "cultural probes" to migrants to help them explore and record their daily environments and used these records to enrich data from more traditional interview methods.

Indirect data that may illuminate or provide insights into participants' experiences and responses can be found in literature, movies, theater, and art. These sources provide interpretations of real life that researchers can use in analyzing dominant discourses or ideologies, historically situated interpretations, or background clues as to what is going on in more direct data.

〰️ WHO MAKES DATA?

In quantitative inquiry, it is very common for research assistants to help investigators in "collecting" data, usually through the use of precoded research instruments. In qualitative inquiry, however, where researchers themselves are more active in making data, the use of research assistants is, if not less common, certainly more often regarded as problematic. Principal investigators who collect their own data argue that by doing so they ensure that the data are of excellent quality and that the interpretive process (such as field note notations about "what is going on") and the possible effect of the researcher on the setting are sufficiently recorded. At the same time, researchers commonly work on projects in loosely or tightly coordinated teams.

Some qualitative researchers do use research assistants to collect data. Indeed, Glaser (1978) has asserted that researchers' conducting interviews by themselves is "a waste of time." His approach is to interview the interviewers to find out what is going on in the data. There is agreement among researchers, however, that when first-level coding is used, the principal investigator should at least do the bulk of the coding.

Conducting an interview or observing in a setting is a task that requires extraordinary interpersonal skills, a firm focus on the project's purposes, and solid theoretical knowledge (because data are representations that need to be interpreted, they are just observations, and the process of recording does not capture everything). If you decide to hire research assistants to help with data collection, be certain that they are theory smart and method wise in their work. More important, ensure that you work with them as a team and that you stay in constant communication with them to discuss interpretations and discoveries.

If your project requires teamwork or collaboration with other projects, build this into the research design; the need for team research should inform your choice of strategies for making and recording data as well as your planning of time and budget.

❋ TRANSFORMING DATA

Preparing data for analysis is a process of transformation. Each research event is transformed from an actual happening to a form that can be handled and manipulated in the process of analysis. Ideally, this process keeps the data as close to the actual events as possible. It may be achieved through the reduction of data in the form of detailed field notes or recordings in other media (audio or video recording, or photography) to text (transcription or a summary description). Be aware of how massive this reduction is and how interpretive the process of making data records is (see Richards, 2009, Chapter 3).

Thus, data ready for analysis are several steps removed from the actual event. The researcher must always remember to interpret data in this context. For example, interviews of participants about their experiences or perceptions of an event should be judged not in terms of the accuracy of the participants' recall of the actual event but in terms of the accuracy of their recall of *how they felt or experienced or perceived the event at the time*.

As Table 5.1 shows, there are limited numbers of ways of recording data used across many strategies of making data. None is inherently superior to any other. Some researchers who are trained as observers assert that the best records come from listening and remembering, with no technology intervening. Others see video recordings as the richest and most lasting records of any given scene (or rather of what was observed), because video recordings allow the researcher to review, examine, and reexamine the scene by replaying the action slowly, even frame by frame. This may assist the researcher in obtaining a more accurate description of the action, particularly if the movement is very fast or if more than one person must be observed at a time. But like all data gathering, reviewing video recordings is an interpretive process. Just as "objective" field notes record what the researcher observed, *not what happened*, a video captures only what was recordable and what was filmed.

How does the recording process influence the reliability and validity of a study? The answer depends on the research question and the type of detail and data needed to answer the question. Strategies for data collection must enable the researcher to gather data at the level needed to answer the questions. If a question addresses types of touch, and touch is silent and transient, then video recorded data are required. If the question addresses the detailed content of conversation, then full transcription of audio recorded dialogues will be needed. If the question addresses relationships, then field notes or recorded interviews may be used, and so forth. In other words, different sorts of interpretive records are relevant for different projects, but all records may be interpreted.

Traditional notions of reliability and validity involve ensuring that the processes of data creation and interpretation record the phenomena of interest as closely as possible and that two researchers working independently obtain data that are as similar as possible. If one considers the process of analysis to be *interpretive*, however, the replication of events is less relevant than a recording that provides insight into exactly what is "going on."

〰 MANAGING DATA

The volume of data that qualitative researchers must manage is enormous. Researchers tell stories of "drowning in data," of stacking piles of data records in their basements, or of not being able to use their dining room tables for several months during the ongoing process of analysis. There are two aspects to this problem—how to manage the *amount* of data and how to manage the data *records.*

In the previous chapter, we asked what amount of data is sufficient. The answer will become clearer during the simultaneous process of making and analyzing data. Theoretical sampling provides *just enough* data. Look for indicators of *saturation* (the replication of data or the verification of incidents/features/facts by several participants) and confidence that adequate data have been obtained. Thus, in a well-designed and well-conducted study, data are not over collected but are well managed.

How do you manage the data records? This involves physical handling of the growing heaps of records as well as intellectual handling of their growing complexity. Physical handling may seem easy, but it requires considerable self-discipline and sometimes considerable clerical duties. You will need a system for storing what is often called "metadata"—information about the records or the participants—as well as the records themselves.

The metadata required will vary with the project, but in all projects, data items must be clearly labeled and easily located. Where anonymity of those you are studying is required (and this is the usual situation), it is important that you create and consistently use a system of pseud-onyms or codes; if you are using and transcribing audio files, you should place these identifier codes on the files and in the headers of the tran-scriptions. If necessary, you may keep, in a secure place, a key that links names with code numbers. Normally, you will want to destroy this list as soon as possible. You should save copies encrypted, in a password-protected computer, and store backup copies of all audio and video files in a locked cabinet. The data records will almost certainly include some paper copies and many computer records. The former should be classified and safely stored, ensuring that during the analysis process they are not decontextualized or broken up. The orderly storage of information and records will not happen automatically.

The computer offers a great deal of help in the physical management of records and the fluid management of ideas. Researchers now normally store and manage data transcripts, written field notes, and other text, audio, or visual documents on the computer, whether or not they use any specialized software. Programs designed for qualitative research offer a wide range of ways of managing data using folders, document names, definitions, memos about documents, and coding. They also offer resear-chers new ways of storing their impressions and ideas from the earliest stages of their research so they can easily locate them again.

Whatever strategies for analysis researchers use, they will always want access to the original documents. So data must be located to facilitate easy and quick retrieval. Most retrieval systems allow researchers to gain access using document identifiers, participant pseudonyms, and, as the coding analysis proceeds or develops, codes or categories. It is essential that you learn your software well before starting to store records and also that you rigorously and consistently store and archive them. It is equally essential that you protect not just your original records but your growing and changing project.

As with all computer records, one copy is not enough. You will need a system to ensure regular backup of the original data files and the growing project you are creating onto another safe medium. A copy of your data records or your project on the same hard disk is not a backup—hardware failure is the most likely cause of data loss. So you need an external storage location for your backups, preferably on another hard disk. The challenges of data management for the data your project needs, and the sort of access to your data records that you will require, should be considered early in your project.

Managing Focus Group Data

Many of these data management issues are clearly shown in the challenges of handling data from focus groups. When records of focus groups are not carefully managed, reports are often very simplistic assertions about what the group supposedly "concluded" or "felt." Such reports waste the data about process and context that made the group interesting.

Unlike an interview, a focus group provides a record created in discussion between participants. Whether this would be an advantage to your project will depend on the research area, the question, and the method you are using. For example, if you are entering a previously unresearched field, groups may be the best way to discover the issues or perceptions that will matter to your project. If the topic is complex, focus groups may help you distinguish between the dimensions that matter to participants.

It is important to recognize that conducting focus groups takes skill and that the data they provide can be difficult to analyze. One of the myths of focus group research is that they are a quick and cheap way of "getting" a lot of data from a lot of people (Morgan, 1993). While any group can make a lot of words, it will require skilled moderation to ensure that these are useful to your project and then skilled data management to use them. If this method appears to fit with your project design, prepare carefully, reading about designing and moderating groups and about managing the resulting data. Focus groups are used differently in different research settings, and you should be clear about the methods developed in yours.

When you record even a short focus group, it transcribes to a *long* record. Even if it did not seem to be a challenging group discussion, you will find you have a record of complex interaction. Reading a transcript, you will immediately want access to information about its context. Who said that? (Was it a woman or a man?) Were they serious in this comment or laughing? (Do we need the voice record, or the video image, to check?) What earlier comment from another participant prompted the response? (And who was that?) Did that earlier remark make them change their minds? (What had they said before on this topic?)

How do you manage such complex data? When confronted by complex, unstructured record, a good first step is to look for *structure*. A well-designed focus group is usually structured by the moderator's input and the participants' interaction. Using computer software, you can automatically gather from all your focus groups all the answers to each of the moderator's questions so they can be read together. Then you can gather everything said by each participant in a group so you can follow their contributions throughout the discussion.

For a second step, look for *context* and how to manage access to it. With focus group data, there are two sorts of context available to you. You have the original audio recording, which captures much more context than the transcript, and from which you could learn, for example, whether that participant was laughing and who was talking behind him. You may wish to plan to use software to code the audio or video recording, or to place links to "clips" of the important moments. The second source of context is the information about participants' characteristics, usually gathered as a group is recruited. If you have gathered and coded everything each respondent said, you can store the relevant information about their characteristics with that coded data. Now it is possible to ask what the women said on a particular topic and to explore whether they had previously held a different view.

〰 THE ROLE OF DATA

The aim of data management in qualitative research is not merely to protect the researcher from overload or data wastage. As you develop a data management system, you will discover that well-managed data inform, even lead, the process of inquiry, so managing data is not merely a clerical but also a first analytical process. When you maintain a balance between data management and data direction, the role of the data can be pivotal and the process exciting.

Data lead inquiry in three ways. First, they may demand to be treated by a particular method, in which case no amount of forcing will permit you to mold the data to fit the originally planned question and method (e.g., you intended to conduct structured interviews, but the respondents talked in stories that demand narrative analysis). Don't force. Data will be wasted if you do not treat them within the most appropriate method.

Second, data may direct you to a new way of working in the next stage of a project. For example, you may discover that you don't understand the processes the participants are discussing in interviews. The interview data are directing you toward a stage of observation. Thus, in her study of outer suburbia, Richards (1990) initially relied on surveys and interviewing, but the data increasingly "directed" her toward observation and detailed analysis of discourse. These strategies provided her with the key to understanding the participants' interlocking ideologies and helped her make sense of interview answers that had appeared to be contradictory.

Third, data may tell you what you can't do. In her suburban study, Richards (1990) discovered that data on conflict among neighbors were not available through direct interviewing in an area where residents were ideologically required to express enthusiasm about their interactions with neighbors. Observation provided quite different results. In such a situation, the researcher must rework the research design, and the report must account for this change of plans.

Expect, then, to be engaged in a dialogue with your data. Recognizing the ways in which data direct the adjustment of research strategies (and sometimes even of research question and study purpose) places the data in a dominant position, one that drives the study. Such realization is sometimes painful, but forcing data into inappropriate studies is more painful and unproductive. This occurs most often when a researcher begins by preparing a proposal while "wed" to a research approach that fits poorly with the topic. The researcher risks making data inappropriate for the method and later may find it impossible to mold the data to the chosen method. Often the only way to proceed is to use the method demanded by the data.

Data can play a definitive role in determining whether a question can be answered. Research into the phenomenon of intuition in nursing has sought data on how nurses can predict a change in a patient's condition before the physiological changes occur and show on the patient's monitor. Nurses are unable to describe the look that patients get, yet researchers have conducted much of their research by interviewing nurses about what they intuit rather than by observing patients to learn the behavioral signs they manifest (Morse, Miles, Clark, & Doberneck, 1994).

Sometimes the data required by a question and method may not be obtainable. At the extreme, one cannot interview infants or aphasic adults; participants with Alzheimer's disease or mental illness often cannot report on their experiences. Participants cannot report on events that occurred when they were unconscious, and they often forget or cannot recall their experiences in agonizing pain or other circumstances. Lorencz (1992) explored the experience of being discharged from a psychiatric hospital by interviewing schizophrenics. As an experienced psychiatric nurse, she discovered she was competing with the patients' multiple voices and multiple realities and often waited more than a minute for participants to respond to her questions. When they did answer, their responses often seemed irrelevant, as though they were responding to other, internal voices; thus, the interviews were characteristically nonsensical, slow, and convoluted, but they offered glimpses of the patients' realities. Studies with less extreme conditions also often have major gaps in data: An important event is missed, finding or gaining agreement from crucial participants proves impossible, or those participants most needed are those most elusive.

Sometimes data may be compromised because of the context, such as when the researcher is denied access for political or ethical reasons and adapts to working with the best available data. But even imperfect data can be amazingly interesting and can produce quite satisfactory results. Morse (1992) found that nurses in trauma rooms insisted they "did not have time to comfort patients" and that the study should be conducted elsewhere. Nonparticipant observation enabled Morse to identify the major types of comfort, but in this setting, recording the confusion—or sorting out the confusion—using participant observation or a stenographer's record proved impossible. Eventually, at another hospital in another country, she and her colleagues received permission to video record, using cameras attached to the wall—"shooting blind," with poor sound quality and the requirement that the patients' faces be obscured. But even these poor data allowed the documentation of the linguistic pattern of speech used by nurses, later dubbed the Comfort Talk Register (Proctor, Morse, & Khonsari, 1996), and of the ways nurses comfort patients (Morse & Proctor, 1998).

YOURSELF AS DATA

Should the researcher be seen as an active participant in the setting studied? It was strenuously argued in early anthropology that researchers should separate themselves from their topics and the people they studied to avoid having their own personal agendas drive the research problem. It was feared that personal involvement made the topic more stressful, that researchers would lose their objectivity, and that the reporting would lose its fairness. Anthropologists argued that researchers could not see a particular culture's values and beliefs if they were immersed in that culture. These objections have now by and large been relaxed, but, as Lipson (1991) has noted, this does not mean it is easy to place yourself in your data:

> It takes a real effort to figure out what is you and what is not you. I think it can be done successfully, but I think it takes a lot of experience and a lot of hard work to get there. And a lot of exposure and a lot of self-explorations to find out where your own values are coming from, what your own behavior is, what you're not seeing, and I think it is a very sticky proposition. (p. 72)

Whether your experience will affect the research is not the question—it will. For all researchers, the big question is how to place that experience. How do you monitor and account for the ways your values, beliefs, culture, and even physical limitations affect the process and quality of data? Two issues are particularly urgent at this early stage. First, what should your relationship be with those you study? And second, what role should you and your experience have in the study? As you read the literature where your project is located, you will find inconsistent answers to both questions.

You and Those You Study

Qualitative methods do not usually advocate depersonalizing those studied and denying the researcher's effects on their behavior. However, you may find that the use of the passive voice in reporting ("An inquiry was made to the group" rather than "I asked the group") and terms such as *informants* and *actors* indicate attempts to depersonalize relationships. (We are wary of these techniques, and we agree that it is best to acknowledge and discuss the researcher's agency rather than elide or deny it.)

Few methods, however, go to the extreme alternative of seeing researchers as a "normal" part of the setting, with no constraints on the ways they may influence it, with their interpretation being just one among many, and with those in the setting regarded as not merely participants but co-researchers. On these issues, the feminist qualitative literature has led an uneven debate since Oakley's (1981) enthusiastic writing about interviewing women and Finch's (1984) more cautious concerns about manipulation of the vulnerable. Most recently, these issues have been expressed in literature on the feminist narrative techniques of memory work (Haug, 1987; for classic and recent references, see Olesen, 2000).

Regardless of the point at which your project is positioned on this range, you must consciously choose, negotiate, and maintain the relationship you have with those you study, and you must record and discuss that relationship throughout your research work and in the final report.

Your Experience as Data

What role should the researcher's personal experience have in the study? When experience brings a particular research problem to the fore, it will drive the study. The researcher's experience may provide a puzzle that leads to a research question. Glaser and Strauss (1968) began their collaborative research on death and dying because both men had experienced the death of a parent in a hospital and both had noted similar features of the experience that were dissatisfying, unexpected, and, in retrospect, "odd." In such a case, the researcher must decide whether or not to disclose to participants this personal interest in the topic (which will make the researcher's experience public). Whether it is disclosed or not, the relevance of the experience must be considered and reported in the study.

There are two approaches you can use to incorporate your own experience in a study. Be forewarned: Both have serious risks and must be done well. The first is to separate your experience from that of others in the study, thus introducing it but segregating it. In this way, Malacrida (1998) explored the experience of having a stillborn child and Karp (1996) investigated the experience of depression. The experiences of others, presented in the main study, can be seen as validating the researcher's own experiences, which will have a major psychological impact on the researcher. The research makes the researcher's own responses and experiences, which had seemed extraordinary, more everyday, more *normal*. But like all aspects of research, the use and reporting of personal experience must be purposeful. The risk of this approach is that it can easily become self-indulgent. Keep asking yourself whether and why your own experience matters to *this study*. Why should you tell the participants or the reader about it? And what will be the effects on the participants and the report of your doing so?

The second way to use your own experience in inquiry is to use it *as data*. You may present your experience as intimately richer and more valid than the reported, secondhand experiences obtained by interviewing or observing others. You can evaluate it by linking your own experience with the experience of others reported in the literature or with concepts that are already well developed in the social sciences. Thus, Arthur Frank (1991) reports on his experience with cancer in his book *At the Will of the Body.*

If you are bringing your own experience into the study, you should go first to the growing and important body of literature on autobiography and autoethnography. Recent works include substantial lists of readings to lead you not only to the excitement of analyzing yourself as data but also to the perils of doing it badly (see, e.g., Ellis & Bochner, 2000).

╲╲ UJING YOUR JOFTWARE FOR MANAGING DATA

Chapter 4 introduced ways in which you can use the computer for creating a project to contain your data and ideas, and immediately for handling the preliminary material that leads to research topic and question. This material is data, and like all the data records you will later create, it must be very carefully and rigorously handled.

As qualitative data records are created, any researcher is challenged to manage their complexity and richness well and responsibly. Software is obviously an aid for certain tasks. Qualitative packages specialize in ways of creating, importing, handling, and managing data records on the computer.

Approaches

Almost all software designed for use by qualitative researchers will handle text. (Most handle "rich text" and/or other formats.) Importantly, programs have different ways of including or linking to nontext records such as audio or video recordings. If you wish to use such records as primary data, without reducing them to representations, explore software that will allow you to retain them whole and to code "streaming" recordings.

All qualitative software will also have some ways to store your reflections on the data, your early ideas as they happen, ensuring that these impressions will not be lost and that you can revisit your account of your data making as the project grows.

Explore your software to get a feel for the processes of making data records and handling them on the computer.

Your software should support all the following processes, which you need to learn:

◈ How to create and edit documents in your qualitative software program

◈ How to import or link to all data files so they can be coded and analyzed in your project

◈ How to store information about the data records and cases they represent (e.g., demographic data)

◈ How to handle nontext records (e.g., photos, videos) so they can be integrated with text

◈ How to store your reflections in memos

◈ How to add annotations and edit

◈ How to link between documents or parts of data records

Advances

The list of software functions above includes much that could not be done before computers. When documents were on paper, storing them and marking them up was awkward and sometimes very time-consuming, but it could be done. On the other hand, changing them, finely annotating them and accessing those comments, storing information about them, and linking that data with statistical analysis were often practically impossible.

Methods change with technology, and these lists offer the first glimpse of the effects of software on qualitative method. You can do much more with your data once they are on the computer, and, of course, you can do it with much more data.

This does not mean you should!

Alerts

Three cautions apply here, and they all concern researchers' tendency to try to fit research to computer programs rather than making the programs work for their projects. Data types, the volume of data, and the data's heterogeneity should be driven by the research goals and method, not by the computer program. Be very careful not to skew your project to what the computer seems to want. If your program won't handle the sort of data your project requires, devise a new strategy using the program's tools (and tell other researchers about it) or move to another program.

1. Don't create bulk data records just because the computer can handle them. Most qualitative projects are hindered by large volumes of data, and some are destroyed by data bulk. In the process of designing your study and fitting your research question to a method and ways of making data, you will have good reasons to predict the volume of data to be created. Always avoid the temptation to make the project impressive by expanding the scale of data.

2. Be discriminating and thoughtful in deciding what qualifies as data. There is security in the computer's ability to store and access all the peripheral and often unexpected material that comes your way—background information, unrelated observations, available documentation, and so forth. But your research design should inform your selection. Never refuse possibly relevant data, but don't assume it must be immediately included in your project.

3. Beware of tidying up your data for the computer. We argued earlier that qualitative research rarely thrives on homogeneous data. Your software does not need homogeneity and, indeed, can do less with homogeneous data than with varied data sources and types. Any computer program is better than a human brain and far better than a filing cabinet at managing complexity. And qualitative projects almost always require complex data.

〰 ſUMMARY

In the preceding chapters, we provided information about the diversity of qualitative research methods. In this chapter, we presented information about strategies for making data that will enable you to meet your research goals and address your research question. Data are not made in isolation but must be linked to plans for analysis. We also discussed the interactive effects of the nature of your data on the project as a whole.

RESOURCES

Mason, J. (2002). *Qualitative researching* (2nd ed.). London: Sage.

Richards, L. (2009). *Handling qualitative data: A practical guide* (2nd ed.). London: Sage.

On Focus Group Data

Carey, M. A., & Asbury, J.-E. (2011). *Essentials of focus groups research.* Walnut Creek, CA: Left Coast Press.

Finch, J. (1987). The vignette technique in survey research. *Sociology, 21,* 105–114.

Krueger, R. (1994). *Focus groups: A practical guide for applied research.* Thousand Oaks, CA: Sage.

Krueger, R., & Casey, M. A. (2000). *Focus groups* (3rd ed.). Thousand Oaks, CA: Sage.

Morgan, D. (1997). *Focus groups as qualitative research.* Thousand Oaks, CA: Sage.

Morgan, D., & Krueger, R. (1997). *The focus group kit.* Thousand Oaks, CA: Sage.

On Interview Data

Cameron, D. (2001). *Working with Spoken Discourse.* London: Sage.

Fontana, A., & Frey, J. H. (2000). The interview: From structured questions to negotiated text. In N. K. Denzin & Y. S. Lincoln (Eds.), *The SAGE handbook of qualitative research* (2nd ed., pp. 645–672). Thousand Oaks, CA: Sage.

Gubrium, J. F., & Holstein, J. A. (Eds.). (2002). *Handbook of interview research: Context and method.* Thousand Oaks, CA: Sage.

Holstein, J. A., & Gubrium, J. F. (2003). *Inside interviewing.* Thousand Oaks, CA: Sage.

Kvale, S. (1996). *InterViews: An introduction to qualitative research interviewing.* Thousand Oaks, CA: Sage.

Morse, J. M., Miles, M. W., Clark, D. A. & Doberneck, B. M. (1994). "Sensing" patient needs: Exploring concepts of nursing insight and receptivity in nursing assessment. *Scholarly Inquiry for Nursing Practice*, 8, 233-254.

Olson, K. (2011). *The essentials of interviewing.* Walnut Creek, CA: Left Coast Press.

Rubin, H., & Rubin, I. (1995). *Qualitative interviewing: The art of hearing data.* Thousand Oaks, CA: Sage.

Spradley, J. P. (1979). *The ethnographic interview.* New York: Holt, Rinehart & Winston.

Wooffitt, R. (2005). *Conversation analysis and discourse analysis: A comparative and critical introduction.* London: Sage.

On Observation Data

Angrosino, M. (2007). *Naturalistic observation,* Walnut Creek: CA: Left Coast Press.

Angrosino, M. V., & Mays de Pérez, K. A. (2000). Rethinking observation: From method to context. In N. K. Denzin &

Y. S. Lincoln (Eds.), *The SAGE handbook of qualitative research* (2nd ed., pp. 673–702). Thousand Oaks, CA: Sage.

Atkinson, P., & Hammersley, M. (1994). Ethnography and participant observation. In N. K. Denzin & Y. S. Lincoln (Eds.), *The SAGE handbook of qualitative research* (pp. 248–261). Thousand Oaks, CA: Sage.

Glaser, B. G., & Strauss, A. L. (1968). *Time for dying.* Chicago: Aldine.

Kaler, A., & Beres, M. (2010). *Essentials of field relationships.* Walnut Creek, CA: Left Coast Press.

Spradley, J. P. (1980). *Participant observation.* New York: Holt, Rinehart & Winston.

On Video Data

Ball, M. S., & Smith, G. W. H. (1992). *Analyzing visual data.* Newbury Park, CA: Sage.

Bottorff, J. L. (1994). Using videotaped recordings in qualitative research. In J. M. Morse (Ed.), *Critical issues in qualitative research methods* (pp. 244–261). Thousand Oaks, CA: Sage.

Farber, N. G. (1990). Through the camera's lens: Video as a research tool. In I. Harel (Ed.), *Constructionist learning* (pp. 319–326). Cambridge: MIT Media Laboratory.

Harel, I. (1991). The silent observer and holistic note taker: Using video for documenting a research project. In I. Harel & S. Papert (Eds.), *Constructionism* (pp. 449–464). Norwood, NJ: Ablex.

Lomax, H., & Casey, N. (1998). Recording social life: Reflexivity and video methodology. *Social Research Online, 3*(2). Retrieved May 8, 2001, from http://www.socresonline.org.uk/3/2/1.html

Margolis, E., & Pauwels, L. (2011). *The SAGE handbook of visual research methods.* London: Sage.

Rich, M., & Patashnick, J. (2002). Narrative research with audiovisual data: Video Intervention/Prevention Assessment (VIA) and NVivo. *International Journal of Social Research Methodology, 5*(5), 245–261.

On Diaries and Indirect Methods

Alaszewski, A. (2006). *Using diaries for social research.* London: Sage.

Drew, S. E., Duncan, R. E., & Sawyer, S. M. (2010). Visual storytelling: A beneficial but challenging method for health research with young people. *Qualitative Health Research, 20*(12), 1677–1688. Retrieved from http://qhr.sagepub.com/content/20/12/1677

Robertson, S. K. (2008). Cultural probes in transmigrant research: A case study. *InterActions: UCLA Journal of Education and Information Studies, 4*(2). Retrieved from http://escholarship.org/uc/item/1f68p0f8

Rolfe, S., & Richards, L. (1993). Australian mothers "construct" infant day care: Implicit theories and perceptions of reality. *Australian Journal of Early Childhood, 18*(2), 10–22.

6

Coding

Any researcher who wishes to become proficient at doing qualitative analysis must learn to code well and easily. The excellence of the research rests in large part on the excellence of the coding.

—Strauss (1987, p. 27)

I n qualitative research, everyone uses the term *coding*, but different researchers mean many different things when they use that term. Why is this variation so rarely discussed? Indeed, researchers often get into difficulties because they are led to coding without a clear picture of its purpose.

There are many ways of coding and many purposes for coding activities across the different qualitative methods. They all share the goal of getting from unstructured and messy data to ideas about what is going on in the data. All coding techniques have the purpose of allowing the researcher to simplify and focus on some specific characteristics of the data. And all of them assist the researcher in abstracting, or "thinking up," from the data. Every qualitative researcher has to be able to code. And it is essential to see that qualitative coding is an entirely different process, with different purposes and outcomes, than coding in quantitative studies. (For a detailed comparison, see Richards, 2009, p. 94.)

But the common use of the term *coding* obscures crucial differences among techniques in the ways they link ideas and data and also in the relative importance of coding (see Coffey & Atkinson, 1996; see also the debate generated by Coffey, Holbrook, & Atkinson, 1996). How you code will depend on the method you are using and the ways that method directs you to analysis.

In this chapter, we start with the techniques of qualitative coding— what researchers *do* to data on the way to abstraction. We distinguish among three kinds of coding, all of which contribute differently to the processes of analysis. The first is the storage of information, sometimes termed *descriptive coding* (Miles & Huberman, 1994); the second is coding in order to gather material by *topic;* and the third is the coding used when the goal is the development of concepts (*analytic coding*). Finally, we discuss the broader goal of the identification of *themes.*

Novice researchers find *topic coding* the most accessible of these techniques. You will need to gather material by topic if you wish to reflect on all the different ways people discuss particular topics, to seek patterns in their responses, or to distinguish dimensions of that experience. When a research design clearly addresses specific topics, coding them is an obvious task. By simply collecting all the answers via a coding technique, the researcher can get a new "cut" on the data.

Before computers, when a researcher coded topics on paper, the technique usually involved bringing copies of passages physically together. In one common method, the researcher identified portions of text as being associated with a particular topic, copied them from the original document, and placed them in a labeled topic file. From that file could be retrieved all the material needed to reflect on a given topic. Alternatively, references to the data segments were kept on topic cards. The process worked fairly well as long as any given text passage was about only one topic. Like a child sorting marbles by color, the researcher could gather data bits into topics and, from there, often see new subdivisions of the topics. (Perhaps marbles come in several shades of green. A child can develop subcategories, separating them according to their lime or turquoise qualities.) Thus, the researcher can create subdivisions within the layers of categories; these can be conceptualized as a treelike structure.

But data are *not* like marbles! Your data documents are multifaceted, and you have precious knowledge about them. You are also likely to want to store information about people, places, sites, and so forth to do *descriptive coding.* If your data are at all interesting, any passage will involve several, even many, topics, so topic coding is not merely a task of sorting into discrete heaps. Working on paper, you will need to copy a passage as many times as there are categories for which you wish to code it, and finding patterns in that coding then becomes a challenge.

Moreover, to return to our discussion in Chapter 3, not much qualitative research consists of description alone. Efficient topic and descriptive coding will be adequate for descriptive projects where the goal might be rigorous summary of the occurrences of complaints, or the ideas for a new project. But where the goals are more analytical, few projects will be adequately served by merely sorting data according to topic and characteristics of participants. The discovery of topics and their occurrences in your data will take you rapidly from merely coding by topic to analytic coding, as you reflect on the themes in the data and your categories for thinking about them.

The use of computers for such research began with these challenges (Richards & Richards, 1994), and the widespread acceptance of software is because it has made them far more manageable. Working in software, you will learn quick ways of doing descriptive coding, storing, and using information. You will also find that once you start topic coding of rich data, it will be rare for you to code a passage only once. Specialized software makes it easy to code data as often as their meanings require and removes clerical delays in doing so. And with software, moving between the tasks of topic coding and analytic coding can be very fluid. (For a detailed account of these processes, see Richards, 2009, Chapter 5.)

Coding always moves you to analysis by a process of creating and developing abstractions from the data. Once this is done, the category, rather than the data gathered in it, is the focus of attention. Researchers often seek more abstract ideas or general themes in data. By a *theme*, we mean a common thread that runs through the data. Just as a theme melody emerges in an opera, recurring at different points, themes in data may keep "emerging"—although their forms may not always be identical. You may identify a theme through processes of coding or by stepping back from the data and asking yourself, "What is this all about?" In the latter case, you then return to the data and code portions relevant to the emerging theme.

The many functions of coding, then, link data with information, topics, concepts, and themes. These help focus and conceptualize data as well as organize data so they are malleable, allowing you to manipulate them as ideas and categories develop. Coding involves many processes, not merely "tagging" data with labels. Below, we address how you can get your data (and yourself) ready for coding and how you can store the ideas generated before and during coding in memos (and how you can manage memos so they work for you). We then describe several different ways of coding. In Chapter 7, we discuss the overall goal of abstraction, returning to memoing and annotating.

※ GETTING INSIDE THE DATA

Coding for any purpose requires that you are familiar with the data and ensures that you get closer to the data. If the person doing the analysis has not conducted the interviews or done the observations, this task is far more difficult and more important.

In Chapter 5, we emphasized the importance of detail in recording data. When reading a data record or a portion of text, the researcher should be able to recall the setting and hear the participant's voice and inflection while reflecting on the meanings and implications of the text. Researchers who write their own field notes and transcribe their own data find "getting inside" the data much easier than do those researchers who have someone else transcribe the data.

Now, as you read a data record, read it purposively. You should be thinking not of that research event alone but of its relevance to your project. As you read, depending on your method and purpose, you will want to do many things. One is to record your ideas in annotations and memos. Another is to create and record categories representing what the text is about.

A Reminder: The Distinctiveness of Qualitative Methods

When starting analysis, do not forget the purpose of your study, its theoretical orientation, and your research goal. Although some analytic strategies (such as theme-ing or categorizing) may appear common to many methods, their application within each method makes the various qualitative methods different from one another. The key to their differences is in the *way the researcher thinks about the data* and subsequently *conceptualizes*—that is, "thinks up" from data. This means that although similar strategies may be used, how these different strategies are applied will produce different analytic forms that fit the particular method used and the question being addressed. Here, we address the generic processes of coding, categorizing, and theme-ing, but while these principles are the same, what you categorize and how you code will vary according to your method. In the next section, we will reintroduce the strategies that make methods distinct from one another.

Storing Ideas

The recording of ideas is necessary in all methods. The process of *writing memos* enables you to reflect on the data record, or on the topic or theme; so your data management system should include an easy way of making and editing memos, which should then become part of the data set. Once you "know" the data, these ideas will come quickly.

In Chapter 7, we discuss the task of recording ideas in more depth. As you start coding, you will often find that you wish to write about the discoveries you are making in the data or the ideas you are developing from the data. Just do it! There are no rules about what a memo should be, or what is not a memo. New researchers often falter because they feel memos should be impressive or professional; experienced researchers use memo writing freely, to record their hunches and to think aloud. There are few examples of such memos in the literature because research reports normally do not cite the memos that contributed to the final product and the processes of writing up the research. Memos may be used in several different ways in order to help you get "up" from the data (Richards, 2009, Chapter 4):

〰 You may use them to record descriptions of events observed, the physical setting, or your memories of the mood or context of a meeting.

〰 You may use them to record your ideas or impressions about portions of an interview and to link the text with the literature, with other data, or with very raw ideas you do not want to forget— reminders of things to check out or watch for in the future.

〰 You may use them to reflect on one word or phrase, on your annotations on discourse, or on your ideas about an entire document.

〰 You may use them to record your ideas about an idea, a category, or a theme for which you are coding data, or a concept you wish to develop.

〰 DOING CODING

Now start coding. Codes, at their simplest, are just labels. Coding data descriptively is like labeling jam or preserves; it will help you later find whatever you are searching for (plum jam or any other variety). If you need somewhere to start, start here. But always ensure that you move beyond mere labeling.

As soon as you think about the labels you assign as a system, you are thinking analytically. If codes are organized in an index system, the labels work like cataloging in a library, allowing the user to find grouped-together material about related topics and showing how they are related. But the labels on jars of jam convey no information about taste, and library cards cannot tell you whether a book is exciting. If you start with simple labels, start also thinking about the codes. During coding, data *make* the categories, in the sense that they alert the researcher to certain patterns and surprise with new meanings.

Coding is *linking* rather than merely labeling. It leads you from the data to the idea and from the idea to all the data pertaining to that idea. For most, but not all, methods, it is important that the links lead both ways. Coding takes you away from the data—"up" from the data to more abstract ideas or categories. Coding will also take you "down" from the idea to all the material you have linked it to, and down from any of those segments to the whole document. Coding, if well done, is the way you monitor occurrences of data about your ideas and the way you test them. It makes resilient links between data and ideas, links you can trace back to find where particular ideas came from and what data are coded there to justify and account for the interpretation of the ideas.

Coding is also a way of *fracturing* data, breaking data up, and disaggregating records. Once coded, the data look different, as they are seen and heard through the category rather than the research event. This is both a great advantage and a danger. The retrieval from a code offers a new focus, the ability to compare and be surprised by things not seen when the data documents were viewed as a whole. But it also wrenches the data segments out of context, distancing you from the original whole.

Descriptive Coding

What Is It Used For?

Descriptive coding is used to store things *known about* data items (e.g., respondents, events, or contexts). The researcher can then access this factual knowledge about the respondent (gender, age, and so on), the setting (in the hospital, clinic, at home), or context (year of interview, which question was being answered, and the like) when seeking patterns, explanations, and theories. In some methods, particularly discourse analysis, codes are descriptive of the text—for example, identifying every hesitation or every "turn taking" in a conversation.

Descriptive codes "entail little interpretation. Rather, you are attributing a class of phenomena to a segment of text. The same segment could, of course, be handled more interpretively" (Miles & Huberman, 1994, p. 57). Descriptive codes are used rarely for simple retrieval but often for asking questions of the data. (Did women and men see an event differently? Did younger women have a different concept of attractiveness than did older women?)

How Is It Done?

Ideally, descriptive codes are incorporated into the data management process, with each new respondent or site allocated all the relevant characteristics. Working manually, you will need a fact sheet or ID card for each. Working electronically, you might put this information in a header or footer. If you are using software designed for qualitative research, you will code data documents with their attributes or, even easier, import the information automatically from a table.

But be forewarned: You should store as much information as you need, but no more. Overcoding confuses. Coding should be sufficient to ask and answer your question. If you are using a computer, you can easily import further information later if you need it.

Where Is It Used?

Descriptive coding is common, if not universal, in all methods, given that qualitative research requires awareness of context. But methods differ in their emphasis on descriptive coding. Researchers using theory construction methods tend to do little such coding because the details about individual cases will be subsumed in the development of an overall theory.

In the earliest stages of research design, you should consider what information you need to store (about people, sites, settings, and so on). What do you want to be able to ask? And if you are intending to work with mixed methods, what data do you want to move between qualitative and statistical analysis?

Topic Coding

Topic coding is the most common and the most challenging sort of coding done in qualitative research, especially since computers make it deceptively easy. In almost any project, the researcher will, at some stage, need to be able to access data by topic. However, you should never allow qualitative topic coding to become what Lyn Richards terms *data disposal* ("This text is about this topic, this is about that . . ."). Topic coding should be an analytic activity; it entails creating a category or recognizing one from earlier, determining where it belongs among your growing ideas, and reflecting on the data you are referring to and how they fit with the other data coded there.

What Is It Used For?

Topic coding is used to identify all material on a topic for later retrieval and description, categorization, or reflection. This sort of coding can be fairly descriptive (the respondent is talking about the headmaster) or more obviously interpretive (hostility, authority figure, role model, and so on).

The purpose of topic coding is seldom merely to allow the researcher to find material according to label. Sometimes its purpose is to provide accurate descriptions of the varieties of retrieved material, and sometimes it is to provide new ways of accessing data by combining codes in sophisticated searches (What did the women say about the headmaster if they were also hostile to traditional formal authority systems?). Think of topic coding as coding *up* from the data. It easily becomes analytic because you can review data coded for a topic in terms of dimensions or patterns, coding *on* from there to new, finer categories.

How Is It Done?

You can achieve topic coding by marking up printed text manually (using colored lines and topics in the margins or, as described above, by cutting and pasting), but this method is satisfactory only for very small projects. It is slow and does not result in material that is easily accessible for you to review and recode. Using index cards or folders for each topic works better, and for some this method provides a useful way to learn how to code. But such coding processes sever data from the context and impede your thinking further about the topic (Did the young women speak differently about class than did older women?). Even such a simple question requires difficult re-sorting of data extracts. Topic coding using manual methods will fracture data by removing it from sequence. This may work against some methodological goals, such as identifying processes in grounded theory.

Using a computer allows you to work directly with the text, selecting passages and doing coding onscreen. You can then immediately view what is coded there "live" or view the context if you wish to return to the original document. You can work on the material gathered by topic to create new categories and to make finer distinctions in the process of "coding on." Or, of course, if the data to be coded can be mechanically identified (e.g., if they consist of any particular series of words), you can use the computer to code words and context automatically.

Where Is It Used?

Topic coding is used in almost all qualitative research methods. It is necessary in any project with an emphasis on finding *all* the data about an aspect of the site or experience studied, or on accurately portraying the distribution of different attitudes, experiences, and so forth. Ethnographers piece together accounts of social processes. Researchers working in both discourse analysis and grounded theory code data using words that occur in the data. In grounded theory, these are termed *in vivo codes*. Narrative analysis requires that the story be seen whole but also that the researcher be able to extract topics. (Thus, you might wish to topic code to gather all the material, for example, on class in a series of life stories.)

All methods benefit from broad topic coding early in a project (What, if anything, do we have on this?). Topic coding may also be useful as a first stage of the analysis, when the researcher is exploring to see "what's here." You may use more finely tuned coding once categories are firmed up and you understand "what is going on." And almost all methods use topic coding as a first step to more interpretive coding. Reviewing all the material on a topic, you may see subtler subtopics or dimensions (e.g., Does *hard life* have different meanings in these narratives?). Create new categories for these on the way to analysis.

Analytic Coding

As you begin to code for more categories, topic coding becomes more analytic. Perhaps you were coding every time "a hard life" was mentioned in the narratives of elderly people looking back over their histories. The stories alert you to the significance of *hard* in this context, and you want to store the insight that *hard* and *easy* may shape memories. Make a special place or a special way of seeing the categories that are growing in complexity, and start writing your queries as memos. Later, if something happens to make you wonder if "having it easy" is always seen as a benefit, you have not preempted this discovery by making it "belong" with "looking back." But what you do with this discovery will of course depend on what you are asking and the method you are using.

What Is It Used For?

Analytic coding is used to make, celebrate, illustrate, and develop categories theoretically. It is labeled *analytic* because in creating categories you go *on*, not just linking them to the data but also questioning the data about the new ideas developing in the new codes. The purposes of analytic coding include the following:

- ☰ To alert you to new messages or themes
- ☰ To allow you to explore and develop new categories or concepts
- ☰ To allow you to pursue comparisons

Usually, the memos you write will contain references to many instances of recurrent themes. The links that connect these to the original sources of the ideas (if they were ever there) may now become unimportant. Think of analytic coding as *taking off from the data*.

How Is It Done?

Analytic coding helps you develop themes or categories. You may make new, more general categories or simply start memos about possible categories. But however you store the ideas, be sure to write about the data and rewrite, linking more data as categories recur or as you see them differently in the process of abstracting. The categories grow in your memos. Date your entries within particular memos, or hyperlinks if you are on a computer; keep a log trail (Richards, 2009, pp. 25–27). Summarize and synthesize data as the categories develop.

Read accounts written by people who have done analytic coding (such as Dey, 1995; Miles & Huberman, 1994; and the highly original account

of coding in grounded theory method by Turner, 1981). Review your codes
for those that may potentially contribute to a higher level of analysis.
Seek to generate new categories and read how others have done so. Vali-
date your development of a conceptual scheme with new data.

Where Is It Used?

Most qualitative researchers who are seeking to develop theory will do
analytic coding. But as methods differ, so too will the processes. If in
doubt, aim at working *up* from topic coding, then working *out* by coding
around the topic to establish its significance and meaning.

When coding is used for category construction, the emphasis is less on
labeling text and more on the evolving categories. Researchers may (but
often do not) identify segments of text as belonging to codes, but what
they emphasize is the ability to discover and develop categories from data.

This is territory that grounded theory method dominates, and, sadly,
it is now much-disputed territory. Coding is central to the arguments
about grounded theory that we mentioned in Chapter 3. Texts from
Strauss's "school" offer techniques of a *coding paradigm*. These provide
the researcher with ways of interrogating categories produced in response
to data, asking how they link to other things the researcher knows. The
terms used suggest the emphases: *open coding* aims at opening up the
data, identifying concepts that seem to fit the data; *axial coding* moves
the focus around a concept; and *selective coding* offers intense analysis
that focuses on one category at a time. This sense of hunting down central themes is very different from the emphasis on the less structured
processes of "theoretical sensitivity" in Glaser's writings, and a central
thrust of Glaser's (1992) attack on Strauss's work with Corbin (1990) is
that their methods involve "forcing data."

If you go on to use the grounded theory method, you will find these
issues hotly debated, and you will need to deal with them. The central
goals of making concepts and theorizing about concepts are, however,
common to both sides. Both Glaser and Strauss emphasized that coding
should start early, a message central to their early work together. Their
works advise researchers to code by building cumulatively on coding and
being strongly aware of the internal development of categories and "changing relations between the categories" (Glaser & Strauss, 1967, p. 114).

Our advice is that you seek an understanding of the purposiveness
of open coding and get a sense of what it can do to data. This is splen-
didly portrayed in Strauss's (1987, Chapter 2) *Qualitative Analysis for*

Social Scientists, which contains transcripts of recordings from team sessions during which researchers worked with data. As so often occurs in qualitative research, the actual performance proves much less rule bound than textbook instruction would lead you to believe, and we are reminded yet again that apprenticeship is the perfect way to learn these skills. (For an adaptation of some techniques of open coding, see Richards, 2009, Chapter 5.)

∭ THEME-ING

Coding to develop themes may occur during any of the processes discussed above, but by *theme,* researchers usually mean something more pervasive than a topic or category. As we have noted previously, a theme runs right through data and is not necessarily confined to specific segments of text. Once a theme is identified, however, you are more likely to see segments of text that are pertinent to it.

Discovery and coding for themes usually involves copious and detailed memos that are abstract and reflective. These memos must be categorized and sorted, as they, too, are data. As you code supporting data, a coterie of codes may develop around the themes. We will return to theme-ing in Chapter 7.

∭ PURPOSIVENESS OF CODING

We have argued that the purposes of coding are very different for different methods, as well as for different stages in a project, but all coding should have purpose. Before you code, ask, "Why am I doing this?" This is a particularly urgent message to those using computers to aid in their research. Because the computer makes coding rapid, researchers who are unclear about what they should do next are tempted to continue coding (and then, perhaps, make more data to code) rather than moving their studies forward conceptually. Coding should never become a routine process of data disposal (considered as something to "get through")—and if you find that it does become routine and mechanical, do something else. Then, after your interest in working has returned, ask yourself why coding became boring.

Note that not all coding is aimed at retrieval of all the material coded. Indeed, of the types of coding described above, only topic coding normally leads to retrieval of all the text coded in a category, and such retrieval is then usually a means to an end, a way toward pattern finding, exploration and reflection, and coding to create new categories. Being able to get back everything coded within a category is rarely an end in itself. Sometimes you can achieve the research goal more simply by comparing two or more codes to locate patterns. For instance, a researcher conducting a focus group analysis to identify areas of concern might create a new code for each topic of concern raised in the group and code it at each segment of the transcript referring to that topic. The researcher's role may be limited to reporting that this is a topic of concern, citing the participants' own words. But even in a very limited study, they will normally aim to say something more useful (e.g., about the range of attitudes on the topic or the ways these attitudes are patterned by individuals' characteristics, such as gender or age group).

Coding may not be primarily for retrieval but for access, as in discourse analysis, where location of segments by keyword is a first step toward gathering all the material where one of a set of related terms occurs. Thus, in a study of a television campaign, Potter and Wetherell (1994) used computer text search to find occurrences of any phrases that referred to cure rates. Retrieval of all such passages together allowed them to reflect further on the discourse used in the campaign. They comment,

> If we were not sure if the sequence was relevant, we copied it anyway, for, unlike the sorts of coding that take place in traditional content analysis, the coding is not the analysis itself but a preliminary to make the task of analysis manageable. (p. 52)

🌄 TIPS AND TRAPS: HANDLING CODES AND CODING

Ways of managing, reviewing, and processing data are typically the stages of research least noticed and least written about. Many texts, and indeed many studies, hardly mention these techniques. Instead, they emphasize ways of making data and the end results—the theories derived from data. Because of this silence on the subject, researchers are offered little instruction about techniques of coding or the different ways of coding that are appropriate for different purposes. Although many authors note that coding can create an enormous clerical load, few add to this warning that because computers code so easily, using computers can put qualitative researchers at risk of what Richards (1998; Richards & Richards, 1994) has called "coding fetishism." Coding is central to analysis, and analysis should never be routine and mundane. So how do you deal with these issues?

Code as You Learn

In all the different methods, coding should be started early. As data come in and you think about them, prepare them for analysis and code them. Avoid letting data build up and then coding in a block. A huge backlog of data makes them seem inaccessible, and should you lose the pacing of data and analysis, it will be harder for you to see thin areas in your data or to use what you find to guide future data making.

Always See Coding as Reflection

Don't allow yourself to see coding as a stage of data preparation *prior to* thinking—coding is a theorizing activity. Even apparently simple topics (such as popularity) may sprout complex ideas. Keep revisiting each category and reviewing what is coded there, and whenever it is surprising or interesting, write a memo.

Never Code More Than You Need

How do you know how much is too much? It helps if you don't see the coding of a document as your last chance to read and think about it. Your data management system should allow you to return easily to the context or the full document—to think and maybe code some more. Not many things in qualitative research are done only once, at one particular stage of the project. Given that you can always revisit what you've done, our best advice concerning descriptive and topic coding is that you code for anything you are likely to want to ask questions about.

For analytic coding, our advice is different: If it moves, code it. Storing and revisiting these categories is likely to be what makes your project come alive. With skilled use of your computer tools, you can flit from the code to the memo about it, to the material coded there, to the original document, and to the all-important theme, altering the coding and reviewing it, creating new memos and coding them.

Manage Your Codes

One commonality among all forms of qualitative research is that analysis does not stop with coding. This is why the early computer programs, when seen basically as coding machines, were widely rejected. "Codes are theoretical directives," Strauss commented in a meeting with Lyn Richards in 1995. "Codes are the crosscuts between talk and biographies. . . . Coding is putting interpretative structure on the data." There is no point in making categories for their own sake—they are for linking to data and to each other.

This returns us to the issue of data management. Good data management is essential in any project in which the number of codes is too great for the researcher to be able to find any given code instantly. To use codes inconsistently, or to shift the interpretation of them, is to invite disaster. Think of coding categories not as receptacles for data but as concepts with which you are working. If you are topic coding, get in the habit of visiting the category when you code into it. Are you being consistent? Are new themes turning up? How much variety is present within the category? Should the category be developed into two finer categories? Do its definition and its memos need revisiting? If you are working in a team, you will want to check from time to time that you and your colleagues are using each category the same way, and discuss it if you are not. Coding is a process of category refinement, even if the coding is solely descriptive. Remembering this will help you avoid treating coding as a substitute for thinking. It will also protect you against the perils of excessive coding and the boredom of unnecessary clerical coding.

When you reflect on a category, locate it in some way that helps you find it again. If you are working manually, you may do this by putting the category file in a logical place in a filing cabinet. If you are using the computer, when you discover categories that seem to go together, use your software's ability to make "trees" of categories and subcategories so that you can see them and manage them efficiently (Richards, 2009, Chapter 6).

Monitor Coding Consistency

Because qualitative coding is primarily interpretive, two researchers will rarely produce identical coding. Why should they? Coding reliability tests can establish reliability of descriptive and simple topic coding (What is her age group? Have I coded every time she has mentioned her treatment?). In quantitative inquiry, researchers seek to have far more confidence in consistency; they want to ensure that they have the right numbers down and have no omissions. But differences in interpretive coding indicate only differences in researchers' purposes and perceptions (Richards, 2009, pp. 108–109).

If you were to observe a quantitative research team at work, you would find that arguments occur (Is this a 3 or a 2?), but inconsistencies are obscured because there is no record, for example, of the wording of the statement interpreted as a 3 on the scale. Good quantitative researchers, aware of this problem, work very hard to clear up inconsistencies in interpretation and to record uncertainties. Good qualitative researchers handle inconsistency in a different but related way. Different interpretations are inevitable, so you must monitor, revisit, and debate them and make them a part of the process of analysis. This process, in itself, can lead you to important insights as you get beneath taken-for-granted meanings.

Under two conditions, however, checking the reliability of your coding is essential:

- ※ You should build into your research design ways of checking your consistency of coding over time and, therefore, your understanding. Document and track your use of these methods.

- ※ If you are working in a team, you need to build in a process for monitoring the consistency of coding by different team members. We would not expect identical coding by different people, and if we found it, we would worry because it probably means nothing interesting or ambivalent is being coded. But it is essential that you know the different ways in which team members interpret categories and handle data and that you monitor and discuss the differences.

※ USING YOUR SOFTWARE FOR CODING

In Chapter 4, we introduced the ways of gathering the preliminary material that lead to research topic and question and using the computer to handle and manage data records as data are made. Now we go on to coding. The computer can take much of the clerical burden from each of the modes of coding—but it leaves you with the task of interpretation.

Approaches

All software packages support coding, but they support it in different ways. Many have a choice of ways of coding. In Chapter 5, we discussed management of data records by "descriptive coding." This is usually done by import of attributes and their values for the relevant documents or cases. Learn to do this routinely, before you start topic and analytic coding.

Software will support the following processes, which you need to learn:

⚜ How to do topic coding by making and defining categories and managing them as they develop

⚜ How to do topic coding automatically, by section or by text search

⚜ How to do analytic coding, which includes discovering and developing categories, linking them to memos, and using the computer to support the discovery and exploration of themes

⚜ How to review the data coded in these categories, online, or away from the computer, whether text or visual data (such as photographs or video segments). Most software will also support rethinking these data segments, recoding them, and developing the concepts they represent or illustrate.

If you wish to try doing coding in software, go to Appendix 1, where there is a guide to tutorials available online.

Advances

You don't need qualitative software to code. As described above, before software, coding was done with pens, index cards, and files. Some instructors insist that students code by hand first, to learn *how to think when coding* without the distraction of the software. Some researchers have used software designed for more general writing purposes (Chenail & Duffy, 2011; Morse, 1991), using varied fonts or color text or highlighters to group text by topic and different windows to sort categories. Text search features may be used and memos put directly into the data files (using fonts or color to differentiate them from the transcript).

So why use specially designed software? For the researcher, there are three critically important differences:

⦚ Computers code easily and swiftly, so coding with software is much faster and more efficient than coding on paper. Your interpretation can be far more easily and immediately stored as coded data.

⦚ Computers can store far more information than can paper files. Effectively, good software has no limit to the number of coding categories you can make or the amount of data you can code at them.

⦚ Coding data—that is, the categories you create and the selections you wish to code into them—are stored by software as pointers to the coded segments, not as marked-up or cut-up extracts of text. This information is much more flexible, and much more easily altered, than are paper records.

⦚ Unlike the filing cabinet, qualitative software can easily take you from the coded segment to the context. Some software can show you "live" all material coded for a topic or concept, allowing you to rethink, revise coding, and "code on" (Richards, 2009, Chapter 5) to further, new dimensions of the concept.

⦚ With specialized software tools, you can ask questions about patterns of coding that were practically impossible with paper records. Qualitative researchers usually need to go beyond their first coding. It's not enough to get in one place everything said about a problem. You are more likely to want to know, for example, when people were coded as saying they had this problem, what they said—anywhere in their interview—about their trust of this advice.

Alerts

The greatest dangers of qualitative coding lie in the facility, capacity, and patience of the computer! Coding is essential to most methods, but it can become a trap if you are not aware of these risks.

1. Never let coding become just a clerical duty; if it's qualitative coding, it has a purpose. Why did you create this category? What are you planning to do with it? Coding is not a substitute for interpretation but, rather, an expression of it.

2. Keep coding in its place. It should not dominate any part of your research timetable. When you are unsure what to do next, or when the meaning is not "emerging" from your data, it is very easy to code some more.

3. Don't overcode. Take care to avoid the dangers of "coding fetishism" (Richards, 2009, pp. 109–110), a compulsive activity of researchers who feel they can't think about data unless it is coded. Coding compulsively can easily replace reflection and exploration of data.

4. Don't allow coding to keep you from other interpretive processes. Whenever you are coding, aim to store changing ideas at the same time and to reach for other tools to write memos, revisit coded data, and ask about what your coding is uncovering.

※ SUMMARY

Coding is the strategy that moves data from diffuse and messy texts to organized ideas about what is going on. According to the researcher's analytic goal, coding may take one of several forms: descriptive coding to identify information according to topics, analytic coding to facilitate interpretation, or coding to identify themes. A researcher may use one or more types of coding simultaneously.

Coding enables data retrieval so you may begin processes of analysis, but analytic coding also enables you to ask questions of the data. Coding is a cognitive activity, not an automatic function—be certain to think as you code. Do not overcode, and be aware that analysis begins with coding—it is not the only component of analysis. In Chapter 7, we discuss the thinking processes that necessitate coding and result from it—categorization, conceptualization, and abstraction.

※ RESOURCES

Bazeley, P. (1999). The bricoleur with a computer: Piecing together qualitative and quantitative data. *Qualitative Health Research, 9,* 279–287.

Bernard, H. R., & Ryan, G. W. (2010). *Analyzing qualitative data: Systematic approaches.* Thousand Oaks, CA: Sage.

Boyatzis, R. E. (1998). *Transforming qualitative information: Thematic analysis and code development.* Thousand Oaks, CA: Sage.

Coffey, A., & Atkinson, P. (1996). *Making sense of qualitative data.* Thousand Oaks, CA: Sage.

Coffey, A., Holbrook, B., & Atkinson, P. (1996). Qualitative data analysis: Technologies and representations. *Sociological Research Online, 1*(1). Retrieved January 24, 2012, from http://www.socresonline.org.uk/1/1/4.html

Dey, I. (1995). *Qualitative data analysis: A user-friendly guide for social scientists.* London: Routledge.

Glaser, B. G. (1978). *Theoretical sensitivity: Advances in the methodology of grounded theory.* Mill Valley, CA: Sociology Press.

Glaser, B. G. (1992). *Basics of grounded theory analysis: Emergence vs. forcing.* Mill Valley, CA: Sociology Press.

Richards, L. (2009). *Handling qualitative data: A practical guide.* London: Sage. [Chapter 5 gives detailed advice on doing coding and using and checking computer coding.]

Richards, T. J., & Richards, L. (1994). Using computers in qualitative research. In N. K. Denzin & Y. S. Lincoln (Eds.), *The SAGE handbook of qualitative research* (pp. 445–462). Thousand Oaks, CA: Sage.

Saldaña, J. (2009). *The coding manual for qualitative researchers.* Thousand Oaks, CA: Sage.

Strauss, A. L. (1987). *Qualitative analysis for social scientists.* Cambridge, UK: Cambridge University Press.

Strauss, A. L., & Corbin, J. (1990). *Basics of qualitative research: Grounded theory procedures and techniques.* Newbury Park, CA: Sage.

7

Abstracting

O ne of the few commonalities among qualitative methods is that all methods urge the researcher to start analyzing as soon as the research begins. There are good reasons for analyzing data as it is made. In earlier chapters, we stressed that all qualitative methods aim to build understanding from the data and that research design adapts to growing understanding. This means that abstracting begins at the beginning of a project. Completing the gathering of all the data and *then* thinking about them is usually highly problematic, because this does not allow the data-gathering process to be data driven. Doing so, however, may be very attractive if you are unsure of what you are doing. Doing more interviews is much easier than confronting the challenge of finding out what is to be learned from those already done. This means that as you start making data, you need a clear idea of how you will analyze it.

All research shares the goal of making the researcher think abstractly. *Abstract thinking* involves transforming data from individual instances by creating, exploring, and using general categories derived from the data. In qualitative research, this is normally a primary goal, even a defining condition for a project to be considered qualitative. As we have shown in our sketches of methods in Chapter 3, all the qualitative methods we are discussing in this book seek a sense of understanding, of things coming together. It is this process that distinguishes description from analysis.

Abstracting from data gets you somewhere else—away from the data and toward the concepts that help you understand them and (sometimes) build theories about them. Consider the qualitative studies you have found satisfying or intriguing—what was satisfying about them was probably an abstraction. Rather than summarizing the experience of all the patients in a cancer ward, Glaser and Strauss (1971) developed the idea of "status passage." After talking to many people in different kinship situations, Finch (1989) wrote not about their individual experiences but about family obligation. Sometimes abstraction is driven by concepts generated from the data. Morse developed the concept of *compathy* to describe the sharing of another's pain experience (Morse, Mitcham, & van der Steen, 1998) when her interviews with nurses who worked with major trauma patients described feelings for patients that did not fit the description of empathy in the literature. Sometimes such abstraction is informed by theory about the phenomenon studied. Richards (1990), in her analysis of neighbor networks, drew on the feminist literature on women's work and ideology of family to interpret conflict in local associations as labor on the border of "private and public" worlds.

How abstracting is done is far too often presented as a mystery. A constant theme in the literature is that the theory "emerges" from the data, but we have never had the privilege of seeing such an apparition. Whether driven by the data or other theory, qualitative abstraction always requires the researcher's active exploration of data. Understanding is developed as a result of the researcher's insight and the researcher's work. As we emphasized earlier, the research process is not passive. The researcher drives it, making informed decisions, thinking, linking, and abstracting. If theory emerges, it is because the researcher "emerged" it.

Understanding the researcher's agency is a first step toward being able to do it. You don't need supernatural powers or the touch of a guru to be able to think abstractly about your data. You do, however, need good research design, good data, skill, and creative and concentrated efforts at thinking. We cannot stress strongly enough that an adequate account of the data or answer to the research question will emerge only if the right conditions exist. For any method, abstraction requires that the data be in the right state, that the researcher be receptive to the emerging ideas, and that the researcher understand and undertake appropriate analytic strategies.

Techniques of abstracting from data vary widely. The terms associated with steps to abstraction include *classifying, coding, distilling,* and *seeking "themes."* To learn specific techniques, go to the specialist literature. Here we focus on what the various techniques have in common: the first steps of abstracting "up" from the data, which are usually called *categorizing* and *conceptualizing.* All qualitative researchers aim to create more general categories, drawing together the complex immediate messages of the data in more abstract topics or groups, and most aim to move from this sorting of data to more theoretical concepts.

〰 THE FIRST STEP: CATEGORIZING

Categorizing is the first, minimal step to abstracting, but it is often also an end goal. For some projects, it is a first step toward creating theory. For others, the goal is *only* categorizing and category exploration, and the analysis process in such a study may require nothing more abstract than giving an accurate account of what is going on. The ability to offer "thick description," or to locate a surprising pattern, may transform complicated data into a story that makes sense—and doing so requires categorization.

It is important to understand that the research question sets the goals for the outcome of the project. In this area, there is a serious lack of fit between what is actually done in the research world and the literature on methods. Either implicitly or explicitly, many texts overlook or devalue studies that do not progress from categorizing to theory construction. This is a major source of confusion for novice researchers, who find it hard to recognize in the texts the sorts of studies they are seeing presented at conferences. As we mentioned in Chapter 3, many such studies seek patterns rather than theories, and there is nothing wrong with seeking patterns. Although doing so may not conform to one of the recognized methods of theorizing analysis, researchers are too often led to believe it must still be labeled with one. If your goal is simply to find out if anything new came from open-ended questions in a survey or to evaluate a pilot focus group, there is no need to pretend that this study is powered by grounded theory or phenomenology, but there is a need for abstracting.

Categorization and Coding

All qualitative research involves categorizing (as does almost all reflective thinking). Only some requires coding—the set of processes described in Chapter 6—for gathering the material *about* the categories. Coding always makes categories, but categorizing only sometimes requires coding.

As we have shown in Chapter 6, in any of the ways of coding, the researcher needs to say, "This is a topic or idea on which I will gather material." In this way, coding generates categories. During coding, the data "make" categories as the researcher is alerted to concepts, themes, patterns, and surprises with new meanings. During coding, new categories seem to "happen" when an existing code doesn't quite fit the data or new data suggest several dimensions of the category. All qualitative methods that involve coding treat it as category creating and at least one way of abstracting *from* data (Richards, 2009, Chapter 6).

Coding also supports development of categories. If paper records are coded, they can be gathered in heaps, reread, and reviewed. If computer software allows "live" display of coded material, the researcher can rework a category, redo coding, and create related categories by further analysis of the material.

But of course it is possible for qualitative researchers to think about the data without coding. As we showed in Chapter 6, "coding" has as many purposes and as many recommended techniques as there are methods. We have warned, then, against coding in the absence of methodological purpose.

Categorization as Everyday Strategy

When our goal is comprehending and learning, seeing or saying something new, predicting or understanding, we categorize. So for most humans, and for some qualitative researchers, category construction is a normal process of comprehending that has nothing to do with coding. Only sometimes is it important to gather material about a category.

Qualitative thinking is very much like everyday thinking. Researchers categorize constantly, creating and using general ideas about particular data items. If you have trouble with the task of category creation in your research project, spend a day watching your own management of the complex data of everyday life. We manage these processes largely by categorizing. If somebody approaches you on the street, you will sometimes move to greet them or offer assistance, or sometimes do your best to avoid contact. Between the approach and the response lie categories—what sort of person is this, what sort of approach, and what sort of attitude? Some answers appear so obvious that we take them for granted. For example, this person is a man (a nonfemale human of mature age). There is no subtle interpretation here (unless the person is heavily disguised or obscured or transgender), but we have categorized this person, rightly or wrongly. Male gender is a category that allows us to think of all males and ask questions about male behavior or male experience. Whether someone is a "homeless man" or a "businessman" will involve more interpretation: How, from physical appearance, do we "know" this person is homeless? In addition, "homelessness" is a category to which people attach stereotypes that may have nothing to do with experience or fact.

Categorizing is how we understand and come to terms with the complexity of data in everyday life. It is our normal sense-making activity, and it is efficient. If one thing is a "sort of" something else, we can respond to *types* of experience, to patterns, to predictable behavior. Categorizing is also always risky because it obscures uniqueness, preempts discovery, and may blind us to the unusual. (Oops, that "homeless man" is an eccentric millionaire!)

It is odd, then, that a process so normal in life and in research can become a major obstruction to doing qualitative research. But category construction can, in our experience, be the earliest obstacle, and sometimes a serious one, for novice researchers. Understanding (properly) that categories are the first step to theories and having learned to treat theories as the products of great minds, new researchers can easily suffer lack of nerve when they think they see something in the data but it seems too trivial to record. Our advice? Record it!

𝒲 THE NEXT STEP: CONCEPTUALIZING

In qualitative research, categorizing is how we get "up" from the diversity of data to the shapes of the data, the sorts of things represented. *Concepts* are how we get up to more general, higher-level, and more abstract constructs. Concepts are mental images. Researchers usually seek ways of moving from categories to concepts and then of building frameworks of concepts that map or image the subjects of research. As Miles and Huberman (1994) note, "Theory building relies on a few general constructs that subsume a mountain of particulars" (p. 18).

Categories may never develop into concepts, but to the extent that they do, you move the study from description to analysis. As you come to understand and go beyond complex data, how far you go beyond is a question decided by your method. Even the simplest categorizing is analytic. The processes of making a category involve discovering a new idea and naming it, storing thoughts about it, managing its relation to other categories, holding it in mind, and linking it to the growing understanding of your work—and all these are theorizing processes. They are the first uncertain steps by which the researcher sets out toward the hazy goal of theory. With categorization, the researcher puts a first foot on what Carney (1990) calls the "ladder of abstraction."

⟨ DOING ABSTRACTION

Qualitative methods of all varieties share a commitment to allowing categories to emerge from the data. For many researchers, this is almost a defining characteristic of qualitative method, and it is certainly one of the few commonalities among methods. (If you were not trying to learn from the data, you probably would not be working qualitatively.) In most methods, some categories are decided in advance, but all methods seek new categories, which emerge as the researcher achieves understanding of the rich data.

There is such a variety in the sorts of categories you are likely to create in a qualitative study, in how and when they arrive in that study, and in the uses to which they are being put that it is at first easy to see them as unrelated tools for different purposes. In the following subsections, we outline the range of ways in which qualitative researchers make and use abstract categories for describing and analyzing data. Not surprisingly, this relates to the range of coding techniques.

The fit of a particular method with a particular research question is often best observed when the researcher considers the ways of abstracting. Methods differ clearly on each of four dimensions relevant to the location of the project and the preparation of the researcher. Each method has its own answers to these questions: When does abstraction happen? Where do abstractions come from? How are abstractions created? What analytic outcome is being sought? Like the other tables in this book offering comparisons among methods, Table 7.1 is a sketch map; it is intended to encourage you to undertake more detailed reading on your selected method and to help you put your method in context. We suggest that you read it in conjunction with the methodological map provided in Chapter 3.

When Does It Happen?

At least some abstraction will always happen early. One of the myths we have challenged is that a good researcher always approaches data with

Table 7.1   Doing Abstraction in Five Different Methods

Method	When Does Abstraction Occur?	Where Does Abstraction Come From?	How Is Abstraction Done?	What Is the Goal of Abstraction?
Ethnography	Prior knowledge of site, situation; understanding develops during field research and data analysis	Knowledge of social and economic setting; observation and learning from the setting	Rich description; combination of qualitative and quantitative patterning; coding, comparing, reviewing field notes	To identify themes and patterns; to explain and account for a social and cultural situation
Grounded theory	Abstraction is from the data but can be informed by previously derived theories	Categories derived from data (observations or line-by-line analysis of texts); constant comparison with other situations or settings	Theoretical sensitivity; seeking concepts and their dimensions; open coding, dimensionalizing, memo writing, diagramming	To identify a core category and theory grounded in the data
Phenomenology	Previous ideas and knowledge are bracketed; data are reflected through the phenomenological concepts	Themes and meanings in accounts, texts	Deep immersion, focus, thorough reading	To describe the essence of a phenomenon
Discourse analysis	Critical approach may present abstract categories for analysis	Categories constructed and texted during detailed analysis of text or talk	Thorough textual analysis by detailed coding	To expose underlying ideology or assumptions
Case study	Prior knowledge of site, situation; if using field research, developing knowledge of site	Depends on the method used for analysis; categories usually derive from previous theory and also from data	Summary and review of cases, comparative analysis	To provide an authoritative account of these cases and generalize from them

an open mind and that this means it should be a mind empty of knowledge about the topic. This myth can seriously hinder the researcher who accepts it and then finds it untrue of his or her situation. If you deny that you know a lot about the situation you are studying (as many researchers do), you are likely to walk those assumptions into your study without acknowledging them.

Qualitative methods—and teachers of qualitative research—differ in their approaches to the handling of prior thinking. You may be advised or urged to assess your prior ideas and theory from the literature at an early stage in the project, as a means of shaping data making and designing access to data. If your method and context require this, the research design will involve reviewing and using this prior knowledge. Using computer software to categorize literature as well as project data will assist you in this task. Be aware, however, that some methods, for good reason, explicitly discourage researchers from categorizing before they explore their data documents. This is because these methods emphasize having the meanings that occur in the data determine the processes of abstracting from those data. This is the reason for the literature on "bracketing" of prior knowledge.

The handling of prior knowledge, then, is a clear example of the need to locate your project methodologically. Nobody approaches any social situation free of categories, and often alongside the categories for thinking about a particular situation come concepts from the literature and beginning theories. So you need to be aware of the pathway to analysis in your chosen method and of the timing of analytical processes. There are strong differences in the acceptability of prior categorization, but in no method is abstraction *entirely* a priori. None of these methods, for example, will achieve abstraction through answers to a "precoded" questionnaire (this term is, in fact, a misnomer, given that the survey researcher is not preemptively *coding* the interview to be conducted but *precategorizing* the answers).

How Is It Done?

This is the area of greatest commonality among the methods. As Table 7.1 shows, all five of the methods described anticipate that abstractions to some extent come "up" from the data rather than "down" from prior theory. This commonality can be a source of confusion. All these methods, for example, rely to some degree on text. Some methods vary in that they use video recordings or photographs, but they all also use text. There are certainly variations in practice—for example, regarding whether an interview is transcribed and, if so, how complete a transcript should be and whether hesitations, tone, and body language should also be recorded—but few would not keep a record of the interview at all. Thus, all require data that can be rich enough to generate interpretation and support abstraction.

Researchers employing different methods have different terms for this qualitative process of category discovery. Watch for accounts of the researcher's agency. Researchers talk of "hearing" themes, "feeling through" meanings, and "seeing" patterns. These phrases hide practical skills—the things the researcher does to data.

When you approach a method, considering its relevance for your project, it is helpful to locate practical, honest accounts of what other researchers have done to their data. These are often missing from published research reports. For examples of some practical accounts that include this information, see the list of resources in Chapter 3.

All the processes of abstraction involve work. It is useful to distinguish, following Turner (1981), between theory emergence and theory construction. Theory emergence is often an event of discovery; theory construction is a craft. The accounts of studies and stories of researchers emphasize the ongoing work of piecing together clues and themes, tiny bits of understanding, and recurrences and links. The qualitative researcher builds a "network of concepts, evidence, relations of concepts, coordinations of data, of hierarchies of grain size where the theory/data/explanation chunks of one grain size are the data for the work of the next grain size up" (Richards & Richards, 1994, pp. 448–449; see also Lofland & Lofland, 1995). (For a more detailed discussion of possible outcomes of your project, and possible aims for your analysis, see Richards, 2009, Chapter 7.)

※ MANAGING ABSTRACTION

The processes discussed so far make another layer of data. You now have not only a growing body of rich data but also a growing body of categories, concepts, and thoughts about them. Almost any qualitative project rapidly acquires a growing task of managing elements so they can be known, viewed, explored, and linked. Some of the literature will assist you in these processes (on manual methods, see especially Miles & Huberman, 1994; if you are using software, see Richards, 2009). Whatever your method, we recommend early attention to ways of managing not just data documents but also ideas, which are your most precious data.

Documenting Ideas: Definitions, Memos, and Diaries

For novice researchers, often the greatest barrier to thinking up from data is the sense that category construction is a majestic and magical performance. The best way to climb over that barrier is to work actively with and within your categories. Make memos about them generously— these can always be deleted later. Even the simplest categories grow and change during a project, and you must record these changes if you are to be able to tell the story of your analysis later.

For any idea, topic, theme, concept, or other abstraction, it is advisable that you store somewhere a description of how it is to be seen and used. When it changes, that description can be changed, and if the change is significant, it can be tracked. As ideas about a category grow, it is useful, sometimes essential, that the category acquire a memo. As your confidence grows, so does the memo, possibly accompanied by or linked to other memos.

Growing Ideas

A theme of this book has been that ideas emerging in a project grow with the data. Whatever your method, it is important that you expect and encourage your ideas to change and be ready to record changes. This means that idea management must be flexible and introspective. As you continue to work with data, you will need ways of revisiting and rethinking categories to develop them further and refine their dimensions (see especially the techniques for "dimensionalizing" in grounded theory, in Strauss, 1987, p. 180). You also need ways of challenging and assessing the themes you are seeing in the data.

> When you're working with text or less well organized displays, you often note recurring patterns, themes, or "gestalts," which pull together many separate pieces of data. Something "jumps out" at you, suddenly makes sense. . . . The human mind finds patterns so

quickly and easily that it needs no how-to advice. Patterns just "happen," almost too quickly . . . [and so] need to be subjected to skepticism—your own or that of others—and to conceptual and empirical testing. (Miles & Huberman, 1994, p. 246)

Unless your colleagues or supervisors are unable to accept this, we urge that you write memos in the first person, firmly reporting "what I did" and "what I saw" in the data. This will later help you avoid passively reporting that a theme "emerged" or a category "appeared." Whatever your chosen method, your study will benefit from your joining the increasing community of qualitative researchers who document, date, and account for their ideas so they can tell a category's story to doubting readers and track back how it has changed and been used. At the end of this chapter, we discuss ways to do this on the computer.

Managing Categories: Index Systems

Most qualitative research methods require some way of gathering and managing ideas and categories (and the definitions and memos attached to them). But few qualitative scholars offer advice on how to do it, and we have seen students tied up for months as they try to establish safe and flexible category management systems. Like any growing body of hetero-geneous materials (correspondence, clothes, library books, recipe cards, addresses, tools, photographs, and more), research ideas will be hard to access, easily lost, and generally problematic if not stored logically. Our advice is that you manage the growing ideas from the start of the project rather than wait and then discover you are losing them. (For detailed advice, see Richards, 2009, Chapter 6.)

However you do it, you will be rewarded for developing a storage system early and reworking it as you go. You can do this manually (with index cards or files) or on the computer. Most specialized qualitative research software now allows you to store categories and subcategories in "trees," which you can manage and view much as you manage and view the structure of your folders and files. A helpful storage system will incorporate what is known prior to the study; will be logical, so you can find ideas again; and will easily accommodate the emerging ideas you are about to put forth. (For help with manual index systems, see Miles & Huberman, 1994; Lofland & Lofland, 1995; for managing categories on the computer, see Richards, 2009; Richards & Richards, 1995.)

Models and Diagrams

Some methods, and within those some researchers, use modeling and displays to assist in the abstraction process. These techniques were given prominence with the publication in 1984 of the first edition of Miles and Huberman's "sourcebook" and with the development since of computer imaging techniques that can relate to the items in a qualitative project. Note that *diagram, model, network,* and related terms have many meanings in this context. Qualitative researchers have always diagrammed, but usually in impressionistic ways. (For ways of "seeing a whole," see Richards, 2005, Chapter 9; for an extended example of the use of diagrams in grounded theory, see Strauss, 1987, Chapter 8; for an extended discussion of modes of display, conceptual frameworks, and models, see Miles & Huberman, 1994.)

※ UJING YOUR JOFTWARE FOR MANAGING IDEAJ

The primary difference between commercial database software and specialized qualitative software is that the latter is designed to help with the processes of analysis and abstraction. Software packages designed for qualitative research will store not only materials but also ideas, concepts, issues, questions, and theories.

The primary difference between using a computer system in qualitative research and using a manual system is that the computer gives a different sort of access, allowing for flexible growth in the webs of ideas the data are producing and enabling the researcher to manage those burgeoning ideas by storing them, defining them, accessing them, and writing about them.

The contribution software can make at the early stages of abstracting is considerable. Most researchers are diffident about first ideas. If scribbled on stick-on labels, the ideas may be lost. The computer makes it easy for the researcher to store them, define them, write about and revisit them, and revise and review them as ideas build up.

Approaches

Your computer software will offer ways to make, manage, and develop categories and to work with them from the early stages of your project.

And all software offers some ways of asking questions about the relations between the categories you are reflecting on.

With your qualitative software, or other software for modeling, explore computer-based diagramming. This allows you to "play" with ideas in ways that are impossible with manual methods, including layering, labeled links, and live access to data.

Software will support the following processes, which you need to learn:

〉〉〉 How to manage and move the categories for abstracting from your data

〉〉〉 How to store definitions and how to describe and write memos about them and log changes

〉〉〉 How to use search and query tools to explore the relations of categories

〉〉〉 How to model your first ideas about the topic and the hunches growing from your exploration of the data

Advances

These are the areas where software has opened entirely new ways of working with qualitative data. As your project progresses, you will learn the uses of these tools to assist your exploration of the data, checking of your hunches, and developing of theories and reporting of patterns and themes.

Category management is much more possible when the researcher is using software. Find how, with your software, you can do the following:

〉〉〉 Flexibly copy, move, and combine coding categories without losing coding

〉〉〉 Link logging of project process

〉〉〉 Search the text of documents

〉〉〉 Expand search results to appropriate context

〉〉〉 Automatically code the results so they can become the basis for another question

〰 Make matrices that demonstrate patterns and allow the researcher to go to each cell to see what *those* people said about *this* issue

〰 Search and query the data (e.g., software supports creating, and optionally saving, questions about patterns of coding)

Models and diagrams were always part of qualitative research, but computer-based modeling offers many advances, for example:

〰 Showing connections you made by coding or linking

〰 Allowing the researcher to open data items from within the model to explore them further

Alerts

Because these new tools are so exciting, be careful to use them thoughtfully and flexibly.

1. Cataloguing and ordering categories can become a passion! Stop when the catalog is good enough for your purposes. Tools for managing, reviewing, and moving categories and for developing ideas about their relationships should be used as indicated by your research goals and design. If unplanned, those processes dominate, since categories can be changed at any time, reordered at any time, and combined or deleted as the data direct your understanding of them. The challenge is to use this flexibility to assist abstraction while avoiding the trap of constantly reworking a workable index system (Richards, 2009, Chapter 6).

2. Learn to conduct and interpret thoughtfully the powerful searches your software supports. When you come to use these tools in your own project, be careful always to prepare the question you are asking in plain language and then interpret the result accurately. (For advice and cautions on using computer-based search tools, see Richards, 2009, Chapter 8.)

3. Modeling with software offers attractive ways of "seeing" and showing your project. But don't assume you need qualitative software for this task. Qualitative software modeling tools offer the advantage of linking items to your data, but their output can be

clumsy and difficult to visualize. A professional drawing package may provide a much more flexible tool.

4. Use your model carefully, as an interpretive tool, with all the caution you bring to any other analysis stage. The risk is that you can "see" in a model a theme or pattern not reflected in your data. Always make the model true to the data.

🕮 SUMMARY

By now you should understand the processes of interpretation that accompany the clerical task of coding and why we code data. Coding is never an end in itself; it is a way of achieving categorization and interpretation, and these, of course, are sought and achieved in ways other than coding. In this chapter, we explained how categories are discovered and used in analysis, as well as the goal of concept development. We looked at some ways of doing abstraction and at the sources and signs of abstract concepts. We emphasized the need for management of ideas and development of categories and how these can be assisted by software. Categorization and conceptualization are processes that will enable you to identify patterns, explore hunches, draw in what you have learned from the literature to inform interpretation and explanation, and derive and justify your understanding. Doing these tasks rigorously is essential for high-quality qualitative research and is also exciting for the researcher.

🕮 RESOURCES

Glaser, B. G., & Strauss, A. L. (1971). *Status passage*. Chicago: Aldine.

Hsieh, H.-F., & Shannon, S. E. (2005). Three approaches to qualitative content analysis. *Qualitative Health Research, 15,* 1277–1288.

Kohlbacher, F. (2005). The use of qualitative content analysis in case study research. *Forum Qualitative Sozialforschung/ Forum: Qualitative Social Research,* 7(1), Art. 21. Retrieved from http://www .qualitative-research.net/index.php/fqs/ article/view/75/153

Mayring, P. (2000). Qualitative content analysis. *Forum Qualitative Sozialforschung/ Forum: Qualitative Social Research,* 1(2), Art. 20. Retrieved from http://nbn-resolv ing.de/urn:nbn:de:0114-fqs0002204

Miles, M. B., & Huberman, A. M. (1994). *Qualitative data analysis: An expanded sourcebook* (2nd ed.). Thousand Oaks, CA: Sage.

Mithaug, D. E. (2000). *Learning to theorize*. Thousand Oaks, CA: Sage.

Morse, J. M. (1994). "Emerging from the data": The cognitive processes of analysis in qualitative inquiry. In J. M. Morse (Ed.), *Critical issues in qualitative research methods* (pp. 23–42). Thousand Oaks, CA: Sage.

Richards, L. (1990). *Nobody's home: Dreams and realities in a new suburb*. Melbourne: Oxford University Press.

Richards, L. (2009). *Handling qualitative data: A practical guide* (2nd ed.). London: Sage.

Richards, T. J., & Richards, L. (1995). Using hierarchical categories in qualitative data analysis. In U. Kelle (Ed.), *Computer-aided qualitative data analysis: Theory, methods, and practice* (pp. 62–68). London: Sage.

Strauss, A. L. (1995). Notes on the nature and development of general theories. *Qualitative Inquiry, 1,* 7–18.

Turner, B. A. (1981). Some practical aspects of qualitative data analysis. *Quality and Quantity, 15,* 225–247.

Van den Hoonard, W. C. (1999). *Working with sensitizing concepts*. Thousand Oaks, CA: Sage.

8

From Method
to Analysis

Revisiting Methodological Congruence

I n Chapter 3, we introduced five major types of qualitative methods, explaining that each method facilitates the achievement of particular analytic goals and each shows a fit of question, data, and outcome. So each method demands that the researcher think about data in a particular way.

Within any method, researchers may incorporate different research strategies and ways of approaching and working with data, but the analytic processes fit together in a coherent way. All these qualitative methods use forms of data that are unstructured and contexted (as discussed in Chapter 5), and all use some sort of coding strategies and procedures for categorizing and/or theme-ing data (presented in Chapter 6). But *how* researchers create data and how they approach analysis differ from method to method and also, sometimes dramatically, within methods. The modes of coding, categorizing, and theorizing are sensitive to the method used and appropriate additional analytic strategies. And each method contains very different approaches, usually ranging from general principles of enquiry to strict rules of procedure.

In Chapter 3, we showed how the differences in methods start from different assumptions, from the researcher's asking and answering different sorts of questions and using different types of data or data in different forms. From method to method, the researcher thinks differently, asking different questions and seeking different data. Whilst there are commonalities across methods, each has its own fit of question, data, and sought outcome.

In this chapter, we revisit the same five methods, focusing now on what it is like to work in each method. For each, we discuss the ways of working with data and the analytic strategies most commonly used in that method, as well as the differences within it.

What follows are sketches of techniques, aiming to provide a feel for what it would be like to work this way and to help you plan your proposal aware of options and alternatives. If you need to use one of these strategies, the literature cited in the text, as well as the resources listed at the end of the chapter, will guide you to more information and examples.

❧ ETHNOGRAPHY

As discussed in Chapter 3, ethnography starts with the assumptions that cultural beliefs, values, and behaviors are learned, patterned, and may change. They may be overt (as ethnic identity is formed) or subconscious, below the level of awareness. The ethnographer, then, needs research designs and strategies for eliciting cultural beliefs and values that are implicit within the culture and strategies that enable the identification, comparison, and contrasting of those characteristics.

The early goals of researchers in ethnography are to learn "what is going on" and to be comfortable in the setting. Researchers achieve these goals by completing first-level description and then, once they have some understanding of the setting, by working to obtain thick description. The strategies described below in each category are not fixed in stone, and each may be used for other analytic goals.

Working With Data

First-Level Description

First-level description is the description of the scene, the parameters/boundaries of the research group, and the overt characteristics of group members. It may include demographic characteristics, the history of the populations, maps of relevant areas, and so forth. First-level description places the reader in the context of the study and sets the stage by providing background information for the subsequent analytic reporting. These data are usually a synthesis of public documents and other publicly available information, along with basic description of the setting through the use of mapping, photography, or other means to illustrate the setting and describe the people. First-level description is usually presented in narrative form and supplemented by tables, maps, or photographs as necessary.

Many strategies for orienting to the setting are described in the literature. "Doing something" can ease the researcher's awkwardness upon entering a setting and help the researcher get to know the participants. Initial strategies include the following:

⁑ Maps/floor plans of the setting or simple line drawings can serve as "memory joggers." Photographs are a quick and effective means for recording the scene.

⁑ Organizational charts can help the researcher learn the formal and informal relationships and chain of command.

⁑ Documents frequently give important clues to the history of the setting; initially, the researcher may simply want to make a list of the kinds of documents available.

⁑ Documenting routines helps give the researcher a feel for the rhythm of the setting. The holistic approach of ethnography is aided by the researcher's inclusion of all routines. For instance, if the setting is a hospital, the researcher should include the routines observed on weekends and nights; if the setting is a community, the researcher should include routines observed in all seasons as well as on special days and holidays; if the setting is an institution, observations should include rush hours as well as slack times.

Other strategies help the researcher assess the status quo:

⁑ A rapid community survey allows teams of researchers to grasp at least the more urgent problems.

⁑ Interviews with key community members, or focus groups, may help highlight issues, allowing the researcher to get a feel for the research domain, obtain relevant items for a questionnaire, or provide a rapid form of evaluation.

⁑ The researcher may study pertinent records and newspaper coverage to supplement and inform participant observation.

The literature also suggests strategies for documenting interpersonal relationships. Researchers interested in informal relations may employ sociograms, network diagrams, and drawings. Many techniques used in social network analysis can help researchers see relations as they are seen by participants. More formal relations may be portrayed in kinship charts and organizational charts.

Thick Description

Researchers develop thick description (see Geertz, 1973) by processing interviews and field notes in which informal conversations and observations are reported and through theoretical insights developed from these materials. These materials are then condensed by summarizing, synthesizing, and extracting the essential features or characteristics of the situation. Synthesizing without losing any significant detail or variation requires skill. There must be consistency between one's observations, reports from the participants, and information in the literature if the study is to achieve generalization, validity, and abstraction. For example, in a study of young mothers in neighborhoods, a researcher might describe how they watch out for one another during the day. Such a description of one case in one neighborhood is context bound. But if the researcher's observations and participants' accounts are placed within the theoretical body of social support literature, the study can be tried against other situations and may move from description to analysis.

All ethnography seeks thick description, usually built by making data: observations, interviews, and diaries. Revisit Chapter 5 to consider why these are central to ethnography.

Ethnographers also often use quantitative surveys early in their studies to establish the base data, or later in the ethnographic fieldwork when they have identified and delineated particular phenomena and need to know how those phenomena are distributed among the groups they are studying. In her ethnographic study on the cultural responsiveness to pain, Morse (1989a) used survey methods and Thurstone's paired comparison technique (Nunnally, 1978) and found that how painful the participants perceived certain conditions to be was culturally taught and varied among cultures. Richards (1990) used statistical analysis of survey results to indicate clusters of neighboring behavior that assisted the development of typologies from the qualitative data. Quantitative measures may supplement qualitative measures: Margaret Mead, for instance, often used psychometric tests as a part of her traditional ethnography.

Comparison

Cultural values are not easily studied or directly reported by participants, so researchers must obtain indicators of such values indirectly. Identification of cultural values and perspectives may be enhanced through the direct comparison of two cultures or through "shadow comparison"—that is, comparison of the results from a given cultural group with those described in the literature or with knowledge of the researcher's own culture.

〰 Comparison of two very different cultural groups can provide information on as wide a range of dimensions as possible.

〰 Before-and-after research design is often less than satisfactory in qualitative work if it requires "blinding" the researcher, collecting baseline data, implementing interventions, and then collecting data to demonstrate the changes that have occurred.

〰 Asking comparative questions can be the key to ethnographic analysis. It involves a stance that constantly asks, "What are the characteristics of . . . ?" "What are the types of . . . ?" and "How does . . . relate to . . . ?"

〰 Researchers may investigate the implicit structural features of concepts and phenomena by using techniques of ethnoscience (see Spradley, 1979; Werner & Schoepfle, 1987a, 1987b).

〰 Researchers may establish commonalities among different types of components through the use of card sorts. In this technique, the researcher writes all the attributes of each component on cards, one attribute per card. The participant is asked to sort the cards into piles and then name each pile and describe how the piles are different. The participants' dominant piles determine the segregates (major categories) and subsegregates. The researcher is able to sort and display the categories as a taxonomy, then search further to determine whether the characteristics are unique to each category and whether further characteristics related to each classification can be identified. (For an example see Morse, 1989b.)

Strategies of Analysis

During analysis, an ethnographer typically works by what has been termed "progressive focusing" (Hammersley & Atkinson, 2007, p. 160). Reading and rereading filed notes and transcripts, the researcher "funnels" the data, selecting and reinterpreting, searching for comparisons, and refining interpretation. Silverman (2010, p. 235) has pointed out that this method has much in common with grounded theory techniques. The segments of data may be considered as pieces of a puzzle that fit together to give a complete, holistic, thick, and rich description of the cultural perspective on the research problem—but this will not happen in one step. Rather, in the ongoing process of interpretation and data collection, the researcher must reflect on what is being found and how, on the role of the researcher in finding it, and on how the original focus is changing and the scope of the question developing. Ethnographic research is inherently flexible. Each time something does not fit, or does not immediately make sense, the researcher is alerted to a challenge to be understood, and in tackling this, the focus is sharpened. Thus, ethnographic research design is malleable but, like any method, only within limits. (Don't forget that if you add new strategies, you will need to notify and obtain permission from your ethics review board.)

Ethnographies are usually presented as giving comprehensive, consistent, and logical portrayals of the groups or phenomena studied (from the emic perspective). Because of the depth of description required and the scope of much ethnography, they are often presented as monographs rather than articles. They may present particular challenges in reporting because the richer the data and the more varied the portrayals, the more identifiable participants may be—regardless of how careful the researchers have been in changing names and details. You should consider these challenges in designing your research.

Ethnography, perhaps more than any other method sketched here, has undergone major changes in recent years. You will find that the literature contains a lively debate about the rival goals of description and theorizing. The results may look like theoretical monographs or like documentary films and articles on some aspect of daily life (e.g., eating, dance, health beliefs), special circumstances (e.g., childbirth, funeral ceremonies), or representation (e.g., use of media such as art, drama, dance).

The result of a traditional ethnography is a rich description (i.e., detailed and comprehensive) of the lives of members of a group as they are lived, frequently published as a monograph. For instance, in *Scripting Addiction*, Carr (2011) examines the question, "Why do addiction counselors dedicate themselves to reconciling drug users' relationship to language in order to reconfigure their relationships with drugs?" She explores the context and conditions of "talk therapy" for addiction, clearly presents assumptions underlying the ritualized form of talk, and describes how addicts' talk is monitored as a sign of progress. Her monograph includes many sources of data to help build her case: genograms with codes depicting the emotional tenor of relationships; ecomaps, to show social networks; ecological models; documents; diagramming; and, of course, interviews and field notes collected over 3 1/2 years of participant observation and fieldwork. The result is a complex depiction of how addiction, language, self-knowledge, and sobriety are manifest in the interactions between the counselors and clients.

In *Violence and Hope in a U.S.–Mexico Border Town*, Glittenberg (2008) explores the underpinnings of violence in a small community in which "levels of homicide have reached new heights; gang warfare, drive-by shootings, and the deadly rampages with adolescents were regular features on the nightly news" (p. 1). Glittenberg and her research assistants lived in the small town, conducting participant observation, focus groups, individual interviews, life histories, and a random household survey. Their research questions were "local": "Why are some communities more violent than others?" and "What is being done to eradicate violence in Esperanza?" While Glittenberg's ethnography is geographically delimited to a small town on the western side of Texas, she clearly states that her project is generalizable, "exposing myths, and inaccurate perceptions, and also giving direction to reducing violence and building hope throughout the country and even internationally" (p. 2).

〰 GROUNDED THEORY

Recall that grounded theory method aims for theory to emerge from data. Its questions explore process, and its outcomes are midrange theories specific to a particular process and a particular situation. The perspective that reality is constantly changing and being negotiated leads the researcher to active inquiry into the event over time. In grounded theory, there is an emphasis on detailed knowledge, constant comparison, and the trajectory of the event. The researcher consistently asks not only "What is going on here?" but also "How is it different?" The method of grounded theory promotes a stance that refuses to accept a report at face value, a sort of methodological restlessness that leads the researcher to seek characteristics, conditions, causes, antecedents, and consequences of events or responses as ways of drawing them together in an integrated theory. Originally, the underlying basis to grounded theory was symbolic interactionism (Blumer, 1986), but, as Charmaz (2006) notes, this is no longer considered essential or even necessary.

As discussed in Chapter 3, acrimonious disputes about approaches to grounded theory have arisen in recent years. In 1987, Strauss stated that the "methodological thrust of the grounded theory approach to qualitative data is toward the development of theory, without any particular commitment to specific kinds of data, lines of research, or theoretical interests" (p. 5). However, the method, as described in Strauss's collaborative work with Juliet Corbin (Corbin & Strauss, 2008), was seen by Glaser as "forcing" data. More recently, differences have been softened. Corbin (2009) sees the main components of grounded theory as including "theoretical sampling, constant comparison and asking some sort of question" (p. 244) and as being "focused on process and structure" (p. 247) located in a larger context of conditions. Glaserian grounded theory continues to develop through the work of methodologists such as Phyllis Stern (Stern, 2009; Stern & Porr, 2011).

Here we emphasize what was central in the method jointly described by Strauss and Glaser. The concept of *theoretical sensitivity* is crucial in grounded theory. The researcher *seeks* theory, constantly working with data records and transcripts, and easing ideas from the concepts and the linkages that might generate theoretical insight. Those emerging concepts are also in constant interplay with the data as the researcher seeks integration and synthesis.

Working With Data

Grounded theory aims for concepts constructed from data, with a goal of understanding process. Data are recorded in detail so the words used and the stages of processes can be examined. These data are usually interviews or observations from field research, or narratives collected retrospectively. Data documents may also include diaries or visual records.

Memos and Their Importance

Whatever the ways of making such primary data, grounded theory method always produces another level of data, in the researcher's memos and other written documentation of insights gleaned during the process of analysis. As theory is constructed, "one can frequently sense the hovering presence of memos which arise out of codes and ideas generated" (Strauss, 1987, p. 109). There is a strong emphasis on dialogue and the challenging of ideas and their development as data accrue. The lone researcher or the team encapsulates this in memos, "a running record of insights, hunches, hypotheses, discussions about the implications of codes, additional thoughts" (p. 110). Memos, in this method, are data.

Data Preparation

Analysis begins with the first exploration of the topic and literature, and is ongoing throughout the study. Hence, it is crucial that the researcher not process data records in bulk and only then consider them. Often a grounded theory study will begin with memos, and then ideas grow from the first field notes of interviews. As researchers explore similar recurring incidents, events, and experiences and begin to develop concepts, they revisit memos written earlier.

Records of interviews or field notes are usually transcribed, and these transcripts are checked for accuracy. At this time, descriptive codes (such as codes for demographic characteristics of the participant) are entered and linked to each transcription. But full transcription is a matter of contention in the literature. Glaser (1998) argues against recording and transcribing on the grounds that this prevents theoretical sensitivity. Conversely, we share a concern that the researcher who does not transcribe relies too much on memory and loses contact with the richly detailed text. Participants' words may be a crucial source of "in vivo" codes and provide a vivid illustration from data that are rich, accurate, and verifiable. Field notes and the researcher's diary should normally also be entered into the computer and treated as data for analysis.

Strategies of Analysis

All the main analytic strategies used in grounded theory are comparative: The founders of the method termed it the constant comparative method. In different representations, subsequently, many terms have been given to techniques, but in all versions, the central strategies are open coding, memoing, categorizing, and the integration of data through diagramming.

Strategies That Facilitate the Identification of Process

Three strategies are particularly useful for facilitating the identification of process:

- The researcher constructs a timeline for each participant—sequencing the major events, emotional responses, or strategies described in the data—and then places the timelines one under the other so that certain events are aligned, rather than in months or other calendar designations. This allows the researcher to use the timelines to compare individual cases.

- The researcher identifies the course or *trajectory* of each participant's story and compares and contrasts major events. Although the stories may not be identical and the participants may not use the same labels for important events, this comparison should make it possible for the researcher to identify common patterns. The researcher then examines data for events in common among participants and similar emotional responses or behavioral strategies of responding to those events. From this comparison, the researcher can develop a rich description of these events and look for common antecedents and consequences.

- Diagramming is recommended by all writers in grounded theory method. Diagrams can be very simple and descriptive or can seek the construction of typologies (Glaser, 1978). At its simplest, the researcher identifies two variables or emerging concepts that appear to contribute to the variations in the phenomenon of interest and, using a two-by-two matrix, explores the effects of the presence or absence of each variable in combinations.

Strategies for Coding

The transcription and analysis of field notes or interviews begins immediately following the events, and there is a continuous and responsive interaction between the collection of data and analysis, with the data directing the coding process and vice versa. In grounded theory, in vivo codes are used alongside, and often in preference to, what Strauss (1987) calls "sociological codes"—that is, such known concepts as social support or coping. The labels for codes are taken directly from the language that participants themselves used. When new categories are created, they are often given new names. Glaser (1978) recommends that to increase their repertoires of codes (and to prevent them from becoming stuck and overusing "pet" codes), researchers should use families of theoretical codes.

In Chapter 3, we recommended thoughtful review of the differences in coding style developed between these two founders of grounded theory. We suggest that you read critically the accounts from both authors to help you understand the processes of coding. Both, in different ways, recommend that the researcher approach coding not as tagging of text by categories but as a way of "opening up" the text to explore its meanings. Whichever recent texts you use as a detailed guide, you will be using the following strategies.

〲 Working with data, you constantly ask a set of questions that will keep the focus on the purpose of the study (e.g., "What are these data a study of?").

〲 Focusing on each data transcript, you will work through it carefully, line by line, highlighting important passages and creating theoretical memos (noting insights, comparisons, summaries, and questions).

〲 Discovering new ideas—phrases used by participants or categories you see in the data—you will be helped in exploring and elucidating each. Each such concept is named, and often a memo is written, as it is "opened" by interrogation. What category is this instance an example of? What is actually happening in these data? What are the *dimensions* of this category? Under what *conditions*, and with what *consequences*, will this occur?

〲 As codes are developed, you will bring together passages of data or memos relating to them, always emphasizing comparison of instances. Thus, *constant comparison* will lead you to comparing indicator with indicator, concept with concept. As you identify patterns, you will be able to label similar incidents as a category and identify the properties of the category. Now you need to write more memos.

❦ The process will lead you up from the data to more *theoretical coding* to follow the "lead" of the data, seeking other instances and related instances to increase the degree of abstraction of the analysis.

❦ In the final step of the coding process, you will seek the linkages connecting the various categories by comparing and contrasting the conditions and consequences of the relationships among categories.

Strategies With Memos

The key component of theory development is the writing of theoretical memos—which are always revisited, constantly growing, and consistently treated as data. While coding, the researcher records in memos information, ideas, insights, thoughts, and feelings about the relationships in the emerging theory. It should be noted that researchers may write memos about other memos. Memos are sorted and compared as the theory becomes more streamlined. If, at any stage, there is a question as to whether personal biases are affecting perceptions of the phenomenon, the researcher should augment observations with informal interviews to clarify perceptions and "ground" the data.

Theory-Building Strategies

As coding and memoing continue, the researcher codes the text in categories and is able to label these categories, alter the memos about them, identify core categories, and note similarities and differences between categories. Transitions or turning points in the data mark the margins between stages. Identifying characteristics, and noting the presence or absence of these primary characteristics, helps the researcher recognize the underlying rationale for participants' chosen decisions and substantially aids the theoretical development of the study. Attention must be paid to the *adequacy and appropriateness* of the data to ensure it is enough to establish saturation—that is, enough so the data begin to "sound familiar" and the researchers begin to feel as though they have "heard it all."

There is constant interaction among sampling, data collection, the emerging analysis, and theory construction. This process of analysis is highly interactive, with the researcher going back and forth between the emerging conceptual scheme or theory and data sorts. As new ideas are identified, continual data making is redirected to elicit further information regarding these ideas. As explained in Chapter 5, during these next stages the researcher probes for more information, or missing data, to develop the theory or repair gaps and address unanswered questions.

The researcher may seek additional negative (i.e., variant) cases or unique cases until these data are saturated and built into the emerging theory. At this point, the researcher seeks confirmation of a growing theory or a specific hypothesis. If the information gleaned from the data is unexpected or unanticipated, it may be necessary to change direction and follow the new leads by interviewing a different group of participants.

As the researcher continues to code, there is active seeking of "integration," the stage of comprehension, an in-depth knowledge of the data, and synthesis—the ability to report, or to tell a "generalized story" ("These people do this and that"). Once the stage of synthesis has been reached, theory development begins. At this point, *critical junctures* may be identified. The researcher now becomes more focused, filling in gaps and thin areas and coding selectively, rather than coding all that once appeared relevant.

In both Glaser's and Strauss's accounts of grounded theory method, there is emphasis on seeking a core category on which local theory will be built. The two describe this differently—but don't allow the dispute to distract you from what is central in the method. In gaining a greater understanding of the research topic, the researcher may be able to identify a primary theme—the core category or the basic social process. This will become a main theme or an emergent fit (Glaser, 1978, p. 107). Core categories are discovered in many ways—through a theoretical code, a process, a condition, two or more dimensions, a consequence. Central to the analysis, they recur frequently in the data and vary with conditions and consequences. Because they are "scattered through many categories," they will become saturated more slowly than other categories and will have theoretical "grab" (see Glaser, 1978, pp. 94–107).

Strauss (1987), quoting the original book and Glaser's work, defines the core category as "a category that is central to the integration of the theory" (p. 21). Note, this is not just your favorite category but one that brings your study together. It is central, appears frequently in the data, and "relates easily to other categories"; it has "clear implications for a more general theory," and as it is explored by open coding techniques, "the theory moves forward appreciably." Importantly, and unusually for qualitative analysis, Strauss points out that it allows for "building in the maximum variation to the analysis. . . . It is one of the hallmarks of the grounded theory mode . . . to seek variation" (p. 36).

Once this core is identified, sampling and coding become more targeted and focused—a process known as *selective coding.* The researcher uses diagramming and mapping extensively to facilitate the analytic process of delineating stages or dimensions of the situation, and the characteristics of each, and to attain an increased level of abstraction and clarify the development of theory.

Changing Grounded Theory

Like other research methods, this one is always changing. We have emphasized here what was central to the original proposal for ways of discovering theory grounded in data and what remains common to the now various schools of grounded theory. Grounded theory will continue to change as it is applied in new fields and as new techniques are explored—and as it leaves behind the acrimony of past disputes. For an overview of the actors in this current stage, see Bryant and Charmaz (2007) and Morse et al. (2009). Recently, "constructivist grounded theory" pointed the method back to its interactionist origins. "Researcher participants' implicit meanings, experiential view—and researchers' finished grounded theories—are constructions of reality and socially produced" (Charmaz, 2006, p. 10). Constructivist grounded theorists get as close as possible "to the empirical realities of the participant" because "we exist in a world that is acted upon and interpreted—by our research participants and by us—as well as being affected by other people and circumstances" (Charmaz, 2009, p. 137).

PHENOMENOLOGY

As described in Chapter 3, phenomenology directs the researcher to understand the meaning of phenomena. With such a goal, expect that instructions as to actual techniques for working with data and analysis may be hard to find. Phenomenological researchers often do not talk about a method per se but, rather, discuss the tradition and the reading, reflection, and writing process that enable the researcher to transform the lived experience into a textual expression of its essence. Van Manen

(1990) notes that "phenomenology differs from almost every other science in that it attempts to gain insightful descriptions of the way we experience the world pre-reflexively, without taxonomizing, classifying, or abstracting it" (p. 9). As discussed in Chapter 3, this reflection takes place within the four existentialisms: *temporality* (lived time), *spatiality* (lived space), *corporeality* (lived body), and *relationality* or *communality* (lived human relation). The end result is not effective theory that enables us to explain reality but, rather, "plausible insights that bring us in more direct contact with the world" (p. 9).

All phenomenologists subscribe to the belief that being human is a unique way of being, in that human experiences and actions follow from their self-interpretation. "The Textatorium," on the Phenomenology Online website (http://www.phenomenologyonline.com/sources/textorium/), provides many examples of phenomenological writing. When new researchers delve into the phenomenological literature, they find a confusing array of methods—many of which are changing and emerging.

Phenomenological methods have evolved in many directions, partly because they are used in widely different disciplines. For example, the hermeneutic phenomenological approach developed by van Manen (1990) and the "human scientific approach" of Giorgi (1997, 2009) differ in both purpose and approach. As an educator, van Manen conducted research primarily on children's learning. As a psychologist, Giorgi (2009, p. 94) aims "to operate in the scientific level of analysis," with analyses that can claim "psychological status" for the method. He aims for a synthesis of phenomenology (modified from Husserl's approach), human science, and psychology.

Working With Data

These data records will be unstructured and will include reflective notes as well as interview or observation records. Recall from Chapter 3 the idea of *bracketing* previous knowledge—that is, placing it aside. Bracketing is relevant to the way the researcher tackles each of the tasks discussed in the preceding chapters: research design, making data, coding, and abstracting. Bracketing—of one's theories, prior knowledge, and experience with the phenomenon—is intended to allow the investigator to encounter the phenomenon "freshly and describe it precisely as it is perceived" (Giorgi, 1997, p. 237). The researcher achieves bracketing by making these notions explicit, writing them down in a diary or memos.

The purpose of this reflection is to find out what is essential in order for the phenomenon *to be*. To grasp an essence, the researcher reflects on concrete experience, trying to imagine it from all aspects.

Other data sources enhance this period of reflection. Phenomenologists obtain descriptions from literature and poetry, explore instances of the phenomena of interest in movies and art, and reflect on the phenomena using the phenomenological literature as a lens. If records of interviews or observation are used, research questions are not predetermined; rather, the researcher follows the cues of the participant and the conversation proceeds thoughtfully.

How to work with such data? Many texts give no direction, but both van Manen and Giorgi provide guidance and contrast.

The process of doing van Manen's phenomenology is essentially one of writing while reading, reflecting, and rewriting. Strategies to ease the process of interpretation include writing about your own personal experience; writing down others' experiential descriptions; tracing etymological sources; using art, diaries, movies, and the experiences of others; discussing with others; and reading other phenomenological writings that stimulate new ways of seeing the text and enable deeper interpretation. By reflecting on the transcribed conversations, phenomenologists identify themes. A theme gives shape and describes the content of the conversation and reduces the description, enabling us to get to the essence. Through reflection we can identify "essential themes"—themes that are an integral part of the phenomenon rather than of the context.

With his emphasis on scientific method, Giorgi (1997) provides more explicit instructions. He proposes five basic steps:

> (1) collection of verbal data; (2) reading of these data; (3) breaking data into some kind of parts; (4) organization and expression of data from a disciplinary perspective; and (5) synthesis and summary of the data for purposes of communication to the scholarly community. (p. 237)

Strategies of Analysis

In all qualitative methods analysis is ongoing from the start of the project, and this is nowhere clearer than in phenomenology. Phenomenological analysis is the process of reading, reflection, and writing and rewriting that enables the researcher to transform the lived experience into a textual expression of its essence (van Manen, 1990, p. 10). Researchers gain insights by using a number of strategies: tracing etymological sources, searching idiomatic phrases, obtaining experiential descriptions from participants, observing and reflecting further on the phenomenological literature, and writing and rewriting (Ray, 1994; van Manen, 1990). They may select words or phrases that describe particular aspects of the lived experience they are studying and reflect on them. They may group and label similar expressions and eliminate expressions they believe are irrelevant, then cluster and label groups of expressions that bear close relationships to one another and check this identified core of common elements against a selection of original descriptors obtained in conversations with participants. For the phenomenological researcher, the value of the process of writing and rewriting cannot be overestimated.

Van Manen (1990) suggests that researchers use their own personal experience as a starting point. From there, they may *trace etymological sources* of the phenomena of interest and search for idiomatic phrases. They may obtain *experiential descriptions* from others, interview for personal life stories, observe to share experiential anecdotes, obtain experiential descriptions from the literature, and consult the phenomenological literature. Through processes of reflection, writing and rewriting, and thematic analysis, the researcher may describe and interpret the essence or meaning of the lived experience. To do so, they seek "essences"—"the thing without which it could not be" (p. 10), or the internal meaning of the lived experience. Attempting to grasp the essence of how people attend to the world, researchers may reflect on four existentialisms: lived space (spaciality), lived body (corporeality), lived time (temporality), and lived human relation (relationality or communality). *Intentionality* is the essential feature of consciousness; the world is already there and we are already a part of it. We cannot both simultaneously experience it *and* reflect on it. We cannot, for instance, at the same time both experience anger and analyze it (van Manen, 1990, p. 182). Thus, intentionality is available only after we have experienced the phenomenon.

Giorgi's (1997) methods consist of three interlocking processes: *phenomenological reduction, description,* and a *search for essences* through the "free imaginative variation" by "analyzing concrete experiences, seeking eidetic invariant meanings that belong to the structure" (p. 100). That is, he is seeking not a universal or a philosophical essence but "pertinent psychological dynamics or the precise uncovering of the psychological nature of the phenomenon." *Presences* are the experience of many phenomena that are not "realistic" but are vital to the understanding of the lived experience. These are such things as dreams and delusions.

Several authors have described the process of doing phenomenology as a series of steps. Seeing the process laid out in steps may help the novice student form an idea of how to proceed. Spiegelberg (as cited in Boyd, 1993) describes seven steps in arriving at essence. The first is *intuition*, which involves developing one's consciousness through looking and listening. This is followed by *analyzing*, which involves identifying the structure of the phenomenon under study and occurs through *dialectic* (i.e., the conversation between participant and researcher, through a joint project in which respondent and researcher are both committed to describing the phenomenon under study). The third phase is *describing the phenomenon*; however, premature description is one of the potential dangers in phenomenology. Insight is communicated through description. The next two steps involve *watching modes of appearing* and *exploring the phenomenon in consciousness*. At this stage, the researcher reflects on the relationships, or *structural affinities*, of the phenomenon. The final two stages are *suspending belief* (phenomenological reduction) and *interpreting concealed meanings*.

As with all qualitative methods, specifying steps and stages is attractive and challenging. Be aware that the research process is not linear but iterative.

※ DISCOURSE ANALYSIS

We introduced discourse analysis in Chapter 3: Like ethnography, grounded theory, and phenomenology, it begins with the assumption that social reality is socially constructed. However, this commonality underlines a stark contrast. As Jennifer Mason (2002) puts it, "the humanist idea of the whole human actor or agent is not a theme here, and neither is the sense of motivations and meanings which characterizes interpretivism" (p. 57). Rather, the focus is entirely on language and text in all versions of discourse analysis.

However, there are also stark contrasts within this method. As explained in Chapter 3, the differences between what is often termed critical discourse analysis and conversation analysis may make them appear unrelated, and conversation analysis is sometimes treated as a separate method. Like all other methods carrying the label "critical,"

critical discourse analysis seeks to deconstruct apparent "reality," disclosing ideological subtexts and motives and seeking to expose power relations. There is considerable literature on the goals and achievements of different approaches, as well as on their relation to critical theory and poststructuralism and, more recently, on gender and discourse (see Crawford, 1995; Wodak, 1997).

Working With Data

For discourse analysis, data are talk—conversations and text. The text may be transcribed conversations but also printed matter, advertisements, and other public presentations. Thus, discourse analysis is concerned with language as it is spoken, considering speech to be an interactive act situated within a larger interpretive frame (Coulthard, 1985, p. viii). Researchers include listeners/audience and pertinent features of the context.

If you are working in discourse analysis, you will usually be handling texts about everyday life; your aim is to subject these texts—all these texts—to detailed examination. Full, broad transcription is required. The text is transcribed exactly, with all the "hmms" and stutters, coughs and pauses. Rather than simply transcribing what is said (as for unstructured interviews), the researcher codes all modes of expression, including laughter, crying, and expletives. Lines are numbered. Coding for conversation analysis follows a set of rules for transcribing and marking up data records, including notation conventions for details such as turn taking, overlapping of speech, interruptions, interjections, and timed pauses. (Most texts cited offer summaries of these notations, and they are also readily available online.)

The point, of course, is not merely to mark up the text but to enable the researcher to interpret its structures and hidden content. The text is not handled in isolation of its context; rather, what the researcher includes and excludes depends on the researcher's question and the argument being brought forward.

If you are working in critical discourse analysis, you will be analyzing language with concern for sequential relationships, as well as the underlying interpretation. For instance, researchers may explore the language of power relations, as well as the underlying exposure and interpretive analysis of power relations and dominance. Not surprisingly, you will work with a much wider range of data documents, making a far more heterogeneous collection of data—such as public debates, press reports, billboards, and brochures. Your study must involve other texts and their social context, and usually historical context as well. Thus, Wodak (1997) insists that while the focus is on the self-contained communicative act,

> this points to a fundamentally more difficult and complex question—
> the extent to which a unit of discourse may be defined as self-
> contained at all. . . . In principle—because of intertextuality—every
> discourse is related to many others and can only be understood on
> the basis of others. (p. 6)

Methods of handling such data work across texts, not within them.

Strategies of Analysis

When doing discourse analysis, the emphasis is on uncovering not only the structure and content of text but its relation to its context. "Social researchers who do discourse analysis often want to make the point that even when we talk 'in our own words,' these words may not actually be 'ours' at all" (Cameron, 2001, p. 13). The researcher is looking not only for people's apparent understanding of their world but also the ways the expression of that understanding is shaped and remade. Following Michel Foucault, they will see discourses as "practices which systematically form the objects of which they speak" (as quoted by Cameron, 2001, p. 13). Emphasis will be on "intertextual" analysis, systematically comparing like or related texts to discover indicators of power, positioning, and the hidden agendas of ideology.

Working in critical discourse analysis, your attention will be focused less on the structure of a text than on recurrent themes and ideological or political implications, and your intent will be on exposing injustices or inequalities of power and, usually, improving the lot of those who suffer from them. Be aware of the challenges here for research robustness. In a passing remark, Wooffitt (2005) contributes a challenge:

> The analytic focus is deliberately skewed. While it is acknowl-
> edged that asymmetries of power, status and opportunity can be
> resisted in various ways, the prime concern is to expose and
> explore the top-down processes of domination. How language can
> be mobilized to resist inequalities and asymmetries of power is
> relatively unexamined. (p. 139)

⟪ CAʃE ʃTUDY METHOD

Case study methods were introduced in Chapter 3 as ways of investigating or illustrating processes via a detailed description of a single case or a few cases. The case may be circumscribed by *spatial unit,* such as one village, one institution, one classroom, one teacher, or one family; by *event,* such as one game or an airplane crash; by *program,* such as one providing Thanksgiving dinner to the homeless or teaching children to swim; or by *particular conditions,* such as one person with a rare illness, a brilliant child, and so forth. Perhaps the particular unit is an excellent instance or contains a pristine example of something; perhaps the disease is rare; perhaps the event seldom occurs and the situation is unique; perhaps the program is successful or remarkably unsuccessful.

Working With Data

As explained in Chapter 3, case study research usually requires detailed data on the case or cases, and this data can be collected and handled by any of the recognized qualitative data-making methods and sometimes also by quantitative techniques. Looked at this way, case study method is more a mode of research design than a particular method of collecting and working with data. If the design indicates an ethnographic approach, for example, the researcher will do field research and work with the data to provide rich descriptions. But an ethnographic approach to case study is likely to start with a theoretical position that will direct the focus to the mechanisms of how things work, the activities of participants, and the function and outcomes of those activities rather than to the culture behind them. The case study researcher may seek the connections between data bits rather than categories of data, the processes over time rather than generalizations. Focus will be on the physical setting and social context and on roles and relationships in the setting.

The reason for seeking a case study will determine how data are handled. For instance, if you are asking a question that entertains a longitudinal design, you will allow for documentation and measurement of variables that will enable change to be detected over time. If you are working on an evaluative question, you must include qualitative data that enable adequate evaluative description and quantitative data that will allow comparison with external norms. If you are asking a descriptive question, it must contain adequate qualitative data that will enable rich description. The goal is to obtain a holistic perspective of the case, describing the phenomena of interest from multiple perspectives or viewpoints, within context. In Stake's (2006) words, "The case has an inside and an outside. . . . Because much of the important activity of the case is recognizably patterned, both coherence and sequence are sought. The researcher tries to capture the experience of that activity" (p. 3).

Case study research uses purposeful sampling according to feasibility and data needs. The case is selected according to the presence of characteristics that meet the researcher's agenda and possibility of access. This means that the site is not chosen randomly but deliberately. Purposeful sampling is also used for data gathered within the case. With qualitative data, data adequacy is ensured as much as possible. If saturation is not possible, researchers seek agreement or confirmation with other types of data until certainty is reached. In this way, qualitative data are considered a set of various types of data, obtained from different perspectives and all shedding light on a single topic. Note that "shedding light on" is not necessarily the same as direct confirmation but may mean additional explanation or further description adding to the evidence the researcher is gathering.

Quantitative data may also be included in the data set. Unless the number of participants available is adequate to use some form of randomized sampling, purposeful sampling is used also for quantitative measurements. In this case the researcher uses the scale's external norms to interpret the case study results.

As with ethnographic studies, the researcher will have many sources of data and a challenge to manage them well so they can be coordinated and compared. Multiple forms of data may be used, including, if necessary, qualitative surveys and questionnaires, but observation will always be important. A case study usually starts with data-gathering techniques that will enable a broad understanding of the setting and ways of working with the data to bring the records from these different techniques together. The researcher may need to coordinate archival records; institutional documents; a map of the setting; unstructured interviews to gain a broad, in-depth understanding; semistructured interviews to determine a wider perspective; perhaps focus group interviews to elicit information and opinions about a certain topic; and surveys. Observations may include nonparticipant observation and/or various forms of participant observation. These different records must be brought together to provide a detailed picture of "what is going on." Usually, the researcher does not have control of the situation or the ability to establish experimental conditions and aims at disrupting the setting as little as possible.

Strategies of Analysis

Is this a likely method for your study? If so, you need to be aware that the literature contains strongly different, even incompatible traditions.

As in each of the methods discussed in this chapter, approaches to analysis technique differ widely. This is important because case study method does not, unlike the other methods considered, contain instructions about the ways theories are used and derived. Theory may be irrelevant, the emphasis being on detailed, accurate description. Or theory may be constructed, emerging from the data, as in grounded theory method. Or, more commonly, the case study may be conducted as illustration of or exploration of an existing theory, or a test of it (Swanborn, 2010, Chapter 4). As McNabb (2010) writes of public administration research:

> The popularity of the case study approach is a result of its great flexibility. Case studies can be written to serve as examples of what a public administrator ought not to do, as well as what should be done. However their primary purpose is to show public administrators what other administrators are doing. Different research objectives call for research designs to be explanatory, interpretive or critical. (p. 39)

In some texts, particularly Yin's (2009), case study method is treated as the alternative to experiment, survey, archival, or historical analysis; thus, "case study" appears to encompass *any* qualitative research. In other texts, a "case study" is a particular way of pursuing qualitative inquiry, distinguished from other qualitative research by its own design rules (for recent examples, see Swanborn, 2010, and Thomas, 2011; see also the collection edited by Gomm, Hammersley, & Foster, 2000).

All approaches seek to portray the case(s) accurately, through examination, pattern identification, and interpretation. They differ in the amount of emphasis placed on prior theory and theory testing, most typified in the work of Yin (2009), whose text is now in its fourth edition. He presents five approaches to different dimensions of data analysis: pattern matching (attained by coding for similarities and content analysis); explanation building; time series analysis (waves of data gathered at predetermined times); logic models; and cross-case synthesis (each case is analyzed separately, then analyses are compared across cases).

By comparison, other streams use more qualitative approaches. Grounded theory is commonly used, for example. When this is the case, the approaches to analysis will be those of one or another grounded theory method. Whatever the approach taken, however, it will be different because the emphasis is on the case: Each type of data collected is analyzed separately, and the results fit together to make a comprehensive and cohesive whole.

☷ SUMMARY

We have stressed how important it is to *think qualitatively* and that each qualitative method requires its own way of thinking and uses a particular perspective and specific strategies to reach its analytic goals. The product of each method, in turn, provides a perspective on reality specific to that method. In this chapter, we explored how researchers work differently with data and vary in their approaches to analysis, depending on which methods they adopt and, moreover, on which approach they take within a method.

Thus, the method you select will provide a distinct perspective and produce a distinct outcome. Each of the methods described offers a way of fitting your research question to data, and ways of working with data and analysis. By now, you should be able to find the right fit for your study.

☷ RESOURCES

The following are resources addressing ways of working in each of the five methods discussed in this chapter.

Ethnography

Agar, M. H. (1996). *The professional stranger: An informal introduction to ethnography* (2nd ed.). San Diego, CA: Academic Press.

Alasuutari, P. (1995). *Researching culture: Qualitative method and cultural studies.* London: Sage.

Atkinson, P., Coffey, A. S., Delamont, S., Lofland, J., & Lofland, L. (2001). *Handbook of ethnography.* London: Sage.

Carr, E. S. (2011). *Scripting addiction.* Princeton, NJ: Princeton University.

Denzin, N. K. (1997). *Interpretive ethnography: Ethnographic practices for the 21st century.* Thousand Oaks, CA: Sage.

Fetterman, D. (2010). *Ethnography: Step-by-step* (3rd ed.). Thousand Oaks, CA: Sage.

Geertz, C. (1973). *The interpretation of cultures: Selected essays.* New York: Basic Books.

Glittenberg, J. (2008). *Violence and hope in a U.S.–Mexico border town.* Long Grove, IL: Waveland.

Hammersley, M., & Atkinson, P. (2007). *Ethnography: Principles in practice* (3rd ed.). London: Tavistock.

Muecke, M. A. (1994). On the evaluation of ethnographies. In J. M. Morse (Ed.), *Critical issues in qualitative research methods* (pp. 187–209). Thousand Oaks, CA: Sage.

Olson, K., Krawchuk, A., & Guddusi, T. (2007). Fatigue in individuals with advanced cancer in active treatment and palliative settings. *Cancer Nursing, 30*(4), E1–E10.

Schensul, J. J., & LeCompte, M. D. (Series Eds.). (1999). *Ethnographer's toolkit* (7 vols.). Walnut Creek, CA: AltaMira.

Van Maanen, J. (1988). *Tales of the field: On writing ethnography.* Chicago: University of Chicago Press.

Werner, O., & Schoepfle, G. M. (1987). *Systematic fieldwork: Vol. 1; Foundations of ethnography and interviewing.* Newbury Park, CA: Sage.

Werner, O., & Schoepfle, G. M. (1987). *Systematic fieldwork: Vol. 2; Ethnographic analysis and data management.* Newbury Park, CA: Sage.

Whyte, W. F. (Ed.). (1991). *Participatory action research.* London: Sage.

Wolcott, H. F. (1995). *The art of fieldwork.* Thousand Oaks, CA: Sage.

Wolcott, H. F. (1999). *Ethnography: A way of seeing.* Walnut Creek, CA: AltaMira.

Grounded Theory

Bryant, A., & Charmaz, C. (Eds.). (2007). *The SAGE handbook of grounded theory.* London: Sage.

Charmaz, C. (2006). *Constructing grounded theory: A practical guide through qualitative analysis.* Thousand Oaks, CA: Sage.

Charmaz, K. (2009). Shifting the grounds: Constructivist grounded theory. In J. M. Morse, P. N. Stern, J. Corbin, B. Bowers, K. Charmaz, & A. E. Clarke (Eds.), *Developing grounded theory: The second generation* (pp. 127–154). Walnut Creek, CA: Left Coast Press.

Chenitz, C., & Swanson, J. M. (1986). *From practice to grounded theory.* Reading, MA: Addison-Wesley.

Corbin, J., & Strauss, A. (2008). *Basics of qualitative research: Techniques and procedures for developing grounded theory* (3rd ed.). Thousand Oaks, CA: Sage.

Corbin, J. (2009). Taking an analytic journey. In J. M. Morse, P. N. Stern, J. Corbin, B. Bowers, K. Charmaz, & A. E. Clarke (Eds.), *Developing grounded theory: The second generation* (pp. 35–53). Walnut Creek, CA: Left Coast Press.

Glaser, B. G. (1978). *Theoretical sensitivity: Advances in the methodology of grounded theory.* Mill Valley, CA: Sociology Press.

Glaser, B. G. (Ed.). (1996). *Gerund grounded theory: The basic social process dissertation.* Mill Valley, CA: Sociology Press.

Glaser, B. G. (1998). *Doing grounded theory: Issues and discussions.* Mill Valley, CA: Sociology Press.

Glaser, B. G., & Strauss, A. L. (1967). *The discovery of grounded theory: Strategies for qualitative research*. New York: Aldine.

Morse, J. M., Stern, P. N., Corbin, J., Bowers, B., Charmaz, K., & Clarke, A. (2009). *Grounded theory: The second generation*. Walnut Creek, CA: Left Coast Press.

Stern, P. N. (2009). Glaserian grounded theory. In J. M. Morse, P. N. Stern, J. Corbin, B. Bowers, K. Charmaz, & A. E. Clarke (Eds.), *Developing grounded theory: The second generation* (pp. 55–84). Walnut Creek, CA: Left Coast Press.

Stern, P. N., & Porr, C. (2011). *Essentials of accessible grounded theory*. Walnut Creek, CA: Left Coast Press.

Strauss, A. L. (1987). *Qualitative analysis for social scientists*. New York: Cambridge University Press.

Strauss, A. L., & Corbin, J. (Eds.). (1997). *Grounded theory in practice*. Thousand Oaks, CA: Sage.

Strauss, A. L., & Corbin, J. (1998). *Basics of qualitative research: Techniques and procedures for developing grounded theory* (2nd ed.). Thousand Oaks, CA: Sage.

Wilson, H. S., & Hutchinson, S. A. (1996). Methodologic mistakes in grounded theory. *Nursing Research, 45*(2), 122–124.

Phenomenology

Giorgi, A. (Ed.). (1985). *Phenomenology and psychological research*. Pittsburgh, PA: Duquesne University Press.

Giorgi, A. (2009). *The descriptive phenomenological method in psychology: A modified Husserlian approach*. Pittsburgh, PA: Duquesne University.

Moustakas, C. (1994). *Phenomenological research methods*. Thousand Oaks, CA: Sage.

Munhall, P. L. (1994). *Revisioning phenomenology* (Pub. No. 41-2545). New York: National League for Nursing Press.

Spiegelberg, H. (1975). *Doing phenomenology: Essays on and in phenomenology*. The Hague, Netherlands: Martinus Nijhoff.

van Manen, M. (1990). *Researching lived experience: Human science for an action sensitive pedagogy*. London, Ontario: Althouse Press.

van Manen, M. (1997). From meaning to method. *Qualitative Health Research, 7*, 345–369.

van Manen, M. (2002). *Writing in the dark: Phenomenological studies in interpretive inquiry*. London, Ontario: Althouse Press.

van Manen, M. (Ed.). (2011). *Phenomenology online: A resource for phenomenological inquiry*. Retrieved from http://www.phenomenologyonline.com/

Discourse Analysis

Cameron, D. (2001). *Working with spoken discourse*. London: Sage.

Coulthard, M. (1986). *An introduction to discourse analysis*. New York: Longman.

Crawford, M. (1995). *Talking difference: On gender and language*. London: Sage.

Fairclough, N. (2003). *Analysing discourse: Textual analysis for social research*. New York: Routledge.

Gee, P. J. (2011). *How to do discourse analysis: A toolkit*. New York: Routledge.

Peräkylä, A. (2004). Conversational analysis. In C. Seale, G. Gobo, J. F. Gubrium,

& D. Silverman (Eds.), *Qualitative research practice* (pp. 165–179). London: Sage.

Ten Have, P. (1999). *Doing conversation analysis: A practical guide*. London: Sage.

Titscher, S., Meyer, M., Wodak, R., & Vetter, E. (2000). *Methods of text and discourse analysis*. London: Sage.

Silverman, D. (2010). *Doing qualitative research* (3rd ed.). London: Sage.

Wodak, R. (Ed.). (1997). *Gender and discourse*. London: Sage

Wodak, R., & Meyer, M. (2009). *Methods for critical discourse analysis*. London: Sage.

Wooffitt, R. (2005). *Conversation analysis and discourse analysis: A comparative and critical introduction*. London: Sage.

Case Study Method

Aldinger, C., & Whitman, C. V. (2009). *Case studies in global school health promotion: From research to practice*. New York: Springer.

Flyvbjerg, B. (2004). Five misunderstandings about case-study research. In C. Seale, G. Gobo, J. Gubrium, & D. Silverman (Eds.), *Qualitative research practice* (pp. 390–404). Thousand Oaks, CA: Sage.

Gomm, R., Hammersley, M., & Foster, P. (Eds.). (2000). *Case study method*. London: Sage.

Hentz, P. (2012). Case study: The method. In P. L. Munhall (Ed.), *Nursing research: A qualitative perspective* (5th ed., pp. 359–371). Sudbury, MA: Jones & Bartlett.

Kinuthia, W., & Marshall, S. (2010). *Educational technology in practice research and practical case studies from the field*. Charlotte, NC: Information Age.

McNabb, D. (2010). *Case research in public management*. New York: M. E. Sharpe.

Platt, J. (1992). Cases of cases . . . of cases. In C. C. Ragin & H. S. Becker (Eds.), *What is a case? Exploring the foundations of social inquiry* (pp. 21–52). New York: Cambridge University Press.

Ragin, C. C., & Becker, H. S. (1992). *What is a case? Exploring the foundations of social inquiry*. New York: Cambridge University Press.

Stake, R. E. (1995). *The art of case study research*. Thousand Oaks, CA: Sage.

Stake, R. E. (2005). Qualitative case studies. In N. K. Denzin & Y. S. Lincoln (Eds.), *The SAGE handbook of qualitative research* (3rd ed., pp. 443–466). Thousand Oaks, CA: Sage.

Stake, R. E. (2006). *Multiple case study analysis*. New York: Guilford Press.

Swanborn, P. (2010). *Case study research: What, why and how?* London: Sage.

Thomas, G. (2011). *How to do your case study: A guide for students and researchers*. London: Sage.

Yin, R. K. (1984). *Case study research: Design and methods* (Applied social research methods series, Vol. 5). Newbury Park, CA: Sage.

Yin, R. K. (2003). *Applications of case study research*. Thousand Oaks, CA: Sage.

Yin, R. K. (2009). *Case study research: Design and methods* (4th ed.). Thousand Oaks, CA: Sage.

Part III

GETTING IT RIGHT

Chapter   9. On Getting It Right and Knowing if It's Wrong

Chapter 10. Writing It Up

9

On Getting It Right and Knowing if It's Wrong

What makes a study solid? How can a researcher convince the readers of the research report of its rigor or demonstrate and communicate its credibility? In this chapter, we discuss the challenges of ensuring and establishing reliability and validity in qualitative research, as well as criteria for evaluating a study. We cover strategies the researcher should use when planning the project, while conducting the study, and while bringing the study to completion. We also look at processes and procedures that continue to establish the legitimacy of the research after the first study has been completed.

Consider the terms we have selected here: *reliability* and *validity*. As discussed in Chapter 5, some authors have argued that these terms have no place in qualitative inquiry (e.g., Lincoln & Guba, 1985). Rather, they insist that because qualitative inquiry is subjective, interpretive, and time and context bound, "truth" is relative and "facts" depend on individual perceptions. Therefore, they argue, *reliability* and *validity* are terms that belong to the positivist paradigm, and qualitative researchers should use different terminology. Others have argued that in the qualitative context, criteria for reliability and validity must be different from those used in a quantitative context. In 1985, Lincoln and Guba recommended that qualitative researchers substitute for the concepts of reliability and validity the following aspects of *trustworthiness: truth value,* which is the *credibility* of the inquiry; *applicability,* which is the *transferability* of the results; and *consistency,* which is the *dependability* of the results.

We have no quarrel with the suggestion that reliability and validity are determined differently in qualitative inquiry than in quantitative work, but we regard it as essential that determining reliability and validity remains the qualitative researcher's goal (see also Kvale, 1989, 1995; Maxwell, 1992; Sparkes, 2001). Briefly, reliability requires that the same results would be obtained if the study were replicated, and validity requires that the results accurately reflect the phenomenon studied.

As one reads the qualitative literature, it becomes evident why these terms have been seen as problematic. Replicating a qualitative study is sometimes impossible and always difficult because the data are richly within the particular context (Sandelowski, 1993). Attempting to judge the representation of "reality" is highly problematic because qualitative researchers always view social reality as a social construction (Altheide & Johnson, 1994). However, to claim that reliability and validity have no place in qualitative inquiry is to place the entire paradigm under suspicion; such a claim has ramifications that qualitative inquiry cannot afford, and it diverts attention from the task of establishing useful and usable measures in the qualitative context. Qualitative researchers can and do defend their own work as solid, stable, and correct. These claims give qualitative research legitimacy and, thus, the right to be funded, to contribute to knowledge, to be included in curricula, and, most important, to inform policy and practice.

For the novice researcher, the critical question is, "How will you know if it is good enough?" (Richards, 2009, p. 147). In this chapter, we offer some ways in which qualitative researchers can ensure, attain, and communicate reliability and validity.

▓ ENSURING RIGOR IN THE DESIGN PHASE

Appropriate Preparation

Any study (qualitative or quantitative) is only as good as the researcher. In qualitative research, this is particularly so because *the researcher is the instrument.* The researcher's skills ensure the quality and scope of data, the interpretation of the results, and the creation of the theory. Therefore, the onus is on the researcher to be maximally prepared in qualitative methods *before* beginning a project. That is why we wrote this book. Research methods are the tools of the researcher, and there is a best (and easiest) way to attack any problem. Methods are continuously being refined and improved, and learning methods is an art that does not stop with the completion of the first project. Preparation requires not only learning of appropriate skills for creating and handling data but also learning the most appropriate techniques of your chosen method. As we have seen in previous chapters, there will be a range of approaches within any method, and changing techniques in all. Learning new methods, developing strategies, improving techniques, and developing skills as an observer, an interviewer, and an analyst are lifelong commitments.

We stress that this advice urgently applies to the apparently simple tasks of choosing and learning software skills. If you as a researcher are the instrument, the software is your tool kit and your working space. Any artisan will tell you that you need the space and the tools *before* you start a skilled job. Compared with the challenge of understanding a setting and designing a project, learning software may seem unimportant. Researchers too often assume they can learn software skills as the project progresses, but doing so ensures data loss and damage, researcher confusion, and a project truncated or misdirected by bad management.

Appropriate Review of the Literature

Surveying the literature allows you to get a grip on what is known and to learn where the holes or weak areas are in the current body of knowledge. New theory never simply renames what has been described and reported previously. You must know what is already known, and when you see it, you must recognize it, acknowledge it, and give it appropriate credit. In short, when you are in the field, you must be able to recognize a previously reported concept or pattern, refer to established explanations and theories, and recognize any variations between what was previously discovered and what you are now seeing.

In earlier chapters, we stressed the different ways in which different methods combine prior knowledge, knowledge gained from the data, and the testing of both against discovery. How you do this in your project will depend on the method you have chosen. All methods, however, require that the researcher balance the use of what is already known with the discovery from the data. The interplay of prior knowledge and discovery is critical in the process of making and developing concepts. "Starting with them (deductively) or getting gradually to them (inductively) are both possible. In the life of a conceptualization, we need both approaches" (Miles & Huberman, 1994, p. 17; for a discussion of deduction and induction in grounded theory, where prior knowledge is often assumed to be irrelevant, see Strauss, 1987, pp. 11–14).

Such knowledge and background do not, however, mean that you go looking for particular information to fit expectations. A common source of invalidity is the researcher's seeking out what the literature suggests he or she should find. Thus, whatever your method, you must bracket and put aside information you have learned about the phenomenon from the literature so that you can learn from the data. Once you have identified and developed what is being observed, you will be able to move the model reported in the literature over it, like a template, and compare the two.

In Chapter 3, we introduced the concept of bracketing as used in phenomenology. Whatever your method, it is a central process. Bracketing means putting your personal knowledge and the knowledge you have gained from the literature aside or making it overt by writing it down so that you can see the research problem, the setting, and the data with fresh eyes and work inductively, creating understanding from data. Several strategies assist with bracketing. One is to write in your diary, before starting the project, your personal assumptions about what is going on, possible relationships, and what you think you will find. If starting in your software, make your first record a "project history" document. (On using this "log trail" to establish validity, see Richards, 2009.) Making the implicit explicit brings your assumptions out into the open and helps you contain them.

Another strategy is to summarize the information you have gathered in your reading to form a literature review, building an argument for you to conduct your study. Then set it aside—but do not put it away. Keep this literature in your mind. Pit it constantly against what you see. If you are confident it is right, use it as a springboard from which to start your inquiry. If you suspect it is incorrect, your constant reviewing and re-reviewing of the literature will allow you to compare and contrast your emerging data with the previous knowledge. You will need to update and discuss that review regularly and return to it at the end of your study, for knowledge must be placed within the context of what is already known. Knowledge builds incrementally or by processes of replacement.

Thinking Qualitatively, Working Inductively

The key to rigorous qualitative inquiry is the researcher's ability to think qualitatively. This is an exhausting process of being constantly aware and continually asking analytic questions of data, which, in turn, regularly address the questions asked. Qualitative inquiry constantly challenges assumptions; questions the obvious; reveals the hidden and the overt, the implicit, and the taken-for-granted; and shows these in a new light. Without such an active mode of inquiry, you risk a shallow, descriptive study with few surprises, reporting the obvious. Neglecting to pursue the real issues in a research topic will result in a weak study—probably one that will not be interesting enough to warrant publication. Yes, missing the essence of phenomena is a fatal validity issue.

Qualitative research does not, and should not, use a rigid prior conceptual framework that dictates the nature of the variables to be collected and the relationships among those variables. We have seen in Chapter 9 that some methods may work with prior theory, but none regard theory as there just to be tested. A rigid framework would naturally guide the interviews so that the researcher would deliberately seek data to fit the framework, showing that whatever the researcher planned to find was found, neat and tidy. Proceeding in such a manner invalidates the study. But there is a difference between using a rigid prior conceptual framework that dictates data collection and adhering to the philosophical basis of the study. Such philosophical paradigms as feminism, postmodernism, and critical theory do not create variable lists; rather, they provide ways of looking and focus the method used in a particular direction for a particular purpose. Overlaying a study with such a theory, provided it is explicit, is not creating a source of invalidity but, rather, a lens to give your project a particular focus.

Let's add one other aspect to this difficult topic. Perhaps you are using nonparticipant observation because it is not possible to use interview data or other verbal data that would give you clues to what is actually going on—for instance, when observing neonates or elderly persons with Alzheimer's disease. In such a case, you need an interpretive framework to transform data into meaningful units. But this is a risk only if other data are not accessible to help you interpret your observations. To return to our supposed study of arrivals and departures (Chapter 2), we could conduct a microanalytic study of types of passengers arriving at the airport. Working inductively without a framework, we could describe the behaviors of the passengers and those waiting by enumerating precategorized movements of touch or nontouch, without attributing any meaning to them at all. The result would be a purely descriptive, but insignificant, study—and a boring read. But if we put the study in a framework of types of attachments according to roles and relationships, it becomes interesting and significant. The bottom line, therefore, is that you must be aware of when using an a priori framework is necessary, know the risk involved with using it, and be prepared to be wrong.

Using Appropriate Methods and Design

We have described, in earlier chapters, how to use an armchair walkthrough to identify the most appropriate method to answer a particular research question. Is using a less appropriate method risking invalidity? Perhaps.

You can drive in a nail with a hammer, a stone, or the heel of your shoe. The goal (of getting the nail in) is achieved no matter which tool you use, albeit clumsily if you use your shoe and awkwardly if you use a stone. But perhaps when you drive the nail, unexpected findings occur— the stone bends the nail or your shoe is damaged. Similarly, you may introduce sources of invalidity into your study by using a less-than-optimal research method. The golden rule of respecting methodological cohesiveness—of ensuring the best fit of the research question with the assumptions, strategies, types of data, and analytical techniques— provides maximal validity. Remember that the different methods have different agendas; they are different ways of thinking about the data, and they produce different results. If you mix and match methods as the study proceeds, you may introduce ways of analysis inappropriate for your data, or data inappropriate for your question.

Validity requires accurate representation of what you are studying (Maxwell, 1992). When you are preparing to do the research, you should design the study to avoid redirecting it away from that goal. For instance, plan to use techniques of theoretical sampling, and plan ways to develop the sample to attain saturation. Plan how you may identify negative cases and seek additional cases. Although such plans are only plans (that is, they may not be followed to the letter), they at least alert the researcher, from the beginning, to the importance of covering the scope of the question, and they help identify possible solutions that will enhance validity.

Proposals are a necessary and essential means of preparing the researcher for doing the project. The armchair walkthrough necessary for developing the proposal prepares the researcher for the project. The proposal may be used to obtain funding for the project, and it informs ethics review boards and the agency or institution in which data are being collected of what the researcher is planning to do. We provide advice on this process in Chapter 11.

﷽ ENSURING RIGOR WHILE CONDUCTING A PROJECT

The most important strategies to enhance and maintain rigor take place during the actual conduct of the study itself (see Meadows & Morse, 2001). Whatever your qualitative method, the major thrust or direction of inquiry must be inductive, and this is crucial for the validity of the study. This is not to say that deduction is never used in qualitative inquiry; deduction is used to develop conjectures and to verify data, but the dominant thrust should be inductive.

Asking *analytic questions* of the data is the key to solid and significant research. The active approach to inquiry is driven by the identification of questions that force the researcher to think, confirm and refute, collect more data, and pursue every avenue.

Using Appropriate Sampling Techniques

Sampling is the key to good qualitative inquiry and also to understanding the dilemmas of qualitative validity. Just as fishermen cast their lines into likely fishing holes, rather than randomly selecting places to fish, so do qualitative researchers deliberately select participants for their studies. Qualitative researchers may seek bias, deliberately choosing the worst case or the best instance of an event rather than the average experience, for the characteristics of a phenomenon are more easily explored in the outstandingly good or bad examples. Average experiences are difficult to explore, as the characteristics of the phenomenon of interest are diluted and mixed in with other characteristics from other experiences.

Therefore, rather than employing random sampling, qualitative researchers seek valid representation with sampling techniques such as the following:

- ﷽ *Purposeful sampling,* in which the investigator selects participants because of their characteristics (*Good informants/participants* are those who know the information required, are willing to reflect on the phenomena of interest, have the time, and are willing to participate; Spradley, 1979.)

- ﷽ *Nominated or snowball sampling,* in which participants already in the study recommend other persons to be invited to participate

░▒ *Convenience sampling,* in which those invited to participate in the study are simply those available to the researcher

░▒ *Theoretical sampling,* in which the researcher deliberately seeks out persons to be invited to participate according to the emerging theoretical scheme

Occasionally, one does see a qualitative project reported in which a random sample has been used; for instance, a researcher might have a large pool of participants and not enough information to use unstructured interviews. Consider the advantages and disadvantages of each way of sampling for your study and the threats of each to validity.

Responsiveness to Strategies That Are Not Working

Sometimes, when you are in the midst of data gathering, the data obtained do not appear as useful as they should be. Data analysis appears to be going nowhere—perhaps the material is not as detailed or as rich or as informative as it should be. When this happens, the response of many inexperienced researchers is to collect more data. But merely continuing to gather more poor data will not usually solve the problem. Rather, more of the same data will dishearten the researcher and, as a result, he or she may risk running out of funding or becoming more bogged down in analysis. The solution is to step back and consider why the data are not fruitful. It may be necessary to change data-making strategies, to select a different group of participants, or to observe or interview participants at different times. This problem particularly affects designs with homogeneous data, and the solution may be to change an interviewing project to observational strategies or to use a different approach to interviewing. The important thing is to stop using strategies that are not working. (Remember: If you do change strategies, you must notify those to whom you are responsible for the project design—partners in an action project, team members, supervisor, or thesis committee—and get any relevant ethics permission.)

Appropriate Pacing of the Project

By *pacing of the project,* we mean the synchrony of data making and analysis, the change of research techniques from obtaining information to verification as the project progresses, and the change of the investigator's conceptualizing process from synthesizing to theorizing. Moving too quickly through a project, or moving to the next analytic task before the first analytic task is completed, will leave the research open to incomplete work, missed analytic opportunities, and possibly having all parts of the project drawn together. Such a study loses validity, credibility, and rigor.

Related to this is the *assessment of saturation*. Data gathering must continue until each category is rich and thick, and until it is replicated. It is saturation that provides the researcher with certainty and confidence that the analysis is strong and the conclusions will be right. If saturation is achieved, *negative cases*—instances that do not fit the emerging model—will be explored. And, using techniques of theoretical sampling, the researcher will deliberately seek other similar negative cases until those categories are also saturated.

How will you know when a data set is saturated? Go back to the literature; read reports of studies that have used your chosen method and look for the ways a *satisfying* explanation is expressed. When data offer no new direction, no new questions, then there is no need to sample further—the account satisfies. Often, the first sign is that the investigator has a sense of having heard or seen it all. When data are saturated, events do not remain as a single instance; they have been replicated at least in several cases, and with that replication comes verification. When writing about the study, the researcher can fully describe not only the phenomenon but also the antecedents and the consequences and the various forms in which the phenomenon occurs.

Coding Reliably

In Chapter 6, we discussed the issue of coder reliability across time and across teams and the issues to be considered when reliability is sought for qualitative coding (Richards, 2009, pp. 108–109). It should by now be evident that the relevance of reliability of coding will depend on the methods used. In semistructured interviews, participants are all asked the same questions in the same order in a search for patterns of answers, so consistency in coding is important. The researcher must develop and record definitions used for particular codes, and if more than one person is coding, the researcher must attend to interrater reliability (i.e., consistency among coders). If using the computer, the researcher can do this rigorously, comparing the patterns of coding in each document in fine detail.

By contrast, when a researcher uses unstructured, interactive interviews, imposing a consistent coding scheme can instead be a source of *invalidity*. If the researcher is learning about the phenomenon as the study progresses, interview content changes as the researcher becomes more informed about the phenomenon. As well, the domain narrows or broadens in scope as the researcher gains understanding and increasingly seeks more detail. Consistency works against the development of a rich interpretive study, the latter being the very reason the researcher decided to use unstructured, interactive interviews. Rather than consistency, malleability is what keeps the coding valid. The key is to keep track of coding decisions, and researchers use memos to track changes in the development of categories, recoding and relabeling the categories as often as necessary. As categories emerge in the process of analysis, the researcher keeps verifying data bits with the categories, verifying as interviews continue, and verifying/confirming with new participants during data collection. If using computers, researchers can easily store records of codes and their meanings at different stages.

∭ WHEN IS IT DONE?

Unseasoned investigators seem to worry a lot about finishing: How will they know when they are done? How will they know when the analysis is good enough? How will they know when they are finished?

You will know. How you know will depend on your goals. For some, the study is finished when they have reached a satisfactory level of explanation, attained their theoretical goals, written up the report, and published it. Some investigators do not consider a study finished until any changes the results indicated as necessary are implemented, evaluated, and moved firmly into practice.

Project Histories

Because the goal of all qualitative research is to produce new understanding from data, researchers always require ways of justifying their analyses. Some projects make limited claims ("I understood what it was like to live in this suburb"), whereas others seek patterns that are easy to justify with rigorous data statements ("This is a problem only for the younger women, and I think I know why"). But even when the goals are limited, the researchers will be helped if they can tell the story of how the understanding was discovered and checked out, or why this explanation fits the participants' accounts better than that explanation.

It is always important, in any qualitative method, that the project design allows the researcher to backtrack to discover and report the history (or development) of the analysis. Most qualitative projects get their claims to validity from the researcher's ability to say how he or she got there. When the record of a project is only in the researcher's memory or an occasionally kept research diary, it is less impressive than a rigorously maintained, dated, and documented history. But the latter, of course, is also more time-consuming. When you are having a brilliant idea, noting the time of its occurrence may be far from your thoughts.

How do you know what sort of a history is adequate? What you should track will depend on what you are going to rely on. If you don't know what that is yet, you will find it helpful to design simple systems to track some important processes:

◈ The gathering of data, how and why samples were selected, the scope of the project determined, and how and why new data were sought by theoretical sampling. Documents may have stories in your project that deserve annotation or memos (for example, your understanding of an interview changed when the participant phoned later to elaborate on his story).

◈ The genesis of a category or idea. When in the project did it happen? Where did it come from? How did it change your research path? Whether you are working manually or on the computer, this usually means recording a quick memo with any significant ideas, or ones that might prove significant.

◈ The story of how an idea develops as you explore more data. (Keep working on that memo—and remember always to date the entries.)

◈ The more complex story of how you explore patterns of ideas and links between data and ideas (for instance, when and how you realized, and then checked, that all the older women's experiences were indeed different, and why you settled for this rather than that explanation of the result). This may include notes on how you chased other hunches and showed them to be wrong or identified cases that didn't fit and developed your theory from studying them. (Write more memos for these insights.)

Audit Trails

The term *audit trail* (or log trail; see Richards, 2009) is used in various ways to refer to evidence that the researcher has kept track of research events and decisions in a way that can be checked by an independent auditor, much as a company's financial books are checked (Guba & Lincoln, 1989). Such a trail is a requirement in some areas and viewed as irrelevant in others; as with many other issues addressed in this book, you need to find out what standards apply in your discipline and method.

What can be audited and what can't? The literature on this subject is still to happen, and the researcher designing an audit process must rely on research principles and common sense. It makes a lot of sense to have someone outside the project review and critique how the researcher arrived at the conclusion. Auditing a project history, either formally or informally, will almost always assist evaluation of the study (by the researcher and by other observers or clients).

On the other hand, it is almost always impossible for an outsider to audit another researcher's coding, because coding, as we discussed in Chapter 6, is a complex process of creation and interpretation of categories and selection of relevant material, and keeping track of that process is impossible. Having an outside auditor code data independently will never justify the coding done. If the coders agree, it must mean that the coding was largely descriptive. If they disagree, we learn something about their different backgrounds and disciplines but not about the study.

Your Findings and the Literature

As a final step in ensuring validity, the researcher must consider whether and how the new findings compare and fit in with the literature—or don't. This consideration may take place in the "discussion" section of the research report. The fit, even of new findings, should be easily accounted for and logical—and never forced.

Where the findings challenge the literature, your task is to develop and account for a framework that is appropriate, consistent, and justifiable. This can be the most exciting stage of reporting and is certainly the most challenging for novices. Resist the temptation to dodge this responsibility to point to gaps in the literature or ways the current conceptual frameworks should be expanded. Forcing a fit with accepted literature dooms your study to irrelevance.

❧ DEMONSTRATING RIGOR ON COMPLETION OF THE PROJECT

Projects are reaffirmed following completion through implementation (the findings work), replication (someone else finds something similar), or incorporation into a metasynthesis (the findings fit into a conceptual scheme). Findings may be moved forward by using them as a conceptual scheme for a new qualitative project using a different approach or to inform a quantitative study. We should stress, however, that this step can determine new questions (for instance, the distribution of the concepts within the population), but it cannot, as is commonly thought, confirm the findings. Qualitatively derived theory is solid if verified in the process of development and, if conducted well, does not require testing quantitatively (and usually cannot be so tested).

Triangulating With Subsequent Research

As discussed in Chapter 4, triangulating related projects after the completion of the first project can provide support for the first project, for if the outcome of the first project were incorrect, the second project could not build on it. Initial findings would not be verified, and the second project would have to correct the first study. With sequential triangulation, the first study is completed and provides a foundation for the second study.

Reaffirming Through Implementation

Implementing changes suggested by the results of the study provides further testing and often an assurance of the correctness of the results. If, for example, the recommendations of a study suggest a particular intervention for a certain problem, and the problem is resolved following the intervention, this provides further credence for the original qualitative study.

What if the intervention does not work? Such a failure does not provide absolute proof that the results of the initial qualitative study were wrong, but it suggests that this could be a possibility. Certainly, careful investigation should follow.

⊗ SUMMARY

Let's now take stock of the variety of ways in which you can ensure that your project is solid:

1. *Asking the right question:* Regardless of what triggered your interest in a particular topic, after you conducted a literature search and critiqued what is known about the topic, did you bracket that information? Once you began making data and conducting observations and interviews, were you receptive to revisiting your question and modifying it as necessary?

2. *Ensuring the appropriate design:* Even if you made an informed choice of method, did you design the study strongly and thoroughly? Once you actually started your study, were you sensitive to the type of data required by your method and the ways data should be handled? Did these data appear to maximize your chances of answering your question?

3. *Making trustworthy data:* Were you responsive to problems that occurred? Did you work to establish trust with participants and verify data both within and among participants? Are your data dependable? Were you careful to code reliably? To categorize or identify valid themes? As you moved forward in your analysis, were you careful to sample theoretically? To saturate categories? To check and verify every relationship?

4. *Building solid theory:* As you moved toward developing and refining a theoretical scheme, did you continue to check and verify developing relationships in the data? Did you triangulate with results from other studies? How did they fit? Did you check the literature again? How did your findings support or extend what is already known? How did your findings fit? Are your new findings a possible logical extension of the literature?

5. *Verification or completion:* Once findings are completed, the processes of verification continue. The peer review process in publication (or your committee's scrutiny before you defend your thesis/dissertation) is the first level of approval. Results are also supported (and perhaps modified) when implemented or used in subsequent projects.

※ RESOURCES

Altheide, D. L., & Johnson, J. M. (1994). Criteria for assessing interpretive validity in qualitative research. In N. K. Denzin & Y. S. Lincoln (Eds.), *The SAGE handbook of qualitative research* (pp. 485–499). Thousand Oaks, CA: Sage.

Bernard, H. R., & Ryan, G. W. (2010). *Analyzing qualitative data*. Thousand Oaks, CA: Sage.

Cho, J., & Trent, A. (2006). *Qualitative Research, 6*(3), 319–340.

Cohen, D. J., & Crabtree, B. F. (2008). Evaluative criteria for qualitative research in health care: Controversies and recommendation. *Annals of Family Medicine, 6,* 331–339.

Guba, E. G., & Lincoln, Y. S. (1989). *Fourth generation evaluation*. Newbury Park, CA: Sage.

Hart, C. (1998). *Doing a literature review: Releasing the social science research imagination*. London: Sage.

Kvale, S. (1989). *Issues of validity in qualitative research*. Lund, Sweden: Cartwell Bratt.

Lincoln, Y. S. (1995). Emerging criteria for quality in qualitative and interpretive research. *Qualitative Inquiry, 1,* 275–289.

Lincoln, Y. S., & Guba, E. G. (1985). *Naturalistic inquiry*. Beverly Hills, CA: Sage.

Maxwell, J. A. (1992). Understanding validity in qualitative research. *Harvard Educational Review, 62,* 279–300.

Maxwell, J. A. (1998). Designing a qualitative study. In L. Bickman & D. J. Rog (Eds.), *Handbook of applied social research methods* (pp. 69–100). Thousand Oaks, CA: Sage.

Meadows, L., & Morse, J. M. (2001). Constructing evidence within the qualitative project. In J. M. Morse, J. M. Swanson, & A. J. Kuzel (Eds.), *The nature of evidence in qualitative inquiry* (pp. 187–200). Newbury Park, CA: Sage.

Morse, J. M., Barrett, M., Mayan, M., Olson, K., & Spiers, J. (2002). Verification strategies for establishing reliability and validity in qualitative research. *IJQM: International Journal of Qualitative Methods, 1*(2), 13–22.

Richards, L. (2009). *Handling qualitative data: A practical guide* (2nd ed.). London: Sage.

Seale, C. (1999). *Quality of qualitative research*. London: Sage.

Sparkes, A. C. (2001). Qualitative health researchers will agree about validity. *Qualitative Health Research, 11,* 538–552.

Thorne, S. (1997). The art (and science) of critiquing qualitative research. In J. M. Morse (Ed.), *Completing a qualitative project: Details and dialogue* (pp. 117–132). Thousand Oaks, CA: Sage.

Whittemore, R., Chase, S. K., & Mandle, C. L. (2001). Validity in qualitative research. *Qualitative Health Research, 11,* 522–537.

10

Writing It Up

Projects end for a number of reasons: Perhaps funds have been spent or the period of time allocated to fieldwork has ended; perhaps it is time to graduate or your family has indicated clearly that it is time for you to find a "real job." Qualitative projects rarely end because all the researcher's questions have been answered. Nevertheless, whatever the practical reasons for stopping, you need to be able to determine when the project is done. Of course, you have been writing consistently throughout the project. You have been writing field notes and memos; you may have kept a diary and a log trail. If you have been using phenomenology, where the writing is the road of reflection, you will have written many, many drafts. But now these drafts are maturing. The end is in sight, and you must prepare to write drafts and then the final version of the report. This chapter is about writing qualitative research reports. It concludes with consideration of the two writing tasks that often dominate novice researchers' views of their future: writing a thesis and writing for publication.

❧ READY TO WRITE?

In qualitative research, the more you learn, the more you write and the more questions arise. The end of your project will not be marked by the end of your questioning. The main indicators that you are finishing are that you feel confident about the data and the findings, that you believe they make sense and can be accounted for, and that you can bring your project together, as a whole (Richards, 2009, Chapter 9). In short, you should have attained the stage of theorizing (Morse, 1994b) and reached your research goals. You should be able to answer your original research question or account for its not being answered by your project (and you probably have answers to other questions that have arisen during the project).

The work of writing, summarizing, synthesizing, and recording field notes or memos will have resulted in piles of papers, many computer files, transcriptions, photographs, and diagrams. A first task is to take stock of these writings and carefully organize how they will be used (for help with this task, see Richards, 2009, Chapter 10). Some of what you have recorded about what you know will already be quite well written, but most will need a lot of work before it can be presented to others. But you know the project is ending because you can make sense of it as a whole. You can *describe* it to a colleague, *write* about it in an e-mail, and see a finish line. Now it is possible to *write it up.*

Who Is It for, and Where Will It Appear?

Once the analysis is completed, your first task is to look at the project as a whole and ask yourself: What do I want to say and to whom? If this project is part of your work toward a graduate degree, the preparation of a dissertation logically comes first and the professional audience is decided. Usually, after the dissertation is finished, there will be new questions: How do you publish your work and where?

First, the audiences: Assume there are many (see Richardson, 1990). At this stage, you need to revisit your earlier commitments. Did you promise a newsletter article, a report in a general meeting, or personal communications about the outcomes? You must honor these obligations. (In Chapter 11, we offer some warnings about making early commitments to later reporting.) Your audience is different from those for which most journalists write. Qualitative researchers most frequently write for other social scientists. They write less often for practitioners or students and even less frequently for the general public.

Writing Qualitatively

What makes qualitative research different from journalism or a novel, different from a biography or autobiography? A good ethnography will orient the reader and flow like a good novel; a phenomenological or grounded theory article has the "grab" (Glaser, 1978) of a good story, entrancing and trapping the reader.

Whereas good journalism and novels may bring new understanding of human interaction and society, good qualitative research does something different. Throughout this book, we have emphasized the features that separate qualitative research from journalism. The purposiveness of qualitative research and the coherence of questions, data, theory, and outcome give skilled writings of qualitative researchers a different character. As you write, aim for an account of your project that is coherent, strong, and elegant. Good reporting is recognized by the nature and type of description, the depth and focus of the descriptive material, the nature of interpretation, and the level of theoretical development.

These goals should inform everything you write and should result in an account that satisfies the reader. Thick description provides contextual background in which the reader can place the study. It ties together analytic pieces, enabling the researcher to present the components of the analysis logically and sensibly. It is the medium in which the actual descriptions of contexts, phenomena, actions, transitions, procedures, and processes are explained, described, explored, revealed, unraveled, compared or contrasted, and linked to other components.

Before you start to write the final article or report, you must complete the analysis so you are clear on what you have to write about. Not knowing what to write is the most common cause of writer's block. Make an outline, select the segments of your analysis to be covered, and edit data quotations accordingly; prepare any tables, diagrams, or photographs to be used as illustrations, and make notes in your outline where they are to be inserted into your article. The skills you have developed from practicing summarizing and synthesizing are vital at this writing-up phase. When writing, be cognizant of "building a case" (for a good example, see Turner, 1994). Put the scene in context with your preliminary description. Now, systematically and logically, develop an argument. We advise you to outline your argument first and then write within the outline. Remember, like qualitative research, qualitative writing is purposive.

Using Your Data

In qualitative reporting, claims to explanation, interpretation, and theories will stand or fall on the adequacy of the researcher's account of the data and the ways they fit the theory. There is no equivalent of the satisfying statistic that establishes that the researcher is unlikely to have arrived at this conclusion by accident. You must show how you arrived at your conclusion and why you stand by it.

When Do You Use Quotations?

An early issue is how and when to incorporate quotations from interviews and descriptions from field notes. The goal is to give credence to your claims about the data and provide enough description to bring the situation you are analyzing alive—without having the analysis diluted by long passages that do not address the point being made.

Carefully monitor the role played by quoted evidence. There are two major ways of presenting data to illustrate your analysis. The first is to present your interpretation of findings and then follow with a quotation to illustrate your description. This gives the reader the information to judge whether or not your interpretation represents the data. Alternatively, you may present a quotation followed by your interpretation. This may show your ability to analyze in fine detail, but it could miss the big picture. Pay attention to the reader's need to know where a quotation is from and what it represents, how representative it is, and how much variety there is in the data you are not quoting. As we noted earlier in this book, critical reading of other studies will assist you in setting standards for making and illustrating claims.

Editing Quoted Material

The goal of editing quotations is to maintain and convey the original expression. Recorded interviews may contain portions that are difficult to hear, and despite instructions to type "as is," transcribers may correct grammar, ignore interjections, lose emphasis, or impose punctuation that alters participants' meanings. The researcher must subsequently correct the text to return it to its original form or to remove irrelevant material. And in writing, we select and edit; a report that is a full transcript of all data collection is not a research report. So the question is not *whether* you edit but how to do it well.

Basic rules for editing quoted material are obvious: In editing, you should avoid distortion or misrepresentation of what was said, and you should always indicate where text has been removed (with ellipses) and where you have substituted words (by enclosing them in square brackets). Use italics, capital letters, or boldface type to represent emphasis and to indicate pauses, exclamations, and emotions (such as laughter or crying). Always attempt to contextualize quotations (Where did she say this? Who else was present? What question was she answering? What did she say before this?). A very important skill is to prune any quoted material that is redundant. Passages you find rich and exciting are hard to prune, but they will almost always have more impact if edited. Keep asking yourself if each phrase is necessary. A briefer quotation may be more vivid and powerful and much more relevant to your argument. If you think the participant is implying something, suggest this in your interpretive commentary.

Using Yourself

In Chapter 5, we discussed the important question of using your own experience as data. As you start writing, this issue will recur. Should you include your personal experience in the reports? As in all questions of qualitative writing, we advise attention to balance. Self-indulgence is to be avoided; keep asking yourself whether your experience is pertinent to your argument, adds evidence or credibility, or merely pads out an unconvincing description. Self-pity is irrelevant; avoid long accounts of how difficult or uncomfortable you found it to gain entry into the field. It's your project and your responsibility. But self-reflection may be very important. We advise you not to dodge responsibility by using the passive voice in your writing. Saying that "the data were analyzed" or "the categories emerged" avoids acknowledgment of your agency.

Brevity and Balance

When you are deeply involved in your data, everything seems to be crucial. How do you decide what is important? A process of distancing is necessary; a reasonable amount of distance will allow you to let go of material that is not pertinent to your argument. This is particularly important when a wonderfully detailed dissertation is being converted to shorter articles. All references may seem relevant, so a first paragraph may contain strings of authors' names interrupting each sentence. Full descriptions of the participants seem deserved, so the reader is given unnecessary detail. The methods section may be too long for an article where the emphasis should be on the results. Attend to these imbalances: You now need to refer only to those works pertinent to this article, describe only those characteristics of participants that matter for this section of the analysis, and briskly outline the methods that contributed to this outcome.

Briefer reports offer the challenge of balancing all these sections with the necessary data. Recall that your categories are masterly compilations of summarizing, synthesizing, and abstracting. The overuse of participants' voices makes the research look like compilations of quotations linked together in a logical way, but with minimal commentary by the researcher. If quotations are overused, the researcher may become silent or be sent into the background, and the readers will be left to interpret the intent and significance of the quotations themselves. This is transcription, not qualitative inquiry. A frequent mistake that novice researchers make in writing is to link together quotations from the same or different participants with minimal commentary and then reiterate the obvious in the commentary between quotations. The resulting description can be shallow, superficial, repetitious, and boring—and, most important, it is unlikely to be analytic.

※ RE-REVISITING METHODOLOGICAL CONGRUENCE

In Chapters 3 and 8, we showed the fit of major qualitative methods with strategies to attain the goals for each method. We stressed that although more than one method may use similar strategies, each method has its unique way of conceptualizing so that the techniques for the various strategies differ and the final products are distinct.

As you write, check your study for methodological consistency and your writing for explanations of how this study, in this method, works. If, for instance, you used grounded theory, are you presenting a robust depiction of a process, an integrated theory developed around a core category and elaborated in stages and phases? If you have conducted an ethnography, does it explicate cultural beliefs and practices? Does your phenomenological study provide a persuasive description of the essence of a lived experience? Does your analysis of discourse really justify your conclusions about power relations? Are your case studies sufficiently strong to support the questions you asked? Check that your language is consistent with your method. When you are writing for the first time, it is a good idea to find and use as a model an excellent published article that reports on a study that employed the same method you have used. Also, you can ask your critical friends to check that what you have written persuades them.

※ PROTECTING PARTICIPANTS

You will need to revisit your ethical commitments before you write. Your writing must, of course, adhere to your agreements (made in the informed consent form) to protect the identities of your participants. We discuss some of these issues in Chapter 11, where we address the processes involved in getting your project started.

Ensuring anonymity for participants usually requires much more than merely changing their names. Most frequently, qualitative researchers provide anonymity by removing as many identifiers as possible and reporting demographic characteristics only as group data. In some, but not all, qualitative reports, this does not hinder the presentation of results. Age, gender, and most characteristics of importance can be reported as means and ranges for the entire group. When demographic characteristics are presented in detailed tables, participants, shown line by line, are at risk of being recognized. Similarly, attaching the same pseudonym to all quotations from a particular participant makes it possible for someone familiar with a person studied (such as a participant's spouse) to go through the manuscript and trace that person's contributions. In such a case, neither confidentiality nor anonymity is respected.

Protecting participants in this way, however, may severely constrain your reporting. Very often, it is important for the reader to know which demographic groups are represented by your account of a response. As you start to write, you may find that protecting your participants exposes your analysis to risk and that subtler and more creative methods are required. (Lyn Richards once "split" a respondent into two people in the published account of a sensitive project!)

Quite often, researchers replace the names of towns or institutions with fictitious names in their writings. Sometimes, however, authorities at research sites agree or request to have their sites named in final reports and in publications; if this is the case in your research, be sure to obtain this agreement or request in writing. Carefully consider the advantages and disadvantages before you agree to name an institution or participants—doing so may place you in an awkward position. If the institution asks to be named, what do you do with any findings that may reflect negatively on that institution? Omitting such findings may result in an invalid report, and including them may leave you open to criticism or, in the worst case, a lawsuit. This is a dilemma that you must consider carefully. On the other hand, Davis (1991) argues that removing too much contextual information (including important identifiers) may render a case study useless and invalid. Clearly, a balance must be attained, but the researcher's primary obligation remains the protection of participants and research sites.

You may be asked by the organization in which you have collected data to present administrators with a draft report for "approval." When negotiating for entry, do not agree to give the organization the opportunity to critique your report, for doing so may result in your conclusions being undermined and invalidated. If you have done your study with care, are confident about your results, and have "cleaned" your findings so that the organization and the participants cannot be identified, you should be able to write results that are insightful and justifiable.

∭ EVALUATING YOUR WRITING

Once you have drafted a chapter, an article, or a report, evaluate it yourself (and perhaps ask your colleagues to review it) to ensure that it is as solid as possible before submitting it. It may be acceptable in your setting to have your writing professionally edited. Many of the works listed in the reference section at the end of this book include discussions of criteria for evaluating qualitative research (for detailed advice and checklists for evaluating your writing, see Richards, 2009, Chapter 10). Evaluation criteria, of course, will vary with the method, but all qualitative methods share three criteria for excellence.

The first, and most obvious, criterion is that a report should show that the study has been competently conducted. It should evidently do justice to the data and clearly provide the basis for its conclusions. Second, the report should offer new knowledge. This does not, of course, mean the report will be entirely new. Researchers who avoid established labels for theory can end up merely relabeling old theory. In the last stage of your analysis, place your findings into the context of the literature, involving the previous theory as you identify unique contributions of your work. But be clear about what you offer that is new, and clearly offer it.

The third criterion involves the nature of the analysis, the coherence of the theory, and the elegance of presentation. If the author's intention is to produce theory, then the criteria for good theory should be applied. Is it clear, logical, and well argued? Is the theory parsimonious—tight and elegant? Is the theory coherent and internally consistent (see Morse, 1997)? Evaluation of the research methods and the contribution of the research as a whole are also in order (Kuzel & Engel, 2001; Thorne, 1997).

※ POLISHING

Once you have written your "final" draft, leave the manuscript alone for a few days to mature; then take it out and read it aloud. It will probably need heavy editing and rewriting. You will be able to identify skimpy pieces or overly wordy parts. If you are writing an article, look again at the criteria for review from the journal to which you are submitting and review the article yourself using those criteria. When the article is as good as you can make it, give your article and the journal's criteria to three colleagues for critique. Then revise again, incorporating their suggestions. Finally, have your article professionally edited. This is essential if English is your second language. Submit the article according to the journal's instructions.

A final word of advice: We argued early in this book that qualitative research is a craft. By now you will have gathered that writing qualitatively is an art. Your reading of published qualitative work will have shown the high proportion of studies that fail to convince because they are presented inadequately. This is because writing up qualitative research, like any other art, requires vision, focus, and hard work—if done well, it is extraordinarily satisfying for both the artist and the audience.

※ USING YOUR SOFTWARE FOR WRITING

Your writing will almost certainly be done on a computer. Writing programs have remade the tasks of composing, editing, and revising.

Approaches

Your writing program will easily receive the data and reflections from your project if it has been created and managed in qualitative software. At any stage of your writing, you should use the ability to make reports of your data or the passages coded or discovered in your analysis.

Advances

Throughout this book we have encouraged you to record your project and your steps in analysis in a "trail." If appropriate, this can include the recording of your checks on coder consistency and sample diversity. This "log" can be efficiently maintained in your software, with links to the relevant data or categories described. (For detailed assistance in setting up a "log trail" in software, see Richards, 2009, Chapters 1–3.)

Your software's search tools have many tasks in this stage (Richards, 2009, Chapter 8). Use them for locating relevant data or quotations, for checking the patterns you are discerning and the adequacy of your coverage of critical issues, or for finding exceptions to a generalization. Don't underestimate the uses of text search to check whether a "dominant" theme really is dominant! As you start the final reporting task, make good use of your software's data management and search tools to take stock of your memos and log trail writings so you can account for all the insights or concerns recorded during analysis (Richards, 2009, Chapter 10).

Alerts

1. Be aware that with your data available online, using too much quoted material is easy. Patchworks of quotation do not substitute for good analytical writing about your subject.

2. Be careful of the language you use as you interpret and discuss the results of software-supported search processes (Richards, 2009, Chapter 8). Software searches are often very powerful and can certainly offer discoveries and checks not possible by manual methods, but they should always be reported for what they are—mechanical searches based on the text *you* provide in your project or the coding *you* do. (You are the weak link!)

3. Schedule your time to include using your software well to provide material and check it out. Your analysis will be much stronger for this work. Readers and reviewers now expect that with software tools, hunches can be tested. Don't be tempted to dodge such tests and merely state your hunch and illustrate it with a juicy quotation—doing so will save time now but will cost time when you are required to resubmit your report.

4. Expect that finishing will be harder when you know there is always another search or report you could do. Plan the processes needed, schedule them sensibly, evaluate, edit, strengthen evidence, check out patterns and explanations claimed—and finish!

◈ WRITING YOUR THESIS OR DISSERTATION

A student's thesis or dissertation is often the first major book-length manuscript, the first piece of completed research. If that is not anxiety provoking enough, a lot hinges on the student's doing a good job—the manuscript will be scrutinized by several faculty members and an outside examiner, and if the research is not up to expectations, an entire career is at stake.

Fortunately, the final examination is not something that happens after several years of working alone—it is usually a "journey" shared by your supervisor. Graduate school is (or should be) a wonderfully mentored situation. During the conduct of your research, guidance should be available and should continue as you write—so consult if you are not certain about any aspect. Furthermore, your department and library should contain many theses/dissertations you can use as models to help you see what the final product should look like. Use also the new resources provided by the Internet for access to help and advice via professional discussion groups and forums.

Another consoling feature is that you may have already written some of your dissertation in the process of doing research. Your proposal may contain a literature review; it may need updating, but this preliminary work could at least form the basis of the literature review for your thesis. Similarly, you may use the methods section for your proposal as the basis of the methods chapter for your dissertation. But do not merely change the tense from the future tense of the proposal to the past or present tense of your thesis/dissertation; also incorporate what you learned as the project unfolded. Qualitative methods chapters (unlike those for survey projects) can never be written in advance of the project, since the method requires that the project design be flexible and data driven. If you have been carefully recording references since your proposal, the bibliography should be in the proper format, automated, and relatively complete. These pieces, no matter how small, are an excellent start for the final document.

This section is a walkthrough of the process of actually *writing the dissertation*. Note that dissertation requirements vary greatly by country, institution, and discipline. In the rest of this section, Morse draws on her experiences. A dissertation is usually organized in a conventional outline, and the form and format, structure, and even style may be dictated by your graduate school's regulations. Obtain these guidelines before you commence. The overall outline may look like the one in Figure 10.1. You could safely use this to frame the details of your own study.

Beginning to Write

While starting at the beginning is tempting and seems obvious, smart writers leave Chapter 1 until later in the project. In qualitative research, writing is a way of analyzing, and the project will continue to take shape as you write. Hence, it is important to write continuously—in memos early in the analytical process and in chapter drafts later—and to take thorough stock of all your writing as you near the end (Richards, 2009, Chapter 10).

Introducing something that is not written yet is difficult, and not knowing exactly *what* to write is one of the most common causes of writer's block, so start writing your dissertation with the "Results" chapter. The easiest chapter to write is the "Methods" chapter, because it is structured and its contents are relatively concrete. Next, write the "Literature Review" chapter followed by the "Discussion" chapter, linking the discussion of the findings with the literature (Chapter 2) and showing clearly what your study has contributed to the literature. While writing, constantly keep the bibliography up to date and accurate. Then, once Chapters 2 through 5 have been written, you will find that writing Chapter 1, the introduction, will come naturally. Write the final summary (of three to four pages), and then further condense that summary for the abstract.

Great! But we are not finished yet. Once you have completed the *draft*, edit it yourself. Read it carefully and slowly, front to back, noting concerns as you go. Now edit your draft—and be particularly critical of your "Results" chapter(s). Make your corrections only when you are satisfied with your draft, and ask your colleagues and friends to review it. Have it professionally edited if appropriate in your setting, and give it to your committee to review if possible. Then prepare for your final examination. Good luck!

1. Descriptive title

2. Front signature/approval pages

3. Abstract

4. Table of contents

5. Preface/foreword

6. Chapter 1: Introduction
   a. Problem statement

7. Chapter 2: Literature Review
   a. Introduction to chapter
   b. Components of the topic reviewed
   c. Summary/framework/research question

8. Chapter 3: Methods
   a. Introduction to methods chapter
   b. Description and justification of method
   c. Setting and sample
   d. Data Collection
   e. Data analysis

9. Chapter 4: Results
   Here, you may systematically describe the results, attending to the previous pointers about writing qualitatively. You may need to break this content into two chapters if it gets too long. Sometimes researchers present the descriptive results in one chapter and then place the content pertaining to building their qualitative theory in a second chapter, titled "Results."

10. Chapter 5: Discussion
    A discussion chapter is often required; here, you would consider how your study fits in with and contributes to the literature. Include a discussion of the strengths and weaknesses of the study, and a discussion of the methods used. How could your study have been improved? What should the next study be? Conclude with a comprehensive summary of the entire dissertation, usually brief (about four pages).

11. Appendices
    If you used any questionnaires or other research guides, they usually are placed here, along with the concept forms, letters of approval, and permissions to conduct the research.

Figure 10.1   Sample Outline for a Dissertation

The International Institute for Qualitative Methodology presents an annual international dissertation award, and the winning dissertations are published by Left Coast Press as monographs. These monographs are a good source for qualitative dissertation models for students.

WRITING AN ARTICLE FOR PUBLICATION

Having written a strong dissertation, and being convinced that all the content is important, it is tempting to write an article by simply cutting sentences and even paragraphs and placing them directly into your article. This seldom works, for the style of writing used in the dissertation is very different from that used in shorter, more succinct articles. If it seems too hard to rewrite your dissertation in article form, start with other articles or conference papers that you used during the dissertation reading (see Box 10.1).

Box 10.1

From Dissertation to Article

Select several studies that you found particularly convincing and well written. Now, critically analyze these as articles, examining how the authors present their studies.

- How do the authors provide their evidence in the space available?
- When and why is the evidence persuasive?
- How do the authors capture their readers' interest?
- Do the authors build their cases convincingly?
- How do they present their interpretations?
- How do they link their findings to the literature?
- What does not satisfy, and how could the authors have rectified these problems?

Return to your own study with the answers to each of these questions. How could you present your study convincingly? Can you do better than these authors did?

When writing an article from a dissertation, the first thing you must do is decide on the content. For instance, will the article be a summary of the entire dissertation or some portion of it? This is not an easy decision, for the most obvious way to partition articles is to sever (note the violent word) the dissertation into concepts, publishing an article from each segment as a meaningful unit. But this means, after carefully arguing in your dissertation for the holistic qualitative perspective, that you are now fracturing your theory into small chunks. Alternatively, you may publish the entire theory intact, but it will be relatively superficial due to the page limitation. Or you may consider publishing the whole study as a monograph. Another common way of dividing a project is by publishing the literature review as a discussion and critique on the topic and then the results as a project report. Sometimes the project will also support an article on the implications for those practicing, such as clinicians or teachers. These decisions should be made early, as editorial rules and copyright regulations often prohibit duplicate publication.

Next, select your audience. Qualitative researchers most frequently write for other social scientists. They write for practitioners or students less often and for the general public even less frequently. Because selected audiences read certain journals and have distinctive styles, select the journal in which you wish your article to appear. Obtain the appropriate author guidelines from the journal, and read back issues of the journal to become familiar with its style (especially its referencing style) and content. If you are writing for practitioners, you will note that the emphasis of such articles is on the application or implications of the results, rather than on the methods and scientific aspects of the study. If you choose to write for a wider public, seek advisors, editors, and readers who can help you translate your academic research project for readers with little concern or interest in the study's methodological origins or specialized concepts or theories.

Beginning to Write

Writing an article requires following the general procedures for writing a thesis/dissertation. First, prepare a detailed outline. Then, prepare and edit all the quotations you plan to use and enter them into the outline. Similarly, prepare any tables or figures you plan to use and temporarily place them in the outline. (Publishers' manuscript formats usually require that the author indicate in the text where the figure or table will be placed and insert the actual table or figure at the end of the document.) Thus, we see in manuscripts instructions such as "Insert Table 1 about here."

The order for article writing is similar to that for dissertation writing: Start writing in the "Results" section, followed by the "Methods," "Literature Review," "Discussion," "Introduction," and "Abstract" sections. Attend to the proportions of text per section as you write. For a 15-page article, "Results" should take up the bulk of the manuscript (at least 7 pages); "Methods," 1 to 1 1/2 pages; "Literature Review" and "Discussion," 2 pages each; and "Introduction," 1/2 a page to 1 page. Cite only references that *deserve to be cited*, and keep them to a minimum. Some journals limit the number of citations (for instance, *Advances in Nursing Science* limits citations to 64, sometimes requiring authors to make difficult choices in providing proper attribution).

Once the writing is finished, put the article aside for a few days so that when you return to edit it, you will see it with fresh eyes. When you do return to it, read it aloud. This will enable you to hear all its faults and then edit carefully.

Most journals have a website with *criteria for review*. These criteria are the components according to which the reviewers will evaluate your article. Print out these criteria and review your own article, making changes accordingly. The criteria for *Qualitative Health Research* are shown in Box 10.2. Note that these criteria resemble the *standards* for qualitative inquiry discussed in the literature. Following these criteria will ensure that you have all the components needed for the publication of an article and that each of these components is as solid as possible.

After these revisions, one more review is necessary: Give your article and the review form to three colleagues whose judgment you trust, and ask them to review your article. Again, make any necessary changes.

While review and revision seem time-consuming, they will save you considerable time in the long run and may make the difference between acceptance or rejection of your article. Also, taking the necessary time to review and revise before submitting will move your article into press as quickly as possible and keep it from being unnecessarily delayed.

Once it has been submitted to a journal, what happens? If you do not receive e-mail notification after a few days, contact the journal editor. Do not sit waiting to hear about a manuscript that vanished into cyberspace and was never received by the journal!

After those weeks of waiting, you will be notified that your article (a) needs further revision, (b) has been rejected (you know what to do—revise and submit it to another journal), or (c) has been accepted. If the article has been accepted, congratulations. Your notification will include a manuscript number that must be used in all correspondence with the editor.

The journal will request the copyright for your article, and this may require that you complete a form. Yes, the publishing company, not the

Box 10.2

Criteria for Review Used by *Qualitative Health Research*

Qualitative Health Research Editorial Review Form

Reviewer: _____

Manuscript no.: _____

Please complete the following: If the categories are not applicable, write N/A. This form will be forwarded to the author.

Importance of submission: What are the manuscript's strengths? Is it significant? Does it contain new and important information?

_____

_____

Theoretical evaluation: Is the manuscript logical? Is it parsimonious? Complete? Useful?

_____

_____

Methodological assessment: Inductive approach? Appropriate methods and design? Is the sample appropriate and adequate? Are data saturated? Theoretical analysis? Linked with praxis and/or theory?

_____

_____

(Continued)

(Continued)

Adherence to ethical standards?

_____

_____

Manuscript style and format? APA format?

_____

_____

Other comments: _____

Please see additional comments: _____

This section will be retained by the Editor: _____

Recommendations: _____

Accept manuscript as submitted: _____

Tending toward acceptance: _____

Tending toward rejection: _____

Reject: _____

Comments for the Editor:

_____

_____

_____

author, usually owns the copyright. Next, after several weeks or months, you will suddenly receive the proofs. Your article will have been edited by a technical editor. As this editing process sometimes changes the meaning of sentences, check every word carefully. You will have been sent a guide of proofreaders' marks, instructing you how to mark any necessary changes on the manuscript. Do this as quickly as possible, as the turnaround time is often short (72 hours or less). Again, there is a wait, until the day you receive by mail several copies of the journal containing your published article. This is one of the most exciting moments. Read your article, and put one copy of the journal away, give one to your dean, and give one to your mother!

〰 AFTER PUBLICATION, THEN WHAT?

Once your study has been published, it may take on a life of its own over which you have little control. It is exciting to see your work cited by others or to hear your writing quoted. But often we wish our findings would be implemented and used by others. We may dream that our research will make a difference, but that rarely happens from a single project. If it does, change usually occurs slowly.

Qualitative research findings may be adopted by others and used in a number of ways. Of course, how your study is used, and what impact it has, depends on the type and relevance of the results themselves. Qualitative inquiry is most commonly used alone or in concert with other findings.

Findings Used Alone

Well-designed qualitative projects create results that are useful, transferable, and generalizable. *How* they may be used, of course, often depends on others. Once the findings are published, as noted above, the original investigator has little control. Possible uses for qualitative findings include the following.

Use the Theory as a Framework for Practice

The theory created in your study may be adopted into teaching, counseling, or professional practice and used to organize the way others teach, counsel, or practice. It may be used to explain outcomes that occur in practice or to provide understanding about what is going on. In evaluation research, it may, for example, be used to indicate what changes should be made in an organization to improve the workplace. Overall, how the findings are trans-ferred and utilized will depend on their presentation during dissemination, how clearly they are understood, and how easily they can be put into practice.

Bring the Implicit and the Informal to the Fore

Qualitative findings often document the unknown or unacknowledged parts of the context or the previously unrecognized actions of partici-pants, making overt what was previously covert. For example, they may show the taken-for-granted assumptions about power in a relationship and allow participants to confront and discuss them. Thus, by bringing such behind-the-scenes actions forward, new understanding about a set-ting, a process, or a procedure may be recognized and, thus, incorporated into the understanding of others.

Delimit Scope or Boundaries of Problems or Concepts

Because qualitative researchers often address problems that have been previously overlooked, the research may allow problems that have seemed insurmountable or not suitable for investigation to become accessible. Qualitative research, therefore, may open up new areas of investigation. In the process of qualitative description, these problems become decon-structed. As problems are partitioned, concepts are identified, and the initial description thus enables others to attempt further inquiry.

Describe the Problem and
Aid in Identification of the Solution

Often, the initial "thick description" from qualitative inquiry may be used to identify possible solutions or interventions for the original problems. If you are studying a certain concept—for instance, the concept of hope—your results will focus on the participants' meaning of the concept and their behaviors working toward whatever they are hoping to attain. You will probably not have, for instance, much data on caregivers and how they fostered, modified, or assessed hope in their patients, because the caregivers may not have been a part of your original study. But you may extend your findings theoretically to create an assessment guide. An observation about the initiation of hope may be "recognizing the threat." This action may be transformed into behavioral indices: "Did the impact of the event 'sink in'?" referring to observable behav-iors that occur when one is grappling with new facts. These behaviors are "reiteration and repetition in speech; connecting with others to talk about the event; and appearing stressed and overwhelmed" (Penrod & Morse, 1997). Thus, an assessment guide may be created by extending the qualitative results to use them as behavioral indicators.

Provide an Evaluation of Nonmeasurable Interventions

In many research areas, traditional methods have insisted that the only adequate way to demonstrate efficacy is to conduct a randomized controlled experimental trial that will give a definitive answer. However, qualitative description, when applied to change models, program implementation, or other dynamic situations, often provides information and results that offer a quite different understanding from that provided by statistical analysis and may enable assessment of significant serendipitous outcomes.

The Cumulative Effect of Research Results

The most common outcome of qualitative study is that the findings fit (agree with/support) the published findings of others. This is the way science progresses, and other investigators will add your study to their literature reviews when preparing the background literature for their own studies. If your study, on the other hand, contradicts others, it may be particularly interesting and something to investigate further. This may be done within your own program of research or by others. One of the most exciting results is that the next study—or series of studies—then appears. Research has a habit, nasty or otherwise, of trapping you in a career trajectory!

⚒ SUMMARY

Qualitative research involves constant writing—of field notes, memos, interpretive definitions, and team notes. We have urged you to see writing as ongoing from the start of a project and "writing up" as something that matures during a project. Use all those materials well as you reach the end of the project. Once you are able to theorize and are confident that you understand what is going on, the writing up of the project commences. First, identify who you are writing for and what you want to write. Plan an outline; prepare data, logs, and diagrams; and insert them into the outline—then write! As you write, consider your audience, purpose, and the possible future outcome of your work, as well as the ways in which you are now reporting it.

╲╲ RESOURCES

Theory

Morse, J. M. (1997). Considering theory derived from qualitative research. In J. M. Morse (Ed.), *Completing a qualitative project: Details and dialogue* (pp. 163–188). Thousand Oaks, CA: Sage.

Strauss, A. L. (1995). Notes on the nature and development of general theories. *Qualitative Inquiry, 1,* 7–18.

Evaluating Qualitative Research

Altheide, D. L., & Johnson, J. M. (1994). Criteria for assessing interpretive validity in qualitative research. In N. K. Denzin & Y. S. Lincoln (Eds.), *The SAGE handbook of qualitative research* (pp. 485–499). Thousand Oaks, CA: Sage.

Cohen, D. J., & Crabtree, B. (2008). Evaluative criteria for qualitative research in health care: Controversies and recommendations. *Annals of Family Medicine, 6*(4), 331–339.

Thorne, S. (1997). The art (and science) of critiquing qualitative research. In J. M. Morse (Ed.), *Completing a qualitative project: Details and dialogue* (pp. 117–132). Thousand Oaks, CA: Sage.

Reliability and Validity

Cho, J., & Trent, A. (2006). Validity in qualitative research revisited. *Qualitative Research, 6*(3), 319–340.

James, N., & Busher, H. (2006). Credibility, authenticity and voice: Dilemmas in online interviewing. *Qualitative Research, 6*(3), 403–420.

Kvale, S. (1995). The social construction of validity. *Qualitative Inquiry, 1,* 19–40.

Morse, J. M., Barett, M., Mayan, M., Olson, K., & Spiers, J. (2002). Verification strategies for establishing reliability and validity in qualitative research. *International Journal of Qualitative Methods, 1*(2), 13–22.

On Writing

Boyle, J. (1997). Writing it up: Dissecting the dissertation. In J. M. Morse (Ed.), *Completing a qualitative project: Details and dialogue* (pp. 9–37). Thousand Oaks, CA: Sage.

Richards, L. (2009). *Handling qualitative data: A practical guide* (2nd ed.). London: Sage. (See, especially, Chapter 10.)

Richardson, L. (1994). Writing: A method of inquiry. In N. K. Denzin & Y. S. Lincoln (Eds.), *The SAGE handbook of qualitative research* (pp. 516–529). Thousand Oaks, CA: Sage.

Part IV

BEGINNING YOUR PROJECT

Chapter 11. Groundwork for Beginning Your Project

Chapter 12. Getting Started

11

Groundwork for Beginning Your Project

Throughout this book, we have aimed to offer an overview of what goes into doing qualitative research. Now that you have a feel for the process, let's go back to the beginning. To start a project, you must first identify a topic of interest, go to the library and learn all about the topic, and, in light of what is already known, refine your research question. An armchair walkthrough will help you think through your question using several methods. This enables you at this early stage to be as certain as possible that you are making informed choices and to foresee any possible problems in selecting your methods and your research design. Most important, it gives you an insight into the type of information you may find in your results.

Once you have decided on a topic, chosen a research question, and put it in the context of the pertinent literature, the usual next step is to work out a research design and prepare a proposal describing your research. Depending on your research setting, this may be a formal proposal to be approved by a supervisory or ethics committee. But even if you are not required to present a proposal, we urge you to prepare one as a step toward clarifying your thinking and your purpose.

※ WRITING YOUR PROPOSAL

What is a proposal? It is a document in which you outline, to the best of your ability, what you plan to study, why, and how you will do it. It serves as a guide to inform your supervisor or dissertation committee; it serves as something to be evaluated by ethics review committees to determine if you will possibly harm participants; it serves to inform interested parties in the institution or community where you will be conducting the research; and it serves as the baseline for the start of your audit trail. Several authors have written guides for qualitative researchers on preparing proposals (see Boyd & Munhall, 2001; Cheek, 2000; Morse & Field, 1995).

A quantitative research proposal normally describes in detail ordered procedures to be adhered to during the research project and promises certain outcomes. By contrast, a qualitative research proposal offers a flexible design by which a research question will be appropriately addressed using a relevant method. As the purpose of the qualitative project is discovery—to find out what is going on—the researcher cannot predict or promise a certain outcome from the research (Boyd & Munhall, 2001). The proposal should make an argument for doing the study and convince the reader that the topic selected is significant and worthy of inquiry. It must specify the method to be used and justify its selection, nominate the research setting and the relevant participants, explain what the researcher will do to gather and handle data, and describe the intended data analysis strategies.

Using the Literature Review

The literature review usually comes first in a proposal, offering an overview of what is known and what is indicated by previous research. It locates the proposed project in the current body of knowledge. The literature review should seek to reveal (rather than conceal) gaps in knowledge and to show areas that are weak and lacking or results that are suspect and perhaps built on assumptions that may be queried. Thus, the literature review leads the reader toward the research question so that, by the end, the question reads as an imperative that must be urgently investigated. If yours doesn't, you need to rethink your question and your rationale for asking it so your project will be useful and contribute new knowledge.

Although the outcome of qualitative research cannot be predicted, the significance of the project itself may be couched in terms of a *theoretical context* derived from the literature (Morse & Field, 1995). The theoretical context is larger than the proposed project, but it places the study in the context of the topic. For instance, if the proposed project is about social support that occurs between patients, literature on the significance and efficacy of peer support in other contexts might locate the study in works on the value of patient–patient support (or factors that impede peer support). Without peer support, we cannot justify many practices, such as support groups. We could even argue that the study will have implications for facilitating patient–patient contact or for hospital design. In essence, the theoretical context is a persuasive argument that extends beyond the proposed research problem and shows the possible ramifications of the study and the way it fits into the greater scheme of things.

Writing the Methods Section

From your armchair walkthrough, you will have a reasonable idea of the method that will best address your question, the setting in which you want to conduct your study, and the types of participants and procedures you need for making and handling data. In your proposal, you must describe these as clearly and with as much detail as necessary for a reader to assess their feasibility and adequacy. Justify your choice of setting and your selection of method. Explain that when sampling, qualitative researchers maximize access to the phenomenon they are studying and select cases in which it is most evident. Obtaining such a "pure" sample is consistent with the principles of science. Build into your plan the expectation that once you have gained an understanding of the phenomenon, you will employ *theoretical sampling* (Glaser, 1978) to seek out particular variations by selecting participants according to the theoretical needs of the study.

Because there are no set requirements for determining sample size in qualitative inquiry, you are unlikely to be able to cite exact numbers for the size of the sample. Instead, explain that the number of participants recruited will be determined by the relevance of the participants' experiences, the ability of the participants to reflect on and report their experiences, and the requirement for further theoretical sampling. Explain how data collection will cease once saturation is reached and what the indicators of saturation may be.

Next, show how you will handle and analyze data. You must present data-handling and analytic procedures in sufficient detail to give reviewers confidence that you will be able to do justice to these data. Indicate your understanding of the sorts of coding and analysis your method requires. If you intend to use a computer program, specify it and justify your choice. (Never merely assert that the "data will be analyzed by" a particular program—software, remember, does not analyze data.) Depending on the detail required, you might illustrate procedures by, for instance, inserting a sample of text with actual coding. Demonstrate how your analysis will proceed with building categories, theme-ing, or using memos and annotations.

Estimating Time (and Related Resources)

Any qualitative project has many stages, and we strongly advise that you consider all these necessary stages from the start. Possibly the most common mistake of novices is to misjudge the time that research will take. Serious crises are created when a researcher plans the use of available time or money by calculating time in terms of data-making events (such as the average length of an intended interview multiplied by the expected number of interviews to be conducted). A more realistic calculation would take into account the usually substantial time needed for each of the many stages before and after interviews (or other data-making events) and also the amount of research work generated by each event. In Figure 11.1, we sketch the demands on your time during a project. Using this formula, you can more clearly see the next year(s) of research time and more realistically view, scope, and rescope a project. You may wish to start by taking the time to revise the scope of your project right now as you face the reality of how much time your original proposal would require.

Developing a Budget

If you are applying for a research grant, you are required to write a budget for the proposal. If you are not seeking a grant, determining expenses is possibly an even more important task. Your salary, stipend, or ability to support yourself through the project will be contingent on your estimation of overall time (above), but other costs must also be estimated. Pay careful attention to the following:

※ *Personnel:* For the salaries of research assistants, estimate hourly rate × duration of employment. Remember to add library time, time for scheduling appointments, travel time, time for listening and checking transcripts, time for involvement in analysis and

Time for research design, critique and discussion of the design, and later for redesign

+

Time for conceptualization, getting into your topic, literature review, and critique

+

Time for preparing, making a reconnaissance, entering the field + time lost by making mistakes, being engaged with the wrong people, misinterpreting early signs, and putting your foot in it

+

Time for choosing, conducting trials, and setting up a data management system, including time to become proficient in it, as well as in underlying skills in the library or on the computer

+

Time for ongoing data management (backing up files, setting up a computer project or labeling boxes, archiving records, descriptive coding)

+

Data creation and interpretation time: time for each event (e.g., an interview) + time for preparing, practicing, learning, rehearsing, and losing your nerve + time making the appointment, finding she isn't home, and remaking it + time for transcribing audio or video files (at least 5 times the time the event took) + time for checking transcripts and researcher time for reading, interpreting, and coding data

+

More data collection and interpretation time for planning theoretical (data-driven) sampling + time for each of these new events and the processing accompanying them

+

Time for ongoing coding, exploring, annotating, categorizing, and, above all, thinking, conducting trials, and establishing explanations, despairing, exalting, talking, consulting, revising, and revisiting

+

Time, from the earliest stages, for analytic work: writing, annotating, memo writing, rewriting, editing, getting it right, discussing, and refining

+

Time for reporting, to participants or professional audiences, in as many ways and contexts as the project deserves

+

Time for the party with your team

Figure 11.1   Estimating Time for Qualitative Research

preparation for subsequent interviews or the next stage, and time for copying, filing, and other clerical work.

☷☷ *Transcribing:* If audio recordings are to be transcribed, this will be a major cost. (Estimate the number of interviews × 4 hours × 60-minute recording × hourly salary.)

☷☷ *Equipment and training:* Present the makes, model numbers, and prices of all audio and video recorders, transcribing machines, computing equipment, and the like. Allow for time and costs of training in interview techniques, computer methods, coding, and so forth.

☷☷ *Payment for participants:* If you plan to pay participants, add costs for focus groups or interviews (usually by time committed), plus reimbursement of expenses for parking, transportation fares, baby-sitting fees, and so on. Allow for expenses for refreshments.

☷☷ *Supplies and travel:* Think ahead to estimate expenses for software, paper, pens, computer external drives, audio and video recorders, printing cartridges, and copying. Also budget for travel for yourself and any research assistants.

☷☷ *Publication costs:* At this stage, publishing may seem a distant dream, but it will eventually entail costs. Plan on expenses for editing, graphics, duplication of reports, mailing, and courier services.

A Note on Dealing With Available Data

Perhaps the data you need are offered ready-made. A preemptive research design, planned before your involvement, or data available for secondary analysis are always a challenge, and sometimes a major risk. This is not to argue that you should refuse to analyze the data already available. Such a situation occurs in many projects. Historians live with it, routinely using documents, diaries, letters, or other data that predate their projects as a way to explore the past. Neither do we urge you to refuse when you are offered data—by an activist group, for example. Some of the great qualitative studies happened that way, with researchers responding to available data. If this is your situation, our best advice is that you take your research design even more seriously than you would if the project were proceeding with data-making processes under your control.

However, available data are highly unlikely to be the data you want or a perfect fit for your question. Your proposal must contain a budget and time for working with the data or possibly gathering additional data. If you want to use a secondary data set, sometimes you will need to think your way into the project and the data set, assess sharply the adequacy of the data available to you by these means, and make claims in the context of the data's limitations.

☰ ENJURING ETHICAL REJEARCH

Qualitative inquiry brings with it special issues pertaining to participant consent and maintenance of participant anonymity. In almost all research settings, formal ethics review committees examine researchers' proposals for inherent risks to participants, specifying the level of consent and permission required from participants and community leaders and the level of anonymity that must be provided to the participants. Before beginning their projects, researchers must obtain permission from their employers (or, in the case of students, from their universities). The institutions in which research will be conducted may also have their own rules regarding access and other issues (as do most schools, hospitals, prisons, and government departments). Researchers often complain about the restrictions placed on them by ethics review committees, but we urge you to give thoughtful consideration to the need for such restrictions. Working outside such a context, you would have the much more difficult challenge of ensuring ethical practice without the assistance of a committee.

Your research institution (and host institution) will have its own ethics procedures and forms; you must use them, but you should also make sure that they adequately cover the requirements of your project. In addition, you must meet the requirements for your country; information about these requirements is generally available on the Internet. See Figure 11.2 at the end of this chapter for a sample participant consent form.

The Challenge of Anonymity

We warned in Chapter 10 how easy it is to breach anonymity by using blocks of quotation and verbatim dialogue in the final report. More extreme risks accompany the use of photographs or videos. Participant consent forms must state the mode of recording and the planned uses of records. Because participants may be recognized in photographs and videos, thus violating promised anonymity, you will need to obtain releases (with separate signature lines) if you are taking photographs or video recording (see the sample consent form addendum at the end of this chapter).

If you have promised your participants anonymity, you will need to check all written material from the start to ensure that persons and places are not recognizable. This is no trivial task, and it is rarely achieved merely through the changing of names. You must make certain that no participant's anonymity is violated indirectly through the linking of his or her demographic characteristics, such as age, gender, marital status, occupation, disease, and even pseudonym.

Unless the participants actively insist on being identified, it is standard practice to change proper names of people, suburbs or villages, and institutions. Even if participants seek identification, you should not identify them unless they have signed releases allowing their names to be used. (And in such situations, you should still be acutely aware of the effects of publishing your research.)

Important to the issue of anonymity is the researcher's responsibility for concealing the names of the institutions or locations in which the research was conducted. We discussed these issues in Chapter 10.

Permissions

Since the 1980s, social science research has been carefully monitored to protect human subjects from certain risks (including invasion of privacy). A researcher cannot undertake a project without first getting a series of permissions and having the research proposal reviewed by university committees and the agencies and communities involved.

First and foremost, you must obtain permission from your employer, for the institution that employs you is considered to be primarily responsible for your actions. Even students (who are not involved in a direct employer–employee relationship) must obtain permission through their universities' ethics review procedures before they can negotiate sites for their research. So your first task, after completing your proposal, is to find out—and follow—your own institution's guidelines. A university's permission is usually reviewed and renewed annually and requires that any incidents and complaints be immediately reported.

The second step is to get support for and permission to conduct your research at the site you have selected. Permissions here are usually obtained on several levels. First, you must obtain approval from the top administrative level, and this often entails a second ethics review. A hospital, for example, will review your proposal to see what you will be asking of staff and patients. Administrators will be concerned about how much staff time is involved in your project (for the institution, staff time is a cost) and what will be asked of patients. They will consider your proposal in light of other ongoing research, for they are also concerned about research burden—the amount of research currently being conducted in the institution and its impact on patients and patient care.

International research is a special case. If your project involves your traveling out of your own country to collect data, you will need special permits and research visas from the host country. These may take some time to obtain, so you should allow ample time for this process in your proposal.

The final level of approval must be obtained from the actual research setting, such as the unit or the classroom where the study will be conducted. Please be aware that getting approval at this level does not mean that the staff will automatically support your research. Once in the setting, you must obtain individual consents and permissions; you must also fit in and win the trust, cooperation, and support of the staff.

Participant Assent and Consent

Covert research (research carried out without the knowledge of participants) is rarely approved by ethics review committees. If it is necessary for research to be conducted without the participants' knowledge, extensive debriefing procedures must be established and consents obtained after the collection of data, with participants given the option of having data referring to them destroyed if they do not wish to participate in the study.

Participants' rights include the following: (a) the right to be fully informed about the study's purpose and about the involvement and time required for participation, (b) the right to confidentiality and anonymity, (c) the right to ask any questions of the investigator, (d) the right to refuse to participate without any negative ramifications, (e) the right to refuse to answer any questions, and (f) the right to withdraw from the study at any time. Participants also have the right to know what to expect during the research process, what information is being obtained about them, who will have access to that information, and what the information will be used for.

We take these rights very seriously and urge you to consider the impact of your research on those you are studying at all times. Having a signed informed consent form does not clear you of this responsibility. When the participant signed that form, they probably did not know what they were going to tell you subsequently, or what emotional issues would surface during a research encounter. The basic rule is that their rights prevail. You have no overriding right to data just because you want it for your project. The richer the data become and the more revealing the accounts you elicit, the more at risk are the rights of those consenting to take part in your research.

Researchers are usually required to obtain formal written consent from participants prior to the commencement of the data-gathering period. Be very clear that this signed form does not permit you to use anything you subsequently obtain, if the participant at a later stage prefers that you not use something. To ensure anonymity, the consent forms are not linked to the data in any way. Researchers commonly keep the forms for a period of 7 years after the study is completed.

If a participant is a minor, usually defined as being under age 18, special conditions apply. If a child is not old enough to understand the concept of research or the required protocol and purpose of the study, then the child's parent or guardian must consent. If the child or adolescent is old enough to understand the purpose of the research and what is being asked, then the child/adolescent gives *assent* and a parent or guardian is still required to give *consent*. However, the child's wishes override those of his or her parent: If the child/adolescent does not want to participate, his or her wishes hold, no matter what the parent desires.

Does this requirement for consent mean that research cannot be conducted in public places? The general rule is that researchers must be careful to inform persons they are studying whenever possible, and if they are conducting studies in a public place, they should not collect identifying data without permission. For instance, if you are conducting a study on a beach, you might announce the study in the local newspaper, place signs on lampposts in the area, and request agreement from anyone approached directly. But because you may observe a number of individuals who have not given their consent to participate, you should not record any information that identifies particular participants.

If you think that participants may object to having their likenesses (in photographs or videos) appear in the public domain but will permit their use for research purposes, you can split the consent form into two parts to get participants for your study so that the prospect of the public use of visual media won't interfere with recruitment. Participants may sign one or both sections (see Figures 11.2 and 11.3 for examples).

[Title of your project]

[Your name, affiliation, contact phone number]

[A brief description of your project: Say what will be required of participants and about how long it will take. If you are providing participants with reimbursement, state that here.]

Consent

I hereby consent to participate in the above research project. I understand that my participation is voluntary and that I may change my mind and refuse to participate or withdraw at any time without penalty. I may refuse to answer any questions or I may stop the interview. I understand that some of the things that I say may be directly quoted in the text of the final report and subsequent publications, but my name will not be associated with that text.

I hereby agree to participate in the above research:

_____	_____ _____	
Participant	Print Name	Date
_____	_____ _____	
Principal Investigator	Print Name	Date
_____	_____ _____	
Witness	Print Name	Date

Figure 11.2   Sample Consent Form

I hereby give consent to be photographed for this research. I understand that my name will not be associated with these photographs. The photographs may be published with the final report and/or articles in professional journals or used for educational purposes.

_____   _____

                                   _____

Participant   Print Name   Date

_____   _____

                                   _____

Principal Investigator   Print Name   Date

_____   _____

                                   _____

Witness   Print Name   Date

Figure 11.3   Sample Addendum to a Consent Form for a Study Using Photographs or Video Recordings

⚞ SUMMARY

Before actually beginning your study, you must do considerable work. You must prepare the proposal, outlining what you intend to do, where, and why, and you must obtain approvals, including from those responsible for enforcing ethics requirements and from those with authority over your research site.

We have noted in this chapter some of the requirements for ethics review committee approval of your proposal, such as information on what will be required of participants and how you intend to use the information obtained. We have also listed the rights of participants, which include the right to be protected from harm and the right to be informed about the research aims.

〰 REſOURCEſ

On Writing Proposals

Boyd, C. O., & Munhall, P. L. (2001). Qualitative proposals and reports. In P. L. Munhall (Ed.), *Nursing research: A qualitative perspective* (3rd ed., pp. 613–638). Boston: Jones & Bartlett.

Morse, J. M. (2003). A review committee's guide for evaluating qualitative proposals. *Qualitative Health Research, 13,* 833–851.

Morse, J. M. (2004). Preparing and evaluating qualitative research proposals. In C. Seale, D. Silverman, D. Gobo, & J. Gubrium (Eds.), *Inside qualitative research: Craft, practice, context* (pp. 493–503). London: Sage.

On Preparing Proposals for Funding

Cheek, J. (2000). An untold story? Doing funded qualitative research. In N. K. Denzin & Y. S. Lincoln (Eds.), *The SAGE handbook of qualitative research* (2nd ed., pp. 401–420). Thousand Oaks, CA: Sage.

Morse, J. M. (1994). Designing funded qualitative research. In N. K. Denzin & Y. S. Lincoln (Eds.), *The SAGE handbook of qualitative research* (pp. 220–235). Thousand Oaks, CA: Sage.

On Ethics Requirements and Approvals

Christians, C. G. (2000). Ethics and politics in qualitative research. In N. K. Denzin & Y. S. Lincoln (Eds.), *The SAGE handbook of qualitative research* (2nd ed., pp. 133–155). Thousand Oaks, CA: Sage.

Mauthner, M., Birch, M., Jessop, J., & Mueller, T. (Eds.). (2002). *Ethics in qualitative research.* Thousand Oaks, CA: Sage.

12

Getting Started

Qualitative research is only as good as the investigator. This is both the good and the bad news. The researcher makes all the analytic decisions—not the data, not the method, not the computer. The researcher, through skill, persistence, patience, and wisdom, earns the trust of participants in the setting, flexibly adapts the strategy, and elegantly balances the design. The researcher makes the necessary data to produce a rich study, ensures methodological congruence, and is meticulous about documentation. The researcher is well informed on the topic, incisively interrogates data, accurately recognizes clues, and sensitively interprets. This is a craft with high standards.

Learning any craft is made easier by knowing the standards of how it is done well. Good researchers set high standards. They are familiar with the relevant theory and studies, so they recognize what is known and what is not known, and they separate these things from those that are new, puzzling, and significant. They can locate an appropriate framework or paradigm to work within, and they have the ability to keep this apart from the data so that inductive work is still possible. They are stimulated, not stopped, by ambiguity or paradoxes but are able to recognize that reality is not simple; rather, it is a complex puzzle, a challenge, to which there may be no best or easy answer. The intellectual work of making sense of their data is a challenge they revel in, because they know the research methods, strategies, and techniques they need. They also know these are only tools to facilitate inquiry—means to the end, not the solution itself. Researchers use strategies and techniques to manipulate data so they may be analyzed; strategies and techniques themselves do not do the analysis.

How, then, do you become a good researcher? The description above might seem daunting for a novice, and it might even be the reason you hesitate to start. But like any craft, qualitative research is learned by doing it. You become a qualitative researcher in the process of doing research, learning from your mistakes as well as your successes. The concern is not how to become a researcher but how to learn best while doing research.

Qualitative research will not mysteriously happen by itself. No project ever self-started. Throughout the research process, the researcher is constantly making choices, asking questions of the data, and asking questions outside of the data. That process starts when you make it start. The corollary, of course, is that it is very easy to postpone starting. So we conclude this book with a focus on this entirely achievable task.

WHY IS IT SO HARD TO START?

If getting started is a problem, it helps to see that this is built into the method. Getting started in any research project, especially a significant one, is always difficult. But qualitative research offers particular challenges that are much easier to deal with if you know they are not your fault.

First, although in a sense qualitative research, like quantitative research, begins when you start thinking about the topic, it *actually* begins when you first enter the setting and conduct your first observation or first interview. The hardest part is walking up to the first participant and explaining your study in two sentences or less. Prepare for this by role-playing and by practicing with your colleagues.

Second, in qualitative research, everything seems to happen at once. At least two things *must* happen simultaneously: the making of data and the exploration of data. This is because the methods are data driven. What you come to understand from early field research or interviewing may change your framing of the research question and, hence, demand changes in the data-construction process. Thus, as data records accrue, you must explore them, code them, discuss them with team members or participants, and question them in the light of the literature; then, in turn, you must explore and record the results of these explorations. So wherever you begin, several processes start at once.

Third, qualitative modes of data collection can be confusing and demanding. Getting accepted as an observer in a strange setting or making it through a first unstructured interview can be nerve-racking even for the most experienced observer or interviewer. For a novice, these first steps can seem a sufficient challenge without the additional need to record impressions, code new discoveries, and diagram connections. These techniques of making data also can have a formidable momentum, making withdrawal and reflection very difficult.

⧟ HOW DO YOU START?

So how do you start? This book is full of answers to that question. If you are ready to start, review them. Determined to gain understanding from the research site or participants, a researcher must begin somewhere.

Start in the Library

Judging whether your research will produce new knowledge involves knowing what is known. There is no alternative to reading extensively and widely on the selected research topic. Start with what is known.

We have argued throughout this book against the myth that prior literature searching and prior theorizing are inimical to theory discovery. If something is known, there is absolutely no point in denying yourself that knowledge and every reason to suppose your study will be better focused and more useful if informed by prior knowledge. Start by finding out what is known and what is still being asked about your research area. Focus on *local* knowledge: What is known about the setting you are studying, the area you are in? Start building up more general knowledge of previous research on the broader topic—but *don't* wait until your knowledge is complete to start.

Starting in the library does not mean you are delaying the research. As you read, treat the outcome of your reading—notes, reviews, memos—as data. These are data records, to be coded and explored along with your interview transcripts or memos. If you are working on the computer, use your qualitative software to analyze literature searches and notes as data as well as alongside your data.

A literature *review* requires techniques similar to those of qualitative analysis—distilling a lot of messy data and finding their story, patterns, or themes. Like most qualitative research, it will start with some questions and generate more. Your first question is "What is known?" As your review progresses, you will discover more specific puzzles ("Why do American studies have results so different from European ones?" or "What theory would be needed to account for this aspect of the topic, and why has it not been developed?").

Reading extensively on the topic is compatible with working inductively. As you read, work on the goal of bracketing knowledge. Good data management will assist with the bracketing process.

◊◊ Always identify material from the literature (type it in a different font, or on colored paper, or code it to a "literature" category). Keep the literature, your ideas about the literature, and any preconceived notions you have about the topic in separate storage areas, each separate from the data.

◊◊ Attach authors' names to ideas, concepts, and theories as a constant reminder of whose ideas are being discussed. Code each piece of text to its citation.

◊◊ As you read, record reminders of preliminary thinking to inform your account of the process of analysis. Remain skeptical of what you find in your reading, and test every assumption.

Start With an Armchair Walkthrough

Reread the ways of systematically thinking out your topic through methodological options. What would your study look like and feel like if it were done by each of the methods sketched there? How would you focus it on a research question, and what sort of data would you seek? Even if, or especially if, you approach this topic committed to a particular method, such a mindful stroll may open possibilities and help define a research design.

◊◊ Record your walkthrough as you think aloud, draw it, or make a matrix form, as we have shown in Chapter 2.

◊◊ Start memos immediately. Projects begin with ideas, not data. Develop a memo-writing routine that you like and will use easily, and record in memos your first thoughts about the project, the appropriate method, the possible routes to take, and the reasons you are studying this topic.

⬟ If you will be working on the computer, start using your software. Store the record of your walkthrough as your first project document and the memos recording your thoughts as more documents.

Start Thinking Method

The walkthrough is a first step toward thinking your way into the appropriate method. It is not a substitute for thorough reading of texts and examples of project reports. Start with the list of references at the end of this book, and branch out from there to immerse yourself in the method and the sort of research it supports. Seek out and *critique* dissertations, books, and conference papers that report on studies using that method.

⬟ Avoid becoming a methodological cultist: Read outside the method and listen to criticisms of it. From the outset, be alert to its challenges as well as its advantages for your project.

⬟ If possible, find a researcher skilled in the method you are studying and work with that researcher, learning as an apprentice does, by observing and following the lead until you can pick up the way to think about data and analysis.

Start With Yourself

Should you include data from personal experience in the study? As we noted in Chapter 5, it is sometimes argued (and was argued strenuously in early anthropology) that researchers should separate themselves from the topics and the people they study to avoid driving their research problems with their own personal agendas. It has been feared that personal involvement makes the topic more emotional, that it leads to researchers' losing their "objectivity" and to less fairness in reporting. Anthropologists argued that researchers cannot "see" a particular culture's values and beliefs if they are immersed in that culture. These objections have now by and large been relaxed, but, as Lipson (1991) has noted, this task is not easy and takes concerted effort.

Where do you place your own experience when your values, beliefs, culture, and even physical limitations affect the process and quality of data? As you read the literature where your project is located, you will find that most researchers are concerned with this question. Adherents of one school of thought aim for objectivity by depersonalizing the data, emphasizing issues of reliability and validity in data collection, and considering those being studied as "informants" or "actors." The extreme alternative is to acknowledge the researcher as a part of the setting. The researcher's interpretation is just one among many, including those of participants—or even co-researchers—in the research process. The researcher must consciously choose, negotiate, and maintain the relationship with the persons being studied.

What Role Should the Researcher's Personal Experience Play?

In Chapter 5, we discussed the pros and cons of using your personal experience or incorporating that experience into the project. We noted that your own experience can be used in two ways: by delineating it and using it as data while separating it from experiences of others in the study, or by using it as legitimate and intimately rich data that are perhaps more valid than the reported, secondhand experiences obtained by interviewing or observing others. Whatever your choice, we advise you to use your experience with care.

Hidden Agendas

Along with the advantages that come with using your own experience—such as making the study richer—there are dangers, and words of caution are needed. Researchers often have hidden agendas—that is, they may have issues they are seeking to resolve and may select these issues as topics for study. Consider the possibility that selecting a problem in which you have personal involvement may make the research project an overwhelmingly distressing experience. Recall that qualitative data collection requires listening to similar stories of those who have also been through the experience, and then dwelling with those stories for months. Do you want to do this to yourself, especially if the material is personally and profoundly disturbing? We do not recommend that you try to understand your own experience of a disturbing event, such as the death of a parent, by conducting a qualitative study.

If you have an ax to grind, similar advice holds. Resolve your problems using the ordinary channels. If you feel you were given a speeding ticket unfairly, do not select attitudes of traffic police toward drivers as your topic. If you feel you were treated unfairly in some other arena, do not attempt to resolve your problem with qualitative research. Above all, you must remember that there is a clear distinction between detective work and qualitative research. You belong with the latter—qualitative research is not a "gotcha" endeavor. Stay clear of high-risk topics that may result in encounters with the law, the subpoenaing of data, and personal risk.

Occasionally in contract research, the contracting agency will have a hidden agenda and will use the qualitative researcher to help make a point, justify its existence, and so forth. The researcher may encounter problems when the agency's agenda is never made explicit, especially when the researcher's results do not meet the agency's expectations. You can avoid such problems, at least in part, if the contracting agreement is clear on certain points, such as to whom the data belong, the limits of confidentiality of the findings and of the host organization, and the publication rights of the researcher.

In summary, you should choose your research topic with care, because selecting something for the wrong reason may result in unnecessary distress and/or poor research. Making your selection may involve some self-reflection ("Why does this topic grab me?") and an assessment of gains or costs to self. Know yourself.

Start Small

Researchers are easily swamped by qualitative data. As in surfing, the challenge is to get on top and stay on top as the volume and momentum of the wave of data build up. When data tower above you, it's too late to get on top. The momentum of qualitative research can be formidable, because modes of sampling and data acquisition are often not under the researcher's control. Once accepted in a fieldwork setting, you are swept up in the events you must observe. Once started on a snowball sample, you can hardly refuse offers of further interviews.

There are serious problems for a project using any qualitative method if the researcher starts data collection without starting analysis, thus allowing data to build up untouched. In 1989, Anselm Strauss memorably described this situation to Lyn Richards: "Students get data crawling up their backs." Qualitative data are, by their nature, rich, complex, and defiant of instant reduction to tidy shapes or numbers. Rapidly acquiring many records without exploring and coding them can be disastrous to your sense of direction and access to the data. We have offered advice on ways of staying on top and processing data records as they come into the project. As for getting started, our advice is simple: Start small.

- ⧄ Start with a limited, relatively self-contained project segment, perhaps with a marginally relevant group, or a documentary analysis of setting the scene. If things go wrong, you can withdraw tactfully without damaging the main project.

- ⧄ From the start, review, consider, and in some way process each item of data as it is brought into the project. On reading it, write a memo recording your memories of the event, first impressions of the interview, and the like.

Start Safe

Maintain control over the research process by strategically planning your entry into the research field or your first interviews. Most projects offer some choice as to where the research starts, and you can use this choice to delay particularly crucial research events or encounters about which you are not confident.

- ⧄ Practice interviewing with friends or family before doing interviews in your research field.

- ⧄ Think out carefully the ethical and courtesy aspects of each research initiative, and consult in the field as widely as possible.

- ⧄ If possible, start in consultation with research confidants or advisors who will talk out with you what happened and what you should do about it.

Start Soon

Delaying the start of a project can have serious effects. Apart from the impact on your self-image and deadline, delaying can lead to a loss of momentum and failure to attain the knowledge level you had planned to reach. The methodological foreplay of reviewing literature, planning, replanning, and consulting is absolutely necessary to any project, but it should not be allowed to take over the research. There is always somewhere you can sensibly start.

Start with caution, especially if you are under pressure to produce results. If clients or supervisors simultaneously demand too much, give them a copy of this book, and while they read it, get on with placing the project, becoming skilled, and designing your entry into the field. These processes need not take long, but you must do them. Before the client has finished this book, you will be ready.

Start With a Research Design

Locating a research question and selecting a method do not provide you with an instant research design. You can't start without a practical outline of a doable project. This is so important that we have devoted an entire chapter to it (see Chapter 4). But you *can* start a project without first making your research design perfect, as long as the design allows for appropriate modification as you learn from the data. And to start it, you must commence with careful consideration of the knowledge you are bringing in, which is the first step in building a good relationship with your research project—a sense that it can be done, that there is a task here you can get your arms around.

Start Skilled

From your armchair walkthrough and your detailed reading on the method to be used, note any skills you will need that you do not yet have and note *when* you will need them. Make it a rule not to commence any stage of the project before you are comfortable with the required skills. If you do not have the research experience with the methods of data collection that your project requires, be sure to learn more about those methods before you begin data collection. Start with the resources listed in this book and read widely on particular methods of making or analyzing data so that you know not only what they entail but also how to know if you are doing them well.

Never test data-collection techniques in real research situations. All qualitative data making is potentially invasive and intrusive, so your mistakes may cause someone else distress. Qualitative data are also cumulative, and informants are likely to communicate, so any mistakes you make are also likely to impede later data-collection efforts.

Start in Your Software

Choose your software early and become competent in computer use and all the relevant software *before* data collection begins. If you wait until you are making data, you will risk damaging or even losing files.

- ⟩⟩ If you are not confident with computers, seek help to ensure that you can manage the operating system and do good housekeeping of your files and backups. You need those skills for any research work, in any software.

- ⟩⟩ Ensure that you are competent in all the software you will be using, including your word-processing software. (Can you format and edit well?)

- ⟩⟩ Now, your qualitative software. You need basic competence in it from the start of research design so that the project can benefit from software from the start. Assess your ability to self-teach. Good software will include self-teaching materials and will be supported by researchers who provide training.

- ⟩⟩ Use others' wisdom! Do not assume self-teaching is best: Seek colleagues or helpers who have the software skills and experience you want. Find what software support is available in your institution and use it. Go to the software maker's website to find workshops, consultants, or virtual courses. Seek out Internet discussion lists devoted to the software so you can pick up tips from other researchers and avoid their mistakes. Learning with others is usually far more productive and often faster and much more fun than learning alone.

⟩⟩ CONGRATULATIONS, YOU'VE STARTED!

Do you remember why you wanted to do qualitative research? Keep this and your project goals in mind as you work, and remain flexible and open to your participants and to your data. Do justice to the richness of your data. And, above all, have fun.

※ RESOURCES

Bilken, S. K., & Casella, R. (2007). *A practical guide to the qualitative dissertation*. New York: Teachers College Press.

Bloomberg, L. D., & Volpe, M. (2008). *Completing your qualitative dissertation: A roadmap from beginning to end*. Thousand Oaks, CA: Sage.

Fitzpatrick, J., Secrist, J., & Wright, D. J. (1998). *Secrets for a successful dissertation*. Thousand Oaks, CA: Sage.

King, N. M. P., Henderson, G. E., & Stein, J. (1999). *Beyond regulation: Ethics in human subjects research*. Chapel Hill: University of North Carolina Press.

Meloy, J. M. (2008). *Writing the qualitative dissertation: Understanding by doing*. Mahwah, NJ: Taylor & Francis.

Piantanida, M., & Garman, N. B. (2009). *The qualitative dissertation: A guide for students and faculty* (2nd ed.). Thousand Oaks, CA: Sage.

Richards, L. (2009). *Handling qualitative data: A practical guide* (2nd ed.). London: Sage. [See, in particular, Part I: Setting Up.]

Appendix 1

Qualitative Software

Where to Go Next

Lyn Richards

We have designed this book to give beginning researchers an understanding of what working qualitatively is like. An important part of this experience now is working qualitatively on the computer. Although we do not assume that all qualitative researchers today will use computers for the handling of qualitative data, many texts and most employers now do make that assumption. Certainly, those who use software can do much with the data that could not be done without a computer. Thus, the researchers who know what specialized software can offer are greatly helped in assessing what they can achieve.

Researchers approaching qualitative software for the first time often find it daunting, but in our experience, their problem usually is simply that they do not know what it would be like to work with qualitative software, or how to start. In this book, and its companion website, we have aimed to show what parts of the researcher's task can be assisted by software tools, and what tools to reach for at each phase of a project.

Each of the chapters of this book covering research design and data and analysis processes has introduced software in the context of the methods issues being considered. In each, I provided a summary of *approaches* to the task with software, *advances* in method because of software, and, importantly, *alerts* to dangers in using software or using it badly.

Go to the companion website to this book (www.sagepub.com/ richards3e) for a précis of these advice sections. This brings those advice sections together as one document for reference as you prepare to use software.

In its second part, the website offers insights into the user experience, to help you learn about common challenges and successful approaches. These observations draw on contributions from some software trainers writing about what they have learned over the decades since the introduction of qualitative software.

So now you are going to use software and will need help in finding a package and preparing to use it. The tables in Chapter 4 summarized what you can expect to get from packages. For more detailed advice, I offer a general introduction to the process of "getting into" software on the companion website (http://www.sagepub.co.uk/richards) to my partner book, *Handling Qualitative Data* (2009). That site advises on the following issues to consider before you go shopping for and start using software:

⬓ Whether you should use qualitative software

⬓ What the state of the art is

⬓ Where to go for unbiased (and some biased) information

⬓ How to go about hunting down and talking to the software developer

⬓ Managing your relationship with software

⬓ A quick online guide to "stepping into software"

Once you've started, do you need specific training in the software package you will be using? Go to the website for that package. All developer sites and many other useful information sources are linked from the home pages of the CAQDAS project (http://www.surrey.ac.uk/sociology/research/researchcentres/caqdas/) at the University of Surrey in the United Kingdom. Many software sites have free downloadable products to trial, with brief tutorials.

Do you learn well by yourself, or do you need a trainer? You may do better to work with an independent trainer than with the developers of the software. Workshops are available in many software products, and trainers working online can give virtual assistance as you learn or as you develop a project. Trainers often provide their own tutorial handbooks. For example, full tutorials for using the current version of one product, NVivo, are available online at http://www.kihi.com.au/.

As the alerts in this book suggest, it is very easy to skew a project toward things that are easy to do in software—and to keep on doing them! It's very disappointing to finish a project and discover how much better it could have been if you had known of the techniques and tools available to you. Unlike many popular software products, qualitative software tools are rarely learned well by just clicking around. The subtler tools of a package, like the subtler processes of qualitative method, are not self-evident. So, before you start to use software, seek accounts of projects conducted in the package you are using, and note the tools that were helpful. Find users and listen to their experience—or, better, watch them work and study their projects online to learn how the analysis was helped (or hindered) by the software tools. Join user groups and share challenges and triumphs openly. Write and present papers not just about your results but about the tools used and how they worked; your experience will help others, and their discussion will help you critique and evaluate your analysis and the software tools you used to get there.

Appendix 2

Applying for Funding

Janice M. Morse

xcellent qualitative inquiry takes time. It must be built on the foundations of literature and the work of others and fit into what is known; therefore, hiring—and, of course mentoring—a research assistant can facilitate many labor-intensive tasks. Excellent qualitative inquiry requires good data, careful transcription, consultation with experienced researchers, and assistance from more junior researchers, which is often expensive. Excellent qualitative inquiry may require equipment (computers and printers, audio and video recorders and transcribers, software, cameras, fax and copy machines), and this equipment is not always available and must be purchased. Good qualitative inquiry must be disseminated at conferences; participants need to be informed of the results, which then must be prepared and submitted for publication. In short, good qualitative inquiry is expensive to do and expensive to disseminate.

Obviously, if the researcher can obtain a grant to assist with or cover these expenses, then the task of doing research is lightened and the chances for success improved. But obtaining a grant is an art, and knowing the tricks of grantsmanship will greatly enhance your chances of success! This appendix offers some advice.

❧ OBTAINING A GRANT

Every granting agency has "terms of reference" or a statement of goals and priority topics describing the types of areas it is interested in funding. It is wise to double-check that your project will be eligible for funding by looking at the lists of projects previously funded, determining whether yours is similar. If still in doubt, phone the agency and ask. While doing so, check the following:

1. Do they fund researchers at your level of expertise? (Do they fund students? New researchers without a track record?)

2. How much funding will they provide? A researcher may require only a small "seed grant"—enough to pay for assistance with transcription and other minor costs—or a larger grant that will also support equipment and staff over a number of years.

3. Do they consider qualitative research? (Check first the titles of previously funded grants.)

Pay careful attention to the application deadlines and other agency requirements, allowing adequate time for the necessary signatures and approvals from your own institution. Note that the grant is normally provided to your institution, not to you as an individual. If you are a graduate student, then your advisor will usually be required to sign the grant as principal investigator.

Can you apply for funding from more than one agency simultaneously? This is usually acceptable, as long as you notify each agency that you have also submitted elsewhere and name the other agency or agencies. Then, if your proposal is rated in the fundable range, the agency will contact the other funding body, and perhaps the agencies will share the costs.

☷ ONCE FUNDED

Once the grant is funded, your timeline begins. Be certain to fulfill all the agency's requirements, including submitting interim and final reports as requested.

Qualitative research, even excellent qualitative work, has an uncertain course and outcome at best. Communicate regularly with the agency's internal research officer responsible for your grant—especially if you deviate from your original proposal. Get official permission if you want to make changes to your proposed design. And, once you complete your work, be certain to acknowledge your funding sources in all presentations and publications.

References

The following is a list of references cited in the text. Many further references are provided in the "Resources" section ending each chapter.

Agar, M. H. (1996). *The professional stranger: An informal introduction to ethnography* (2nd ed.). San Diego, CA: Academic Press.

Altheide, D. L., & Johnson, J. M. (1994). Criteria for assessing interpretive validity in qualitative research. In N. K. Denzin & Y. S. Lincoln (Eds.), *The SAGE handbook of qualitative research* (pp. 485–499). Thousand Oaks, CA: Sage.

Atkinson, P., & Hammersley, M. (1994). Ethnography and participant observation. In N. K. Denzin & Y. S. Lincoln (Eds.), *The SAGE handbook of qualitative research* (pp. 248–261). Thousand Oaks, CA: Sage.

Baig, A. A., Wilkes, A. E., Davis, A. M., Peek, M. E., Huang, E. S., Bell, D. S., et al. (2010). The use of quality improvement and health information technology approaches to improve diabetes outcomes in African American and Hispanic patients. *Medical Care Research and Review, 67*(5, Suppl.), 163s–197s.

Bates, G., & Mead, M. (1942). *Balinese character: A photographic analysis.* New York: New York Academy of Sciences.

Bazeley, P. (2010). Computer assisted integration of mixed methods data sources and analyses. In A. Tashakkori & C. Teddlie (Eds.), *Handbook of mixed methods research for the social and behavioral sciences* (2nd ed., pp. 431–467). Thousand Oaks, CA: Sage.

Beatty, A. (2010). How did it feel for you? Emotion, narrative and the limits of ethnography. *American Anthropology, 112*(2), 430–443.

Benner, P. (Ed.). (1994). *Interpretive phenomenology: Embodiment, caring, and ethics in health and illness.* Thousand Oaks, CA: Sage.

Blumer, H. (1986). *Symbolic interactionism: Perspective and method.* Berkeley: University of California Press. (Original work published 1969)

Bowers, B., & Schatzman, L. (2009). Dimensional analysis. In J. M. Morse, P. N. Stern, J. Corbin, B. Bowers, K. Charmaz, & A. E. Clarke (Eds.), *Developing grounded theory: The second generation* (pp. 107–125). Walnut Creek, CA: Left Coast Press.

Boyd, C. O. (1993). Phenomenology: The method. In P. L. Munhall & C. O. Boyd (Eds.), *Nursing research: A qualitative perspective* (2nd ed., pp. 99–132). New York: National League for Nursing.

Boyd, C. O., & Munhall, P. L. (2001). Qualitative proposals and reports. In P. L. Munhall (Ed.), *Nursing research: A qualitative perspective* (3rd ed., pp. 613–638). Boston: Jones & Bartlett.

Bryant, A., & Charmaz, C. (Eds.). (2007). *The SAGE handbook of grounded theory.* London: Sage.

Bryman, A. (2006). Integrating quantitative and qualitative research: How is it done? *Qualitative Research, 6*(1), 97–113.

Cameron, D. (2001). *Working with spoken discourse.* London: Sage.

Carney, T. F. (1990). *Collaborative inquiry methodology.* Windsor, Ontario: University of Windsor, Division of Instructional Development.

Carr, E. S. (2011). *Scripting addiction.* Princeton, NJ: Princeton University.

Carspecken, P. F. (1996). *Critical ethnography in educational research: A theoretical and practical guide.* New York: Routledge.

Cassell, J. (1992). On control, certitude and the "paranoia" of surgeons. In J. M. Morse (Ed.), *Qualitative health research* (pp. 170–191). Newbury Park, CA: Sage. (Original work published 1987)

Charmaz, K. (2006). *Constructing grounded theory: A practical guide through qualitative analysis.* Thousand Oaks, CA: Sage.

Charmaz, K. (2009). Shifting the grounds: Constructivist grounded theory. In J. M. Morse, P. N. Stern, J. Corbin, B. Bowers, K. Charmaz, & A. E. Clarke (Eds.), *Developing grounded theory: The second generation* (pp. 127–154). Walnut Creek, CA: Left Coast Press.

Cheek, J. (2000). An untold story? Doing funded qualitative research. In N. K. Denzin & Y. S. Lincoln (Eds.), *The SAGE handbook of qualitative research* (2nd ed., pp. 401–420). Thousand Oaks, CA: Sage.

Chenail, R. J., & Duffy, M. (2011). Utilizing Microsoft Office to produce and present recursive frame analysis findings. *Qualitative Report, 16*(1), 292–307.

Clark, L., Bunik, M., & Johnson, S. L. (2010). Research opportunities with curanderos to address childhood overweight in Latino families. *Qualitative Health Research, 20*(1), 4–14.

Clarke, A. (2005). *Situational analysis: Grounded theory after the postmodern turn.* Thousand Oaks, CA: Sage.

Clarke, A. (2009). From grounded theory to situational analysis: What's new? Why?

How? In J. M. Morse, P. N. Stern, J. Corbin, B. Bowers, K. Charmaz, & A. E. Clarke (Eds.), *Developing grounded theory: The second generation* (pp. 194–234). Walnut Creek, CA: Left Coast Press.

Clarke, M. (1992). Memories of breathing: Asthma as a way of becoming. In J. M. Morse (Ed.), *Qualitative health research* (pp. 123–140). Newbury Park, CA: Sage. (Original work published 1990)

Coffey, A., & Atkinson, P. (1996). *Making sense of qualitative data.* Thousand Oaks, CA: Sage.

Coffey, A., Holbrook, B., & Atkinson, P. (1996). Qualitative data analysis: Technologies and representations. *Sociological Research Online, 1*(1). Retrieved January 24, 2012, from http://www.socresonline.org.uk/1/1/4.html

Corbin, J. (2009). Taking an analytic journey. In J. M. Morse, P. N. Stern, J. Corbin, B. Bowers, K. Charmaz, & A. E. Clarke (Eds.), *Developing grounded theory: The second generation* (pp. 35–54). Walnut Creek, CA: Left Coast Press.

Corbin, J., & Strauss, A. (2008). *Basics of qualitative research: Techniques and procedures for developing grounded theory* (3rd ed.). Thousand Oaks, CA: Sage.

Coulthard, M. (1985). *An introduction to discourse analysis.* New York: Longman.

Crawford, M. (1995). *Talking difference: On gender and language.* London: Sage.

Davis, D. L. (1983). *Blood and nerves: An ethnographic focus on menopause.* St. John's: Memorial University of Newfoundland.

Davis, D. L. (1992). The meaning of menopause in a Newfoundland fishing village. In J. M. Morse (Ed.), *Qualitative health research* (pp. 145–169). Newbury Park, CA: Sage. (Original work published 1986)

Davis, D. S. (1991). Rich cases: Ethics of thick description. *Hastings Center Report, 21*(4), 12–17.

Denzin, N. K., & Lincoln, Y. S. (Eds.). (2005). *The SAGE handbook of qualitative research* (3rd ed.). Thousand Oaks, CA: Sage.

Dey, I. (1995). *Qualitative data analysis: A user-friendly guide for social scientists*. London: Routledge.

Drew, S. E., Duncan, R. E., & Sawyer, S. M. (2010). Visual storytelling: A beneficial but challenging method for health research with young people. *Qualitative Health Research, 20*(12), 1677–1688.

Ellis, C., & Bochner, A. P. (Eds.). (1996). *Composing ethnography: Alternative forms of qualitative writing*. Walnut Creek, CA: AltaMira.

Ellis, C., & Bochner, A. P. (2000). Autoethnography, personal narrative, reflexivity: Researcher as subject. In N. K. Denzin & Y. S. Lincoln (Eds.), *The SAGE handbook of qualitative research* (2nd ed., pp. 733–768). Thousand Oaks, CA: Sage.

Fairclough, N. (2010). *Critical discourse analysis: The critical study of language*. Harlow, UK: Longman.

Finch, J. (1984). "It's great to have someone to talk to": The ethics and politics of interviewing women. In C. Bell & H. Roberts (Eds.), *Social researching: Politics, problems, practice* (pp. 70–87). London: Routledge & Kegan Paul.

Finch, J. (1989). *Family obligations and social change*. Cambridge, UK: Polity.

Frank, A. W. (1991). *At the will of the body: Reflections on illness*. Boston: Houghton Mifflin.

Gee, P. J. (2011). *How to do discourse analysis: A toolkit*. New York: Routledge.

Geertz, C. (1973). *The interpretation of cultures: Selected essays*. New York: Basic Books.

Germain, C. (1979). *The cancer unit: An ethnography*. Wakefield, MA: Nursing Resources.

Giorgi, A. (1997). The theory, practice, and evaluation of the phenomenological methods as a qualitative research procedure. *Journal of Phenomenological Psychology, 28,* 235–281.

Giorgi, A. (2009). *The descriptive phenomenological methods in psychology: A modified Husserlian approach*. Pittsburgh, PA: Duquesne University Press.

Glaser, B. G. (1978). *Theoretical sensitivity: Advances in the methodology of grounded theory*. Mill Valley, CA: Sociology Press.

Glaser, B. G. (1992). *Basics of grounded theory analysis: Emergence vs. forcing*. Mill Valley, CA: Sociology Press.

Glaser, B. G. (1998). *Doing grounded theory: Issues and discussions*. Mill Valley, CA: Sociology Press.

Glaser, B. G., & Strauss, A. L. (1967). *The discovery of grounded theory: Strategies for qualitative research*. Chicago: Aldine.

Glaser, B. G., & Strauss, A. L. (1968). *Time for dying*. Chicago: Aldine.

Glaser, B. G., & Strauss, A. L. (1971). *Status passage*. Chicago: Aldine.

Glittenberg, J. (2008). *Violence and hope in a U.S.–Mexico border town*. Long Grove, IL: Waveland.

Goffman, E. (1989). On fieldwork. *Journal of Contemporary Ethnography, 18,* 123–132.

Goldman-Segall, R. (1998). *Points of viewing children's thinking: A digital ethnographer's journey*. Mahwah, NJ: Lawrence Erlbaum. (See also website at http://www.pointsofviewing.com)

Gomm, R., Hammersley, M., & Foster, P. (Eds.). (2000). *Case study method*. London: Sage.

Greenwood, D. J., & Levin, M. (2007). *Introduction to action research: Social research for social change* (2nd ed.). Thousand Oaks, CA: Sage.

Guba, E. G., & Lincoln, Y. S. (1989). *Fourth generation evaluation*. Newbury Park, CA: Sage.

Gubrium, J. F. (1975). *Living and dying at Murray Manor*. New York: St. Martin's.

Hammersley, M., & Atkinson, P. (2007). *Ethnography: Principles in practice* (3rd ed.). London: Tavistock.

Haug, F. (1987). Female sexualization: A collective work of memory (E. Carter, Trans.). London: Verso.

Holstein, J. A., & Gubrium, J. F. (2003). *Inside interviewing.* Thousand Oaks, CA: Sage.

Hughes, C. C., Sherman, S. N., & Whitaker, R. C. (2010). How low-income mothers with overweight preschool children make sense of obesity. *Qualitative Health Research, 20*(4), 456–478.

Jean, R. T., Bondy, M. L., Wilkinson, A. V., & Forman, M. R. (2009). Pubertal development in Mexican American girls: The family's perspective. *Qualitative Health Research, 19*(9), 1210–1222.

Karp, D. A. (1996). *Speaking of sadness: Depression, disconnection, and the meaning of illness.* New York: Oxford University Press.

Kelpin, V. (1992). Birthing pain. In J. M. Morse (Ed.), *Qualitative health research* (pp. 93–103). Newbury Park, CA: Sage. (Original work published 1984)

Knoblauch, H. (2005). Focused ethnography. *Forum Qualitative Sozialforschung/ Forum: Qualitative Social Research, 6*(3), Art. 44. Retrieved from http://nbn-resol ving.de/urn:nbn:de:0114-fqs0503440

Kools, S., McCarthy, M., Durham, R., & Robrecht, L. (1996). Dimensional analysis: Broadening the conception of grounded theory. *Qualitative Health Research, 6,* 312–330.

Kuzel, A. J., & Engel, J. D. (2001). Some pragmatic thoughts about evaluating qualitative research. In J. M. Morse, J. M. Swanson, & A. J. Kuzel (Eds.), *The nature of qualitative evidence* (pp. 114–139). Thousand Oaks, CA: Sage.

Kvale, S. (1989). *Issues of validity in qualitative research.* Lund, Sweden: Cartwell Bratt.

Kvale, S. (1995). The social construction of validity. *Qualitative Inquiry, 1,* 19–40.

Kvale, S. (1996). *InterViews: An introduction to qualitative research interviewing.* Thousand Oaks, CA: Sage.

Lee, R. M., & Fielding, N. G. (1996). Qualitative data analysis. Representations of a technology: A comment on Coffey, Holbrook and Atkinson. *Sociological Research Online, 1*(4). Retrieved January 17, 2012, from http://www .socresonline.org.uk/1/4/lf.html

Lincoln, Y. S., & Guba, E. G. (1985). *Naturalistic inquiry.* Beverly Hills, CA: Sage.

Lipson, J. G. (1991). On fieldwork in your own setting. In J. M. Morse (Ed.), *Qualitative nursing research: A contemporary dialogue* (pp. 72–89). Newbury Park, CA: Sage.

Lofland, J., & Lofland, L. H. (1995). *Analyzing social settings: A guide to qualitative observation and analysis* (3rd ed.). Belmont, CA: Wadsworth.

Lorencz, B. J. (1992). Becoming ordinary: Leaving the psychiatric hospital. In J. M. Morse (Ed.), *Qualitative health research* (pp. 259–318). Newbury Park, CA: Sage. (Original work published 1988)

Madison, D. S. (2005). *Critical ethnography: Method, ethics, and performance.* Thousand Oaks, CA: Sage.

Malacrida, C. (1998). *Mourning the dreams: How parents create meaning from miscarriage, stillbirth and early infant death.* Edmonton, AB: Qual Institute Press.

Mason, J. (2002). *Qualitative researching* (2nd ed.). London: Sage.

Maxwell, J. A. (1992). Understanding validity in qualitative research. *Harvard Educational Review, 62,* 279–300.

McNabb, D. (2010). *Case research in public management.* New York: M. E. Sharpe.

Meadows, L., & Morse, J. M. (2001). Constructing evidence within the qualitative project. In J. M. Morse, J. M. Swanson,

& A. J. Kuzel (Eds.), *The nature of qualitative evidence* (pp. 187–200). Thousand Oaks, CA: Sage.

Miles, M. B., & Huberman, A. M. (1994). *Qualitative data analysis: An expanded sourcebook* (2nd ed.). Thousand Oaks, CA: Sage.

Morgan, D. (1993). *Successful focus groups: Advancing the state of the art.* Newbury Park, CA: Sage.

Morse, J. M. (1989a). Cultural responses to parturition: Childbirth in Fiji. *Medical Anthropology, 12*(1), 35–44.

Morse, J. M. (1989b). Gift-giving in the patient-nurse relationship: Reciprocity for care? *Western Journal of Nursing Research, 13,* 597–615.

Morse, J. M. (1991). Analyzing unstructured interviews using the Macintosh computer. *Qualitative Health Research, 1,* 117–122.

Morse, J. M. (1992). Comfort: The refocusing of nursing care. *Clinical Nursing Research, 1,* 91–113.

Morse, J. M. (1994a). Designing funded qualitative research. In N. K. Denzin & Y. S. Lincoln (Eds.), *The SAGE handbook of qualitative research* (pp. 220–235). Thousand Oaks, CA: Sage.

Morse, J. M. (1994b). "Emerging from the data": The cognitive processes of analysis in qualitative inquiry. In J. M. Morse (Ed.), *Critical issues in qualitative research methods* (pp. 23–42). Thousand Oaks, CA: Sage.

Morse, J. M. (1996). Is qualitative research complete? *Qualitative Health Research, 6,* 3–5.

Morse, J. M. (1997). Considering theory derived from qualitative research. In J. M. Morse (Ed.), *Completing a qualitative project: Details and dialogue* (pp. 163–188). Thousand Oaks, CA: Sage.

Morse, J. M. (1999). The armchair walkthrough [Editorial]. *Qualitative Health Research, 9*(4), 435–436.

Morse, J. M. (2001). Using shadowed data [Editorial]. *Qualitative Health Research, 11*(3), 291.

Morse, J. M. (2010). Procedures and practice of mixed methods design: Maintaining control, rigor and complexity. In A. Tashakkori & C. Teddlie (Eds.), *Handbook of mixed methods in social and behavioral research* (2nd ed., pp. 339–352). Thousand Oaks, CA: Sage.

Morse, J. M., & Bottorff, J. L. (1992). The emotional experience of breast expression. In J. M. Morse (Ed.), *Qualitative health research* (pp. 319–332). Newbury Park, CA: Sage. (Original work published 1988)

Morse, J. M., & Field, P. A. (1995). *Qualitative research methods for health professionals* (2nd ed.). Thousand Oaks, CA: Sage.

Morse, J. M., Miles, M. W., Clark, D. A., & Doberneck, B. M. (1994). "Sensing" patient needs: Exploring concepts of nursing insight and receptivity in nursing assessment. *Scholarly Inquiry for Nursing Practice, 8,* 233–254.

Morse, J. M., Mitcham, C., & van der Steen, W. (1998). Compathy or physical empathy: Implications for the caregiver relationship. *Journal of Medical Humanities, 19*(1), 51–65.

Morse, J. M., & Niehaus, L. (2009). *Mixed methods design: Principles and procedures.* Walnut Creek, CA: Left Coast Press.

Morse, J. M., & Proctor, A. (1998). Maintaining patient endurance: The comfort work of trauma nurses. *Clinical Nursing Research, 7,* 250–274.

Morse, J. M., Stern, P. N., Corbin, J., Bowers, B., Charmaz, K., & Clarke, A. (2009). *Grounded theory: The second generation.* Walnut Creek, CA: Left Coast Press.

Moustakas, C. (1990). *Heuristic research: Design, methodology, and applications.* Newbury Park, CA: Sage.

Moustakas, C. (1994). *Phenomenological research methods.* Thousand Oaks, CA: Sage.

Muecke, M. A. (1994). On the evaluation of ethnographies. In J. M. Morse (Ed.), *Critical issues in qualitative research methods* (pp. 187–209). Thousand Oaks, CA: Sage.

Nunnally, J. C. (1978). *Psychometric theory* (2nd ed.). New York: McGraw-Hill.

Oakley, A. (1981). Interviewing women: A contradiction in terms? In H. Roberts (Ed.), *Doing feminist research* (pp. 30–61). London: Routledge.

Olesen, V. L. (2000). Feminisms and qualitative research at and into the millennium. In N. K. Denzin & Y. S. Lincoln (Eds.), *The SAGE handbook of qualitative research* (2nd ed., pp. 215–255). Thousand Oaks, CA: Sage.

Olson, K. (2011). *The essentials of interviewing.* Walnut Creek, CA: Left Coast Press.

Penrod, J., & Morse, J. M. (1997). Strategies for assessing and fostering hope: The hope assessment guide. *Oncology Nurses Forum, 24*(6), 1055–1063.

Peräkylä, A. (2004). Conversational analysis. In C. Seale, G. Gobo, J. F. Gubrium, & D. Silverman (Eds.), *Qualitative research practice* (pp. 165–179). London: Sage.

Phillips, N., & Hardy, C. (2002). *Discourse analysis: Investigating processes of social construction.* Thousand Oaks, CA: Sage.

Platt, J. (1992). Cases of cases . . . of cases. In C. C. Ragin & H. S. Becker (Eds.), *What is a case? Exploring the foundations of social inquiry* (pp. 21–52). New York: Cambridge University Press.

Potter, J., & Wetherell, M. (1994). Analyzing discourse. In A. Bryman & R. G. Burgess (Eds.), *Analyzing qualitative data* (pp. 47–67). London: Routledge.

Proctor, A., Morse, J. M., & Khonsari, E. S. (1996). Sounds of comfort in the trauma centre: How nurses talk to patients in pain. *Social Science & Medicine, 42,* 1669–1680.

Ray, M. A. (1994). The richness of phenomenology: Philosophic, theoretic, and methodologic concerns. In J. M. Morse (Ed.), *Critical issues in qualitative research methods* (pp. 117–133). Thousand Oaks, CA: Sage.

Reason, P., & Bradbury, H. (2008). *The SAGE handbook of action research: Participative inquiry and practice* (2nd ed.). London: Sage.

Rich, M., & Patashnick, J. (2002). Narrative research with audiovisual data: Video Intervention/Prevention Assessment (VIA) and NVivo. *International Journal of Social Research Methodology, 5*(5), 245–261.

Richards, L. (1990). *Nobody's home: Dreams and realities in a new suburb.* Melbourne, Australia: Oxford University Press.

Richards, L. (1998). Closeness to data: The changing goals of qualitative data handling. *Qualitative Health Research, 8,* 319–328.

Richards, L. (1999). Qualitative teamwork: Making it work. *Qualitative Health Research, 9,* 7–10.

Richards, L. (2000, September). *Pattern analysis and why it isn't grounded theory.* Paper presented at the Conference on Strategies for Qualitative Research Using QSR Software, University of London.

Richards, L. (2005). *Handling qualitative data: A practical guide.* London: Sage.

Richards, L. (2009). *Handling qualitative data: A practical guide* (2nd ed.). London: Sage.

Richards, L., & Richards, T. J. (1994). From filing cabinet to computer. In A. Bryman & R. G. Burgess (Eds.), *Analyzing qualitative data* (pp. 146–172). London: Routledge.

Richards, L., Seibold, C., & Davis, N. (1997). *Intermission: Women's experiences of midlife and menopause.* Melbourne, Australia: Oxford University Press.

Richards, T. J., & Richards, L. (1995). Using hierarchical categories in qualitative data analysis. In U. Kelle (Ed.), *Computer-aided qualitative data analysis: Theory, methods, and practice* (pp. 62–68). London: Sage.

Richardson, L. (1990). *Writing strategies: Reaching diverse audiences.* Newbury Park, CA: Sage.

Robertson, S. K. (2008). Cultural probes in transmigrant research: A case study. *InterActions: UCLA Journal of Education and Information Studies, 4*(2). Retrieved from http://escholarship.org/uc/item/1f68p0f8

Rolfe, S., & Richards, L. (1993). Australian mothers "construct" infant day care: Implicit theories and perceptions of reality. *Australian Journal of Early Childhood, 18*(2), 10–22.

Sandelowski, M. (1993). Rigor or rigor mortis: The problem of rigor in qualitative inquiry. *Advances in Nursing Science, 16*(2), 1–8.

Sandelowski, M., & Barroso, J. (2007). *Handbook for synthesizing qualitative research.* New York: Springer.

Schatzman, L. (1991). Dimensional analysis: Notes on the alternative approach to the grounding of theory in qualitative research. In D. R. Maines (Ed.), *Social organization and social process* (pp. 303–314). New York: Aldine.

Silverman, D. (2010). *Doing qualitative research* (3rd ed.). London: Sage.

Smith, D. E. (2005). *Institutional ethnography: A sociology for the people.* Toronto, Canada: Alta Mira.

Smith, J. A., Flowers, P., & Larkin, M. (2009). *Interpretative phenomenological analysis: Theory, method and research.* Los Angeles: Sage.

Smith, S. J. (1992). Operating on a child's heart: A pedagogical view of hospitalization. In J. M. Morse (Ed.), *Qualitative health research* (pp. 104–122). Newbury Park, CA: Sage. (Original work published 1989)

Sparkes, A. C. (2001). Qualitative health researchers will agree about validity. *Qualitative Health Research, 11,* 538–552.

Spradley, J. P. (1979). *The ethnographic interview.* New York: Holt, Rinehart & Winston.

Stake, R. E. (1995). *The art of case study research.* Thousand Oaks, CA: Sage.

Stake, R. E. (2005). Qualitative case studies. In N. K. Denzin & Y. S. Lincoln (Eds.), *The SAGE handbook of qualitative research* (3rd ed., pp. 443–466). Thousand Oaks, CA: Sage.

Stake, R. E. (2006). *Multiple case study analysis.* New York: Guilford Press.

Stern, P. N. (1994). Eroding grounded theory. In J. M. Morse (Ed.), *Critical issues in qualitative research methods* (pp. 212–223). Thousand Oaks, CA: Sage.

Stern, P. N. (2009). Glaserian grounded theory. In J. M. Morse, P. N. Stern, J. Corbin, B. Bowers, K. Charmaz, & A. E. Clarke (Eds.), *Developing grounded theory: The second generation* (pp. 55–84). Walnut Creek, CA: Left Coast Press.

Stern, P. N., & Porr, C. (2011). *Essentials of accessible grounded theory.* Walnut Creek, CA: Left Coast Press.

Strauss, A. L. (1987). *Qualitative analysis for social scientists.* New York: Cambridge University Press.

Strauss, A. L., & Corbin, J. (1990). *Basics of qualitative research: Grounded theory procedures and techniques.* Newbury Park, CA: Sage.

Strauss, A. L., & Corbin, J. (1994). Grounded theory methodology: An overview. In N. K. Denzin & Y. S. Lincoln (Eds.), *The SAGE handbook of qualitative research* (pp. 273–285). Thousand Oaks, CA: Sage.

Strauss, A. L., & Corbin, J. (1998). *Basics of qualitative research: Techniques and procedures for developing grounded theory* (2nd ed.). Thousand Oaks, CA: Sage.

Swanborn, P. (2010). *Case study research: What, why and how?* London: Sage.

Tashakkori, A., & Teddlie, C. (Eds.). (2010). *Handbook of mixed methods research for the social and behavioral sciences* (2nd ed.). Thousand Oaks, CA: Sage.

Tesch, R. (1990). *Qualitative research: Analysis types and software tools.* London: Falmer.

Thomas, G. (2011). *How to do your case study: A guide for students and researchers.* London: Sage.

Thomas, J. (1993). *Doing critical ethnography.* Newbury Park, CA: Sage.

Thorne, S. (1997). The art (and science) of critiquing qualitative research. In J. M. Morse (Ed.), *Completing a qualitative project: Details and dialogue* (pp. 117–132). Thousand Oaks, CA: Sage.

Thorne, S. (2008). *Interpretive description.* Walnut Creek, CA: Left Coast Press.

Titscher, S., Meyer, M., Wodak, R., & Vetter, E. (2000). *Methods of text and discourse analysis.* London: Sage.

Turner, B. A. (1981). Some practical aspects of qualitative data analysis: One way of organising the cognitive processes associated with the generation of grounded theory. *Quality and Quantity, 15,* 225–247.

Turner, B. A. (1994). Patterns of crisis behaviour: A qualitative inquiry. In A. Bryman & R. G. Burgess (Eds.), *Analyzing qualitative data* (pp. 195–216). London: Routledge.

van Manen, M. (1990). *Researching lived experience: Human science for an action sensitive pedagogy.* London, Ontario: Althouse.

van Manen, M. (2011). Orientations in phenomenology. Retrieved January 17, 2012, from http://www.phenomenology online.com/inquiry/orientations-in-phenomenology/

Wax, R. H. (1971). *Doing fieldwork: Warnings and advice.* Chicago: University of Chicago Press.

Weitzman, E., & Miles, M. B. (1995). *Computer programs for qualitative data analysis.* Thousand Oaks, CA: Sage.

Werner, O., & Schoepfle, G. M. (1987a). *Systematic fieldwork: Vol. 1; Foundations of ethnography and interviewing.* Beverly Hills, CA: Sage.

Werner, O., & Schoepfle, G. M. (1987b). *Systematic fieldwork: Vol. 2; Ethnographic analysis and data management.* Beverly Hills, CA: Sage.

Westphal, L. M. (2000). Increasing the trustworthiness of research results: The role of computers in qualitative text analysis. In D. N. Bengston (Ed.), *Applications of computer-aided text analysis in natural resources* (General Technical Report No. NC-211, pp. 1–6). St. Paul, MN: USDA Forest Service, North Central Research Station.

Wodak, R. (Ed.). (1997). *Gender and discourse.* London: Sage

Wooffitt, R. (2005). *Conversation analysis and discourse analysis: A comparative and critical introduction.* London: Sage.

Yin, R. K. (2009). *Case study research: Design and methods* (4th ed.). Thousand Oaks, CA: Sage.

Author Index

Agar, M. H., 56
Altheide, D. L., 216
Atkinson, P., 130, 149, 190

Baig, A. A., 102
Barroso, J., 101
Bates, G., 61
Bazeley, P., 100, 111
Beatty, A., 99
Bell, D. S., 102
Benner, P., 71
Blumer, H., 61, 192
Bochner, A. P., 60, 143
Bondy, M. L., 102
Bottorff, J. L., 62
Bowers, B., 67, 198
Boyd, C. O., 70, 202, 256
Bradbury, H., 61
Bryant, A., 198
Bryman, A., 111
Bunik, M., 102

Cameron, D., 73, 128, 204
Carney, T. F., 174
Carr, E. S., 190
Carspecken, P. F., 60
Cassell, J., 55
Charmaz, C., 198
Charmaz, K., 65, 66,
    192, 198
Cheek, J., 256
Chenail, R. J., 165
Clark, D. A., 139
Clark, L., 102
Clarke, A., 66, 67, 198
Clarke, M., 69

Coffey, A., 149
Corbin, J., 62, 64, 65, 159, 192, 198
Coulthard, M., 203
Crawford, M., 73, 203

Davis, A. M., 102
Davis, D. L., 55, 88
Davis, D. S., 238
Davis, N., 88
Denzin, N. K., 95
Dey, I., 158
Doberneck, B. M., 139
Drew, S. E., 132
Duffy, M., 165
Duncan, R. E., 132
Durham, R., 67

Ellis, C., 60, 143
Engel, J. D., 239

Fairclough, N., 75
Field, P. A., 56, 256
Fielding, N. G., 63
Finch, J., 132, 141, 170
Flowers, P., 42
Forman, M. R., 102
Foster, R., 77, 207
Frank, A. W., 143

Gee, P. J., 72
Geertz, C., 58, 188
Germain, C., 59
Giorgi, A., 70, 199, 200, 201
Glaser, B. G., 42, 62, 64, 65, 89,
    133, 142, 159, 169, 193,
    194, 195, 197, 232, 257

Glittenberg, J., 190
Goffman, E., 102, 103
Goldman-Segall, R., 61
Gomm, R., 77, 207
Greenwood, D. J., 61
Guba, E. G., 215, 226
Gubrium, J. F., 59, 126

Hammersley, M., 77, 130, 190, 207
Hardy, C., 73, 74
Haug, F., 142
Holbrook, B., 149
Holstein, J. A., 126
Huang, E. S., 102
Huberman, A. M., 150, 155, 158,
    173, 178, 179, 180, 217
Hughes, C. C., 102

Jean, R. T., 102
Johnson, J. M., 216
Johnson, S. L., 102

Karp, D. A., 142
Kelpin, V., 69
Khonsari, E. S., 140
Knoblauch, H., 59
Kools, S., 67
Kuzel, A. J., 239
Kvale, S., 126, 216, 218

Larkin, M., 42
Lee, R. M., 63
Levin, M., 61
Lincoln, Y. S., 95, 215, 226
Lipson, J. G., 141, 273
Lofland, L. H., 97, 177, 179
Lofland, R. M., 97, 177, 179
Lorencz, B. J., 62, 140

Madison, D. S., 60
Malacrida, C., 142
Mason, J., 126, 130, 202
Maxwell, J. A., 95, 216, 220
McCarthy, M., 67

McNabb, D., 207
Mead, M., 61, 189
Meadows, L., 221
Meyer, M., 74
Miles, M. B., 106, 150,
    155, 158, 173, 178,
    179, 180, 217
Miles, M. W., 139
Mitcham, C., 170
Morgan, D., 137
Morse, J. M., 36, 37, 42, 56, 62, 80,
    90, 100, 132, 139, 140, 165,
    170, 188, 189, 198, 221, 231,
    239, 251, 256
Moustakas, C., 72
Muecke, M. A., 59
Munhall, P. L., 256

Nunnally, J. C., 188

Oakley, A., 141
Olesen, V. L., 142
Olson, K., 126

Patashnick, J., 132
Peek, M. E., 102
Penrod, J., 251
Peråkylå, A., 74
Phillips, N., 73, 74
Platt, J., 78
Porr, C., 65, 192
Potter, J., 161
Proctor, A., 140

Ray, M. A., 70, 201
Reason, P., 61
Rich, M., 132
Richards, L., 9, 46, 55, 80, 88, 95,
    97, 103, 104, 122, 132, 134,
    139, 149, 151, 153, 158, 160,
    162, 163, 164, 166, 167, 170,
    172, 177, 178, 179, 180, 182,
    188, 216, 218, 223, 226, 231,
    232, 238, 240, 242, 282

Richards, T. J., 151, 162, 177, 179
Richardson, L., 232
Robertson, S. K., 132
Robrecht, L., 67
Rolfe, S., 132

Sandelowski, M., 101, 216
Sawyer, S. M., 132
Schatzman, L., 67
Schoepfle, G. M., 188
Seibold, C., 88
Sherman, S. N., 102
Silverman, D., 190
Smith, D. E., 59
Smith, J. A., 42
Smith, S. J., 68
Sparkes, A. C., 216
Spradley, J. P., 59, 127, 188, 221
Stake, R. E., 76, 77, 78, 79, 206
Stern, P. N., 64, 65, 192, 198
Strauss, A. L., 42, 62, 64, 65, 67, 142, 149, 159, 163, 169, 178, 180, 192, 193, 195, 197, 217, 275
Swanborn, P., 77, 207

Tashakkori, A., 100
Teddlie, C., 100
Tesch, R., 106
Thomas, G., 77, 79, 207
Thomas, J., 60
Thorne, S., 42, 239
Titscher, S., 74
Turner, B. A., 62, 159, 177, 233

van der Steen, V., 170
van Manen, M., 67, 68, 69, 70, 71, 198, 199, 200, 201
Vetter, E., 74

Wax, R. H., 56
Weitzman, E., 106
Werner, O., 188
Westphal, L. M., 131
Wetherell, M., 161
Whitaker, R. C., 102
Wilkes, A. E., 102
Wilkinson, A. V., 102
Wodak, R., 73, 74, 203, 204
Wooffitt, R., 74, 75, 128, 204

Yin, R. K., 76, 77, 207

Subject Index

Abstracting, 169–184
  about, 169–170
  categorizing step of, 171–173
  conceptualizing step of, 173–174
  diagrams in, 180, 181, 182
  ideas, documenting, 178
  ideas, growing, 178–179
  index systems for, 179
  managing, 177–180
  models in, 180, 181, 182–183
  process of, 175 (table), 176–177
  resources for, 183–184
  software use for, 109 (table),
    180–183
  summary of, 183
  timing of, 174, 175 (table), 176
"Abstract" section, writing, 246
Action research (AR), 40–41, 61
Agendas, hidden, 274–275
Aim of qualitative research, 46
Analysis:
  in case study method,
    32, 33 (table), 207–208
  conversation, 73–74, 74–75,
    124 (table), 128, 202
  in discourse analysis,
    32, 33 (table), 204
  in ethnography, 32, 33 (table),
    57, 190–191
  in grounded theory, 32, 33 (table),
    193–198
  integrity of qualitative research
    and, 32–33, 33 (table)
  in phenomenology, 32, 33 (table),
    200–202
  project pacing and, 98

Analytic coding, 150, 151, 157–160,
    162–163
Analytic questions, 221
Anonymity, 136, 237–238,
    261–262
AR. See Action research
Armchair walkthrough:
  integrity of qualitative research
    and, 24, 35–36, 37 (table)
  starting with, 272–273
Articles:
  about, 244–245, 244 (box)
  audience for, 245
  beginning to write, 245–249,
    247–248 (box)
  from dissertation, 244–245,
    244 (box)
  review criteria, sample,
    247–248 (box)
Assent and consent, participant,
    45, 262, 263–265,
    265 (figure), 266 (figure)
Assessment of saturation, 223
Audience, 232, 245
Audit/log trails, 226, 240
Autoethnography, 43, 60
Awareness of self, 57
Axial coding, 159

Bad data/good data, 122–123
Basic social process/basic social
    psychological process,
    42, 62, 64, 197
Bibliography, 241
Bracketing, 176, 199, 218, 272
Budget, developing, 258–260

CAQDAS Networking Project
   (University of Surrey), 9, 282
Card sorts, 189
Case study method:
   about, 76
   abstraction in, 175 (table)
   analysis in, 32, 33 (table),
      207–208
   approaches in, 79
   armchair walkthrough of
      hypothetical project,
      37 (table)
   data, working with, 205–207
   data making and, 31–32
   data types and, 31 (table), 77–78
   as descriptive method, 51
   methodological congruence and,
      205–208, 211
   questions suited to,
      30, 30 (table), 76
   researcher's stance in, 77
   resources for, 86, 211
   results of, 78
Categories:
   core, 64, 196, 197–198
   managing, 179
Categorization, 171–173
Change, scoping for, 91
Chicago School, 77, 78
Classification systems/
   taxonomies, 59
Coding, 149–168
   about, 149–151
   amount needed, 162–163
   analytic, 150, 151,
      157–160, 162–163
   axial, 159
   categorization and, 171–172
   consistency of, 164
   data, getting inside the, 152–153
   data management and, 163, 165
   descriptive, 150–151,
      154–155, 165
   discourse analysis, 161
   doing, 153–160
   grounded theory, 157, 159,
      194–196
   ideas, storing, 153
   of interviews, 224
   in vivo codes, 157, 193, 195
   managing codes, 163
   open, 65, 159–160
   purposiveness of, 160–161
   as reflection, 162
   reliability of, 164, 223–224
   resources for, 167–168
   selective, 159, 198
   sociological codes, 195
   software use for, 108 (table), 151,
      155, 157, 163, 164–167
   summary of, 167
   theme development through,
      151, 160
   theoretical, 196
   tips and traps, 161–164
   topic, 150, 151, 156–157
   validity of, 224
   as you learn, 162
Coding paradigm, 159
Cognitive ethnography, 59
Collective case studies, 79
Comfort Talk Register, 140
Communality/relationality
   (lived human relation),
   68, 199, 201
Comparative design, 102
Comparison, 189
Concepts, core, 62, 64
Conceptualizing, 17–18, 96, 173–174
Congruence, methodological. *See*
   Methodological congruence
Consent and assent, participant,
   45, 262, 263–265, 265 (figure),
   266 (figure)
Constructivist grounded theory,
   66, 198

Context:
  research, 41–45
  theoretical, 256–257
Contract research, 275
Convenience sampling, 222
Conversation analysis, 73–74,
    74–75, 124 (table), 128, 202
Cooperation and acceptance phase,
    in ethnography, 57
Copyright, 246–249
Core categories, 64, 196,
    197–198
Core concepts, 62, 64
Corporeality (lived body),
    68, 199, 201
Covert research, 263
Criteria for review, journal,
    246, 247–248 (box)
Critical discourse analysis,
    75, 202–203, 204
Critical ethnography, 60
Cultural probes, 132–133

Data:
  dealing with, 260–261
  determining, 120–123
  forcing, 139, 159, 192
  fracturing, 154
  getting inside, 152–153
  good *versus* bad, 122–123
  linking, 154
  method and, 30–32, 31 (table)
  nature of, 91–93, 94
  online sources of, 122,
      125 (table), 130
  preparing, 193
  quantitative, 206
  requirements, determining, 120
  researcher as, 140–143
  researcher experience as, 142–143,
      235, 273–275
  researcher in, 121–122
  role of, 138–140

software, choosing, 106 (table)
transforming, 134–135
using in writing, 233–235
See also Data making; Data
    making techniques
Data analysis. *See* Analysis
Data disposal, 156
Data files, external storage of,
    136–137
Data making, 119–147
  about, 119–120
  case study method and, 31–32
  data, determining, 120–123
  data, good *versus* bad, 122–123
  data, requirements for, 120
  data, researcher as, 140–143
  data, researcher experience as,
      142–143, 235, 273–275
  data, researcher in, 121–122
  data, role of, 138–140
  data, transforming, 134–135
  focus groups and, 31
  methods for, 123–133
  research assistants in, 133
  researcher/participant relationship
      and, 141–142
  resources for, 146–147
  responsibility for, 133–134
  rigor and, 228
  strategies that aren't working,
      rethinking, 222
  strategy use and, 222
  summary of, 145
  team research in, 134
  as term, 119
  See also Data; Data making
      techniques; Data
      management
Data making techniques, 123–133
  about, 123, 124–125 (table), 126
  conversations, 124 (table), 128
  diaries and letters, 125 (table), 132
  documents, 125 (table), 132

indirect strategies, 42–43,
    125 (table), 132–133, 147
interviews, group, 124 (table),
    128–129
interviews, interactive/
    unstructured, 124 (table),
    126–127
interviews/questionnaires,
    semistructured, 124 (table),
    127–128
observations, 124 (table),
    129–130
online sources, 122,
    125 (table), 130
photography, 125 (table), 131
video recording, 125 (table), 131
    See also Data; Data making
Data management:
    about, 135–137
    coding and, 163, 165
    focus group, 137–138
    getting started, 275–276
    setting up/managing, 97–98
    software use for, 143–145
    See also Data making
Description:
    first-level, 186–188
    thick, 58, 188–189, 233, 250
Descriptive coding, 150–151,
    154–155, 165
Descriptive methods, 41–42, 50–51
Design, 87–116
    about, 87
    appropriate, 228
    comparative, 102
    doing, 93–94, 114
    getting started, 277
    levels of, 88
    mixed method, 99–101, 115
    multiple method, 99, 101, 115
    multiple studies in, 98–104
    overview, taking an, 104–105
    planning, 88–93

preemptive, 87
project pacing, 88, 96–98
resources for, 114–116
rigor and, 216–220
software, choosing, 105–109
software, using for, 110–113, 116
summary of, 113
topic to researchable question,
    move from, 45
triangulated, 103–104
validity of, 94–95
Diagrams, 180, 181, 182, 194
Diaries:
    data making from, 125 (table),
        132, 147
    for documenting ideas, 178
    in ethnography, 58
Dimensional analysis, 66
Discourse analysis:
    about, 72
    abstraction in, 175 (table)
    analysis in, 32, 33 (table), 204
    approaches in, 75
    armchair walkthrough of
        hypothetical project, 37 (table)
    coding specific to, 161
    critical, 75, 202–203, 204
    data, working with, 203–204
    data types and, 31 (table), 74–75
    methodological congruence and,
        202–204, 210–211
    questions suited to, 30, 30 (table),
        72–74
    researcher's stance in, 74
    resources for, 85–86, 210–211
    results of, 75
    transcription in, 203
"Discussion" chapter/section, writing,
    242, 243 (figure), 246
Diversity, scoping for, 91
Documents, 107 (table), 125 (table),
    132, 187
Doing, learning by, 7–9

Editing quotations, 234–235
Emic/insider perspective, 56
Employer, permission from, 262–263
Entering the field, 96–97
Equipment/training budget, 260
Ethical issues:
    about, 261
    anonymity, 136, 237–238, 261–262
    online sources, 130
    participant assent and consent, 45, 262, 263–265, 265 (figure), 266 (figure)
    permissions, 45, 262–263
    privacy, 43, 44–45
    research setting, 43
    resources for, 267
Ethnography:
    abstraction in, 175 (table)
    analysis in, 32, 33 (table), 57, 190–191
    approaches in, 59–61
    armchair walkthrough of hypothetical project, 37 (table)
    autoethnography, 43, 60
    cognitive, 59
    critical, 60
    data, working with, 186–189
    data types and, 31 (table), 57–58
    as descriptive method, 51
    focused, 59–60
    methodological congruence and, 186–191, 208–209
    questions suited to, 29, 30 (table), 54–55
    researcher's stance in, 55–57
    resources for, 81–83, 208–209
    results of, 58–59
    visual, 61

Etic/outsider/researcher perspective, 56
Evaluation:
    comparative qualitative research in, 102
    of nonmeasurable interventions, 251
    of qualitative research, resources for, 252
    of writing, 238–239
Existential phenomenology, 71

Field, entering the, 96–97
Field notes, 57–58, 193
Field research, 54, 56
    See also Ethnography
Findings. *See* Results
First-level description, 186–188
First person, writing memos in, 179
Focused ethnography, 59–60
Focus groups:
    data making and, 31
    data management and, 137–138
    as descriptive method, 51
    group interviews *versus*, 128–129
    resources for, 146
Focusing, 15–16, 45, 190
Forcing data, 139, 159, 192
Funding, applying for, 285–286

Getting it right. *See* Rigor
Getting started, 269–279
    about, 269–270
    armchair walkthrough, 272–273
    data management, 275–276
    design, 277
    literature review, 271–272
    with personal experience, 273–275
    as problem, 270–271
    resources for, 279
    safety in, 276

skills required for, 277–278
with software, 278
"start thinking" method, 273
timing of, 276–277
See also Groundwork for beginning
    your project
Glaserian grounded theory, 64–65,
    192, 195, 197
Goals, research, 43–44, 52
Good data/bad data, 122–123
Grand tour/opening
    questions, 127
Grants, obtaining, 285–286
Grounded theory:
    abstraction in, 175 (table)
    analysis in, 32, 33 (table),
        193–198
    approaches in, 64–67
    armchair walkthrough of
        hypothetical project,
        37 (table)
    changes in, 198
    coding and, 157, 159, 194–196
    constructivist, 66, 198
    data, working with, 192–193
    data types and, 31 (table), 63
    diagrams in, 194
    Glaserian, 64–65, 192,
        195, 197
    methodological congruence and,
        191–198, 209–210
    questions suited to, 29–30,
        30 (table), 61–62
    researcher's stance in, 62–63
    resources for, 83–84, 209–210
    results of, 63–64
    Straussian, 64–65, 192,
        195, 197–198
Groundwork for beginning
    your project, 255–267
    about, 255
    ethical research, ensuring,
        261–266, 267

proposal, writing, 255–261, 267
    resources for, 267
    summary of, 266
    See also Getting started
Group interviews, 124 (table),
    128–129

Heuristic phenomenology, 72
Hidden agendas, 274–275

Ideas:
    documenting, 178
    growing, 178–179
    managing, 180–183
    software, choosing,
        107 (table)
    storing, 153
    See also Abstracting
Implementation, reaffirming
    legitimacy through, 227
Index systems, 179
Indirect data making strategies,
    42–43, 125 (table),
    132–133, 147
Informants, 58
    See also Participants
Insider/emic perspective, 56
Instrumental case studies, 79
Integrity, methodological, 4–5
Integrity of qualitative research,
    23–48
    about, 23
    aim and, 46
    armchair walkthrough to ensure,
        24, 35–36, 37 (table)
    methodological congruence and,
        34–35
    methodological purposiveness
        and, 23–33
    research context and, 41–45
    resources for, 47–48
    summary of, 46–47
    topic, 36, 38–41

Interactive/unstructured
  interviews, 32, 124 (table),
  126–127, 224
International research, 263
Interpretive methods,
  42, 51–52
Interviews:
  coding of, 224
  data making from, 124 (table),
    126–129, 146
  in ethnography, 58
  group, 124 (table), 128–129
  interactive/unstructured, 32,
    124 (table), 126–127, 224
  semistructured, 124 (table),
    127–128, 223
Intrinsic case studies, 79
"Introduction" chapter/section,
  writing, 242, 243 (figure), 246
Invalidity. *See* Validity
In vivo codes, 157, 193, 195

Journals:
  criteria for review, 246,
    247–248 (box)
  qualitative research, 48

Key informants, 58

Learning by doing, 7–9
Letters, 125 (table), 132, 147
Linguistical phenomenology, 71
Literature review:
  findings and, 226
  getting started, 271–272
  in proposal writing,
    256–257
  rigor and, 217–218
  in thesis/dissertation, 241
  topic and, 39–40
  writing up, 242, 243 (figure), 246
Lived body (corporeality),
  68, 199, 201

Lived human relation (relationality/
  communality), 68, 199, 201
Lived space (spatiality),
  68, 199, 201
Lived time (temporality),
  68, 199, 201
Location, methodological, 94
Log/audit trails, 226, 240

Maps, 125 (table), 187
Memos:
  documenting ideas with, 178
  getting started, 272
  importance of, 193
  strategies with, 196
  writing, 153, 160, 162,
    163, 179
Metadata, 135–136
Metasynthesis, 53, 99, 101–102,
  115–116
Methodological congruence,
  185–211
  about, 185–186
  case study method approach to,
    205–208, 211
  defined, 34
  discourse analysis approach to,
    202–204, 210–211
  ethnography approach to,
    186–191, 208–209
  grounded theory approach to,
    191–198, 209–210
  integrity of qualitative research
    and, 34–35
  phenomenology approach to,
    198–202, 210
  resources for, 208–211
  summary of, 208
  writing and, 236
Methodological integrity, 4–5
Methodological location, 94
Methodological purposiveness,
  23–33

Methods:
  data making, 123–133
  defined, 2, 10–11
  descriptive, 41–42, 50–51
  interpretive, 42, 51–52
  quantitative, 25–26, 28–29
  "start thinking," 273
  See also Qualitative methods;
    Qualitative method selection
"Methods" chapter/section, writing,
  241, 242, 243 (figure),
  246, 257–258
Method selection. *See* Qualitative
  method selection
Minor age participants, 264
Mixed method designs,
  99–101, 115
Models and modeling, 109 (table),
  180, 181, 182–183
Multiple method designs,
  99, 101, 115

Negative cases, 90, 223
Negotiating entry phase, in
  ethnography, 56
Nominated/snowball sampling,
  89, 221
Nonparticipant observation, 130

Observation:
  data making from, 31, 124 (table),
    129–130, 146–147
  nonparticipant, 130
  participant, 31, 55–56, 130
  resources for, 146–147
  simulated, 132
Online data sources, 122,
  125 (table), 130
Open coding, 65, 159–160
Opening/grand tour questions, 127
Outline, sample, 243 (figure)
Outsider/researcher perspective, 56
Overview, taking an, 104–105

Pacing, project, 88, 96–98, 222–223
PAR. *See* Participatory action
  research
Participant observation,
  31, 55–56, 130
Participants:
  assent and consent, 45, 262,
    263–265, 265 (figure),
    266 (figure)
  budget for paying, 260
  finding, 44
  minor age, 264
  protecting, 237–238
  researchers and, 121–122,
    141–142
  rights of, 263–264
Participatory action research (PAR),
  60–61
Pattern analysis, 80
Permissions, 45, 262–263
Personnel budget, 258–260
Perspectives, 56
Phenomenological nod, 70
Phenomenology:
  about, 67–68
  abstraction in, 175 (table)
  analysis in, 32, 33 (table),
    200–202
  approaches in, 70–72
  armchair walkthrough of
    hypothetical project,
    37 (table)
  data, working with, 199–200
  data types and, 31 (table), 70
  existential, 71
  hermeneutical, 67–68, 71, 199
  heuristic, 72
  as interpretive method, 52
  linguistical, 71
  methodological congruence and,
    198–202, 210
  questions suited to, 30, 30 (table),
    68–69

researcher's stance in, 69–70
resources for, 84–85, 210
results of, 70
transcendental, 71
Photographs:
  consent for, 262, 266 (figure)
  data making from, 125 (table), 131
  in first-level description, 187
Preemptive research design, 87
Privacy, 43, 44–45
Progressive focusing, 190
Project histories, 224–225
Project pacing, 88, 96–98, 222–223
Proposals:
  about, 255–256
  budget, developing, 258–260
  data, dealing with, 260–261
  literature review, 256–257
  methods section, 257–258
  as preparation, 220
  quantitative *versus* qualitative
    research, 256
  resources for, 267
  thesis/dissertation, using
    information in, 241
  time, estimating,
    258, 259 (figure)
Pseudonyms, 136, 237, 262
Public administration research, 207
Publication costs, 260
Public places, research in,
  264–265
Purpose, research, 27–29, 93–94
Purposeful sampling, 206, 221
Purposiveness:
  of coding, 160–161
  methodological, 23–33

Qualitative method integrity. *See*
  Integrity of qualitative research
Qualitative methods:
  competence in, developing, 16
  data and, 30–32, 31 (table)

demystifying, 7
distinctiveness of, 152
diversity of, 5–6
evolution of, 5
quantitative methods, combining
  with, 25–26, 29
question and, 29–30, 30 (table),
  80–81
rigor and, 220
See also Methods; Qualitative
  method selection; Quantitative
  methods
Qualitative method selection,
  49–86
about, 49–50
case study method as selection,
  75–79, 86
descriptive *versus* interpretive
  methods, 50–52
discourse analysis as selection,
  72–75, 85–86
ethnography as selection, 54–61,
  81–83
grounded theory as selection,
  61–67, 83–84
phenomenology as selection,
  67–72, 84–85
resources for, 81–86
starting simple, 52–53
summary of, 79–81
See also Qualitative methods
Qualitative research:
  aim of, 46
  as challenge, 9–10
  as craft, 7–9
  reasons for, 25–29
  resources for, by discipline,
    47–48
  See also specific topics
Qualitative research design. *See*
  Design
Qualitative research
  proposals, 256

Qualitative research steps,
14–19
about, 14–15
conceptualizing and theorizing,
17–18
focusing, 15–16
methodological competence,
developing, 16
molding and writing, 18–19
shaping the study, 17
Qualitative studies:
combining, 99–100
combining quantitative studies
with, 100–101
Quantitative data, 206
Quantitative methods, 25–26,
28–29
Quantitative research
proposals, 256
Quantitative studies, 100–101
Questionnaires/interviews,
semistructured, 124 (table),
127–128, 223
Questions:
addressed by case study method,
30, 30 (table), 76
addressed by discourse analysis,
30, 30 (table), 72–74
addressed by ethnography,
29, 30 (table), 54–55
addressed by grounded theory,
29–30, 30 (table), 61–62
addressed by phenomenology,
30, 30 (table), 68–69
analytic, 221
asking right, 228
grand tour/opening, 127
method and, 29–30, 30 (table),
80–81
qualitative methods and,
25–26
topic and, 45
Quotations, 234–235, 240

Random sampling, 221, 222
Readme First (present book):
about, 1–4
goals of, 4–10
shape of, 11–14
terminology used in, 10–11
Reflexivity, 74
Relationality/communality (lived
human relation), 68, 199, 201
Reliability:
coding, 164, 223–224
importance of, 215–216
resources for, 252
See also Rigor
Research:
contract, 275
covert, 263
field, 54, 56
international, 263
public administration, 207
in public places, 264–265
team, 134
See also specific research types
Research assistants, 133
Research context, 41–45
Research design. *See* Design
Researchers:
as data, 140–143
in data, 121–122
experience as data, 142–143, 235,
273–275
good, 269–270
as instrument, 216–217
participants and, 121–122,
141–142
perspective of, 56
stance in case study method, 77
stance in discourse analysis, 74
stance in ethnography, 55–57
stance in grounded theory, 62–63
stance in phenomenology,
69–70
Research goals, 43–44, 52

Research method selection. *See*
    Qualitative method selection
Research purpose, 27–29, 93–94
Research questions. *See* Questions
Research settings, permission
    from, 263
Research sites, 237–238, 262, 263
Research strategies. *See* Strategies
Resources:
  abstracting, 183–184
  case study method, 86, 211
  coding, 167–168
  data making, 146–147
  design, 114–116
  diaries and indirect methods, 147
  discourse analysis, 85–86, 210–211
  ethical issues, 267
  ethnography, 81–83, 208–209
  focus group data, 146
  getting started, 279
  grounded theory, 83–84, 209–210
  groundwork for beginning your
    project, 267
  integrity of qualitative research,
    47–48
  interview data, 146
  metasynthesis, 115–116
  methodological congruence,
    208–211
  mixed method designs, 115
  multiple method designs, 115
  observation data, 146–147
  phenomenology, 84–85, 210
  qualitative method selection,
    81–86
  qualitative research, by discipline,
    47–48
  qualitative research,
    evaluating, 252
  reliability, 252
  rigor, 229
  software, using for research
    design, 116

  theory, 252
  validity, 252
  video data, 147
  writing, 252
Results:
  case study method, 78
  cumulative effect of, 251
  discourse analysis, 75
  ethnography, 58–59
  grounded theory, 63–64
  literature and, 226
  phenomenology, 70
  rigor and, 228
  used alone, 249–251
  writing up, 242, 243 (figure), 246
Review criteria, journal, 246,
    247–248 (box)
Rigor, 215–229
  about, 215–216
  on completion of project, 227
  in conducting a project, 221–224
  in design phase, 216–220
  finishing, 224–226
  resources for, 229
  summary of, 228
Routines, documenting, 187

Sample, scope of the, 89
Sampling:
  convenience, 222
  nominated/snowball, 89, 221
  principles of, 89–90
  project pacing and, 98
  purposeful, 206, 221
  random, 221, 222
  rigor and, 221–222
  theoretical, 89–90, 98, 222, 257
Saturation, assessment of, 223
Scope and scoping, 89–91, 94, 250
Scoping for change, 91
Scoping for diversity, 91
Scripting Addiction (Carr), 191
Search tools, 108 (table), 240

Selective coding, 159, 198
Self, awareness of, 57
Semistructured interviews,
    124 (table), 127–128, 223
Sensitivity, theoretical, 62–63, 159,
    192, 193
Simulated observation, 132
Sites, research, 237–238, 262, 263
Situational analysis, 66–67
Snowball/nominated sampling,
    89, 221
Sociological codes, 195
Software:
    abstracting, 109 (table), 180–183
    coding, 108 (table), 151, 155, 157,
        163, 164–167
    data management, 143–145
    design, 110–113, 116
    getting started with, 278
    learning about, 9, 217
    qualitative, 281–283
    writing, 239–241
    See also Software selection
Software selection:
    about, 105–106, 217
    abstracting, modeling, questioning,
        and reporting, 109 (table)
    coding and text search, 108 (table)
    data documents, ideas, and links,
        107 (table)
    project and first data, 106 (table)
    See also Software
Spatiality (lived space), 68, 199, 201
Starting. See Getting started
"Start thinking" method, 273
Strategies:
    data making and, 222
    defined, 11
    indirect data making, 42–43,
        125 (table), 132–133, 147
    responsiveness to, 222
Straussian grounded theory, 64–65,
    192, 195, 197–198

Studies:
    multiple, synthesizing, 53, 99,
        101–102, 115–116
    nature of, 41–42
    qualitative, combining,
        99–100
    qualitative and quantitative,
        combining, 100–101
    shaping, 17
Substantive scope, 90–91
Supplies/travel budget, 260
Surveys, 28
Synthesizing multiple studies,
    53, 99, 101–102, 115–116

Taxonomies/classification
    systems, 59
Team research, 134
Techniques, defined, 11
    See also specific techniques
Temporality (lived time),
    68, 199, 201
Terminology, 10–11
Text search, 108 (table), 240
Theme development, 151, 160
Theoretical coding, 196
Theoretical context, 256–257
Theoretical sampling, 89–90, 98,
    222, 257
Theoretical sensitivity, 62–63, 159,
    192, 193
Theory:
    building, 17–18, 196–198, 228
    emergence versus construction
        of, 177
    as framework for practice, 249–250
    resources for, 252
Thesis/dissertation writing:
    about, 241–242
    beginning to write, 242, 244
    outline, sample, 243 (figure)
Thick description, 58, 188–189,
    233, 250

Thin areas, 90
Thinking ahead, 94
Thinking qualitatively, 218–220
Time, estimating, 258,
    259 (figure)
Timelines, in grounded theory, 194
Topic, 36, 38–41, 45
Topic coding, 150, 151, 156–157
Training/equipment budget, 260
Transcendental phenomenology, 71
Transcription, 193, 203, 260
Trauma care recording, 45
Travel/supplies budget, 260
Triangulation, 103–104, 227

Unstructured/interactive
    interviews, 32, 124 (table),
    126–127, 224

Validity:
    coding, 224
    design, 94–95
    importance of, 215–216
    methods, design and, 220
    qualitative and quantitative
        studies, combining, 100–101
    resources for, 252
    See also Rigor
Video recordings:
    consent for, 262, 266 (figure)
    data making from, 125 (table),
        131, 147
    data transformation from, 134
    in ethnography, 61
Vignettes, 132
*Violence and Hope in a U.S.-Mexico
    Border Town* (Glittenberg), 191
Visual ethnography, 61

Withdrawal phase, in
    ethnography, 57
Word processing, 239–241
Writing, 231–252
    about, 18–19, 231
    "Abstract" section, 246
    articles, 244–249
    audience for, 232, 245
    brevity and balance in,
        235–236
    data, using your, 233–235
    "Discussion" chapter/section,
        242, 243 (figure), 246
    evaluating, 238–239
    in first person, 179
    "Introduction" chapter/section,
        242, 243 (figure), 246
    "Literature Review"
        chapter/section,
        242, 243 (figure), 246
    memos, 153, 160, 162,
        163, 179
    methodological congruence
        and, 236
    "Methods" chapter/section, 241,
        242, 243 (figure), 246,
        257–258
    participants, protecting,
        237–238
    polishing, 239
    publication and use of findings,
        249–251
    qualitatively, 232–233
    resources for, 252
    software for, 239–241
    summary of, 251
    thesis/dissertation, 241–244
    See also Proposals